Sir Samuel Hood and the Battle of the Chesapeake

New Perspectives on Maritime History and Nautical Archaeology

UNIVERSITY PRESS OF FLORIDA

Florida A&M University, Tallahassee
Florida Atlantic University, Boca Raton
Florida Gulf Coast University, Ft. Myers
Florida International University, Miami
Florida State University, Tallahassee
New College of Florida, Sarasota
University of Central Florida, Orlando
University of Florida, Gainesville
University of North Florida, Jacksonville
University of South Florida, Tampa
University of West Florida, Pensacola

LORD HOOD.

Published May 31, 1784, by W. Bent, Paternoster Row.

Samuel Hood, 1st Viscount Hood. Line engraving published by William Bent. Courtesy of the National Portrait Gallery, London.

Sir Samuel Hood and the Battle of the Chesapeake

COLIN PENGELLY

Foreword by James C. Bradford and Gene A. Smith, series editors

University Press of Florida
Gainesville/Tallahassee/Tampa/Boca Raton
Pensacola/Orlando/Miami/Jacksonville/Ft. Myers/Sarasota

Copyright 2009 by Colin Pengelly
Printed in the United States of America on acid-free paper
All rights reserved

13 12 11 10 09   6 5 4 3 2 1

Library of Congress Cataloging-in-Publication Data
Pengelly, Colin.
Sir Samuel Hood and the Battle of the Chesapeake/Colin Pengelly;
foreword by James C. Bradford and Gene A. Smith.
p. cm.—(New perspectives on maritime history and nautical archaeology)
Includes bibliographical references and index.
ISBN 978-0-8130-3313-6 (alk. paper)
1. Chesapeake, Battle of the, Va., 1781. 2. Hood, Samuel Hood, Viscount,
1724–1816—Military leadership. 3. Admirals—Great Britain—Biography.
4. Great Britain. Royal Navy—History—Revolution, 1775–1783. 5. United
States—History—Revolution, 1775–1783—Naval operations, British.
6. United States—History—Revolution, 1775–1783—British forces. I. Title.
II. Series.
E241.C515P46 2009
973.3'379–dc22   2008044557

The University Press of Florida is the scholarly publishing agency for the
State University System of Florida, comprising Florida A&M University,
Florida Atlantic University, Florida Gulf Coast University, Florida Interna-
tional University, Florida State University, New College of Florida, Univer-
sity of Central Florida, University of Florida, University of North Florida,
University of South Florida, and University of West Florida.

University Press of Florida
15 Northwest 15th Street
Gainesville, FL 32611-2079
www.upf.com

CONTENTS

FOREWORD

Water is unquestionably the most important natural feature on earth. By volume the world's oceans compose 99 percent of the planet's living space; in fact, the surface of the Pacific Ocean alone is larger than that of the total land bodies. Water is as vital to life as air. Indeed, to test whether the moon or other planets can sustain life, NASA looks for signs of water. The story of human development is inextricably linked to the oceans, seas, lakes, and rivers that dominate the earth's surface. The University Press of Florida's series New Perspectives on Maritime History and Nautical Archaeology is devoted to exploring the significance of the earth's water while providing lively and important books that cover the spectrum of maritime history and nautical archaeology broadly defined. The series includes works that focus on the role of canals, rivers, lakes, and oceans in history; on the economic, military, and political use of those waters; and upon the people, communities, and industries that support maritime endeavors. Limited by neither geography nor time, volumes in the series contribute to the overall understanding of maritime history and can be read with profit by both general readers and specialists.

Although the American War of Independence was largely fought on land, its outcome was determined at sea. For six years following the outbreak of hostilities in 1775, Great Britain enjoyed all the advantages of a dominant sea power. The British transported a large army to North America, and supported it, along supply lines that stretched across 3,000 miles of ocean. In American waters the Royal Navy gave military commanders a flexibility envied by patriot leaders. Naval transport and gunfire support allowed British commanders to evacuate Boston in 1776 and seize New York City as a new center of operations, to occupy virtually at will posts as far afield as Penobscot in Maine, Newport in Rhode Island, and Savannah in Georgia. When British strategists concluded that capture of the American capital at Philadelphia could end the rebellion, they sent an army by sea to the head of the Chesapeake Bay to outflank American defenses on the Delaware River and then approached the city from the west. The English shift to a "southern strategy" meant transporting army troops to Georgia and South Carolina for campaigns that captured Savannah and Charleston.

Only during the Yorktown campaign of 1781 did sea power fail to provide a margin for victory. Indeed, while the Royal Navy lost no ships at the battle of the Virginia Capes, the French navy so badly mauled the van of the British fleet that Admiral Sir Thomas Graves decided to break off action and retire with his fleet to New York. This decision made the engagement a strategic defeat for the British because the Royal Navy left the French in control of the Chesapeake Bay and the York River. Momentary naval supremacy allowed the French to land siege artillery to support American and French troops, blocked resupply of British forces hemmed in at Yorktown, and prevented the extraction of Lord Cornwallis's army by sea. Cornwallis's surrender, accompanied by reverses in the Caribbean, Florida, and India, led political leaders in London to abandon offensive action and to seriously negotiate a peace treaty that recognized American independence.

Few conflicts are as fraught with suppositions and "what if's" as the American War of Independence. Among these is "What if the Royal Navy had prevailed in the battle of the Virginia Capes?" This leads to the subsidiary question "Would the outcome have been different had Graves's second in command, Admiral Sir Samuel Hood, brought the rear of the British fleet into battle?"

A military loss of such magnitude invariably prompts a search for individuals to fault. British army commanders escaped serious criticism; hadn't they been failed by the navy? But who in the Royal Navy should assume responsibility? Indeed, who was to blame for the British loss at Yorktown? Some contemporaries compared the engagement off the Capes in September with one in the same area the previous March in which the strategic positions of the two sides were reversed. Then a French squadron under the command of Captain the Chevalier Destouches approached the Chesapeake carrying 1,200 French troops and siege artillery to augment the American army commanded by the marquis de Lafayette. Learning that seven French ships of the line had departed Newport accompanied by transports, Admiral Arbuthnot sailed in pursuit from New York with an equal force. When the two squadrons met off the Chesapeake on 16 March, the British ships suffered greater damage, but Destouches withdrew from the area without landing the troops or siege artillery, and the British subsequently reinforced their army in Virginia. Six months later, during the second battle of the Virginia Capes, it was the British who drew off, leaving the French in control of the Chesapeake at a crucial time.

Did Thomas Graves deserve the bulk of blame in the strategic loss? Should he have been cast as the scapegoat? How much of the blame should be assigned to Hood for not bringing his ships into action? Why did Hood not engage the enemy? These questions are the focus of Colin Pengelly's study, which is both an analysis of the engagement and a biography of Admiral Sir Samuel Hood. Though he was a major figure in the Royal Navy of the last quarter of the eighteenth century—no less a naval commander than Horatio Nelson is quoted as calling Hood "the greatest Sea-officer I ever knew"—Hood has lacked a full-length biography. Plumbing the character of Hood, Pengelly deftly places him in the context of the Royal Navy and of British politics during the late eighteenth century. This is a nuanced study of a fascinating personality which tells the reader much about both Hood and his times.

James C. Bradford, Texas A&M University
Gene A. Smith, Texas Christian University

ACKNOWLEDGMENTS

The origins of this book go back to my earlier research into the life of Lord Hood. It was a long-nurtured project to convert that research into a book. When Paul Wilderon of the United States Naval Institute Press considered my partially finished manuscript on Hood, he suggested that I draw from the information in it to write the story of the battle of the Chesapeake and the part Hood played in it. This I did, and this book is the result of his suggestion.

I made use of the original sources from the National Maritime Museum, the British Museum (now the British Library), and the Public Record Office (now the National Archives), as well as the private collections of the Sandwich Papers and the Thomas Smith Papers. I am indebted to their staffs for their assistance in producing documents for me and answering questions by telephone and e-mail. In particular I would like to mention Andrew Davis of the National Maritime Museum, who was always willing to pursue any point I raised. I am grateful for the assistance which I received from the late Lord Cobham in researching the Smith Papers and to the late Victor Montagu for the Sandwich Papers. As well as these main sources, I was aided by the staff of the Dorset, Gloucester, and Worcestershire Record Offices; by the Bristol Central Reference Library, which produced copies of articles from the *Mariners Mirror* for me; the staff of the Weston Central Library, who obtained for me many out-of-print books; and J. Webber, chief archivist at Belvoir Castle, who assisted me in connection with the papers of Lord Robert Manners. Bernard Horrocks of the National Portrait Gallery in London was helpful in producing the frontispiece from the NPG Collection.

I am grateful to my brother-in-law Dr. Lawrence Scales for his translation of my letters into French for submission to the Musée de la Marine and to Dave Leishman and Dean Gargano, who translated the replies. Dr. Michael Duffy read parts of the final manuscript and made suggestions for improvements. Any errors which now remain are my responsibility.

I was fortunate while in contact with the United States Naval Institute Press to make the acquaintance of James Bradford, who was to put me in contact with the University Press of Florida, which took on the task of putting the book into print. I am grateful for all the staff at UPF but in particular Meredith Morris-Babb, my editor, and my personal liaison contact, Heather Romans. I owe special thanks to the copy editor, Ann Marlowe, who with her deep understanding of the eighteenth century read the manuscript with a sharp eye to detail.

Finally I would like to mention my wife, Evelyn, who has supported and assisted me and who has lived, and suffered with, my writing activities for the last forty years. If anyone deserves to have a book dedicated to them it is Evelyn! This one is duly so dedicated.

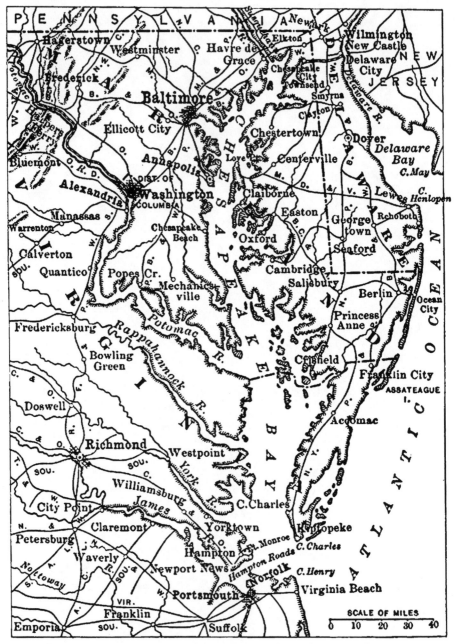

Chesapeake Bay Region, 1916. Used with permission of the Florida Center for Instructional Technology, University of South Florida, ©2007.

INTRODUCTION

The second battle of the Chesapeake (or the second battle of the Virginia Capes, as it is known in the United States) was fought on the fifth of September 1781. On the British side were the combined squadrons of Rear Admiral Sir Thomas Graves,[1] Sir Samuel Hood, and Francis Samuel Drake.[2] They faced a superior French fleet commanded by the comte de Grasse.[3] The day's action produced only an indecisive skirmish, yet it operated as a defeat for the British. Though they lost no ships, they had had two objectives when they sailed from New York: to defeat the French fleet and to relieve the besieged British army at Yorktown. The British had enjoyed naval superiority on the American coast since the start of the war and had used it in carrying out a number of successful amphibious operations. But the equivocal outcome at the Chesapeake left the French undefeated and the two objectives of the British thwarted, and its ultimate effect, the surrender at Yorktown, destroyed the government of Lord North. The battle carried no glory for the Royal Navy and became largely forgotten as the navy went on to better times starting with the Saintes and culminating with Trafalgar.

George Washington[4] had long recognized that his own operations would be immensely enhanced if the French could achieve naval dominance on the American coast and use it in his favor. The operations of the first French squadron in 1778 had been unsuccessful and disappointing to Washington. Now, in conjunction with the French, the American commander had brought a superior army to Virginia and had persuaded the French to bring a superior naval force to the Chesapeake, though this destination was not the first choice of Washington, who favored an attack on New York. The stakes were high, for the French and Americans aimed at a decisive defeat of the British forces at Yorktown and an end to British operations in Virginia.

It is doubtful if Rear Admiral Graves realized the desperate situation, partly of its own making, in which the British army now was. Samuel Hood did not have that knowledge either, but he had the capacity to do what Wellington called "seeing the other side of the hill." He did not know the strength of the French detachment from the West Indies, but he did know that the British had to find, engage, and defeat it to maintain their superiority on the American coast. He realized that time was important and had hastened Graves out of New York to join his own squadron. The strategy of detachment, which the British used for their army in America, required naval superiority if these detachments were not to be defeated and forced to surrender or evacuate their positions. So far this requirement had been maintained.

Graves was the senior of the three rear admirals and had the command of the fleet. He faced a difficult task in fighting an enemy fleet of unknown strength when his own fleet comprised two squadrons drawn from different command areas and used to different signaling and tactical systems. Graves has since borne the weight of the subsequent failure of the British attack and the surrender at Yorktown. This interpretation was first propagated by Hood in his letters home after the battle and then later supported by historians, but I believe it to be faulty and not in accordance with the historical facts. If Hood had been in command, it is said, things would have been different.

If Hood had been in command! It is a point worth debating that, if Hood had joined the navy at the age of thirteen or fourteen, as was common, then he would have been senior to Graves; and America, or at least the British army at Yorktown, would have been saved! It can certainly be postulated that, if Hood had joined the navy in 1737 or 1738, he would, with the patronage he enjoyed, have reached the rank of master and commander (that is, the command of a ship rated lower than a frigate) before the War of the Austrian Succession ended in 1748, rather than having to wait until 1754. Promotion to post captain would have followed in a few years, with his flag coming before the outbreak of the American War. If he *had* been in command at the action, would the result have been different?

No one would claim that Hood was inferior to Graves in his ability to handle a fleet, though when he arrived in North America he still had a lot to prove. He would still have had a fleet that had not had time to operate together and to practice a common system of maneuvers. These were the factors that lowered the quality of the British fleet. Some individual ships may have been superior fighting units to their French opposite numbers—the performance of the *Princessa* and the *Intrepid* was outstanding—but as a whole the British fleet was made up of captains who did not know their commander or, in many cases, each other and it had two senior officers who had experience in different systems.

I think there is no doubt that Graves realized the shortcomings of his fleet and that he could not take risks with a precipitate attack in which all his captains might not understand his intentions. He had come from the Channel Fleet, the fleet in which the proponents of the new tactical ideas were most prominent, and he must have been familiar with the ideas then under discussion. His intention was to bring all of his fleet against part of the French. This intention was ruined by the actions of two officers who had come from the West Indies: the commander of the leading ship of the line, the *Shrewsbury*, who misunderstood the signal to engage the French ship opposite him to mean the leading ship of the French fleet, and the commander of the van squadron (albeit he was now in the rear of the fleet), Sir Samuel Hood!

Hood claimed for the rest of his life that the signal for the line was still flying from the *London*, Graves's flagship, so he could not bear down and attack the French without disobeying, and disregarding, the order for line of battle. There seems to have been no place in Hood's mind for the principle that he should put his ship alongside that of the enemy, the "Nelsonic" interpretation.

There are just two explanations for Hood's actions, even granting that the flag for the line was flying. First—and this is the case most commonly put forward—that he came from under the command of Rodney[5] and was used to a regime of complete obedience to the orders of the commander in chief, or, second, that he acted out of jealousy of Graves and was glad of the chance to see his plan of attack fail. The first scenario is now generally accepted as the more likely. Of all his virtues and vices as an admiral, the one quality that Hood prized most of all was duty. Duty to your king and country; duty to your superiors and duty to your subordinates. Given this belief, it is difficult to see Hood acting out of malice towards Graves on the day of the action, though his behavior afterwards is another matter.

Hood was one of the few officers to come out of the American War with his reputation enhanced. King George III thought highly of him, and he was able to share in the reflected glories of the Saintes, in which he played a significant part, as well as reaping glory from his own tactical masterpiece at St. Kitts. With Lord Howe[6] he became one of the most influential figures in the navy in the ten years following the end of the American War. To truly assess the position of Hood in the naval pantheon we must compare him to his two contemporaries (though both were senior to him in rank) Rodney and Howe.

Richard Howe, who was two years younger than Hood, had already held independent commands in the Seven Years' War. When the American War came, he was a natural selection for the North American station. Further, the Howes were a family with Whiggish sympathies at a time when the command structure was highly politicized—to such an extent that Richard, in accepting the naval command, was paired with his brother William as commander of the land forces. The two brothers also agreed to serve as peace commissioners in a final attempt to negotiate a settlement with the colonists. The idea did not work, and the dual role of the brothers was at cross-purposes with the desire of the government to seek a quick military solution. When Howe returned home in October 1778 he was offered both the position of first lord and the post of commander in chief of the Channel Fleet, a post for which he was well suited by talent and aptitude. He refused both, not for the political reasons that he implied had affected his decision but for personal reasons, one of which was the refusal of the government to bestow an honor on his brother.

He had, while on the American station, conducted a notable defensive campaign against the superior fleet of d'Estaing[7] and at the end of the war had carried out a successful relief of Gibraltar. The defensive nature of both these successes seemed to fit his persona. The dashing ship commander who had led the fleet into Quiberon Bay had become a defensive-minded admiral. After a spell at the Admiralty he commanded the Channel Fleet again at the commencement of the French Revolutionary Wars. He won the victory of the Glorious First of June, in which his idea was for the British ships to break through the French line and engage from the leeward. The victory was incomplete because most of the British ships did not achieve this position and the French were not pursued vigorously after the victory.

Howe was a favorite of the king and widely respected both in and out of the profession for his technical competence and his personal quality of undoubted courage. He was, unfortunately, convoluted in both his writing and his speech (he was a poor and infrequent speaker in Parliament) and often had great difficulty in making himself understood. Yet he was a favorite with the crews he commanded, and it was to Howe that the government turned when a figurehead was needed to persuade the suspicious mutineers at Spithead that all their grievances had been met.

Howe has to be judged on two fronts: his actions in the American War and the tactical plan for the First of June, and also his interest in signaling and tactics to improve the handling of his fleets. On these grounds he stands very high among British fleet commanders of the eighteenth century. But his declining the Channel command when offered in 1779 must remain a black mark against him. Howe was more interested in the "intellectual" side of his profession than Rodney or Hood, but he lacked the attacking flair shown by Rodney at the Moonlight Battle and by Hood at St. Kitts.

Where Hood is directly compared with Howe as a commander, he can be recognized as superior to his great contemporary by the incisiveness of his orders. As Nelson said, "His orders are so clear there is no misunderstanding them."[8] This intelligibility probably made Hood a more popular commander than Howe. He also stressed duty and was severe on those who failed in it. He court-martialled the first lieutenant of the *Nymphe* when she collided with the *Alfred* on the passage to St. Kitts. This side of his character did not make him universally popular. Cuthbert Collingwood, unlike his friend Nelson, did not admire Hood, believing that his ambitions exceeded his abilities. After his dismissal from his Mediterranean command, Lord Hugh Seymour told the First Lord of the Admiralty that many officers had expressed satisfaction that Hood had been brought to heel by the Admiralty.[9]

The commander with whom Hood is mostly associated was his immediate superior in the West Indies, Sir George Rodney. In Rodney there were marks of real ability, approaching genius. He had proved himself in more and more responsible positions in the Seven Years' War. His absence from Britain at the time of the French declaration of war in 1778 was due to debt: he had long been an inveterate gambler and was sheltering from his British creditors in France when war came. In a chivalrous gesture the duc de Biron paid all his debts in France so that Rodney could return to Britain to offer his services.

The government was hard pressed for commanders for the Channel Fleet following the resignation of Keppel. The veterans Sir Charles Hardy[10] and Francis Geary[11] had been given the command, and both had performed creditably. When Rodney arrived home, the command immediately available was in the Leeward Islands following the resignation of Hon. John Byron.[12] This command was offered and accepted but, given the suspicions concerning Rodney and the misuse of public money, an arrangement was put in place to prevent any recurrence.

Rodney's command started brilliantly. On his way to the relief of Gibraltar he intercepted and took a Spanish convoy and its escort and then destroyed the squadron of Lángara in the Moonlight Battle. His methods of command, however, showed what would now be called "zero tolerance" for his subordinates. When his first action against de Guichen at the battle of Martinique was unsuccessful owing to his captains' failure to understand his intentions, he undertook the task of drilling them into obedience and made the comment that to him was left the painful duty of thinking! It is this rigidity of command that is said to have affected Hood's failure to act on his own initiative at the Chesapeake.

As a commander Rodney took more ships than any other admiral during the American War. His victory at the Saintes, though not as complete as it might have been, enabled Britain to end the war on reasonable terms. He had been at his peak two years earlier in 1780 when his first engagement with de Guichen might have produced the much-wanted naval victory and altered the course of the war. In 1781 failing health and his preoccupation with St. Eustatius led to his decision to go home and not take his full force to North America—another critical decision with long-term consequences. He returned in 1782 to win the action at the Saintes as a finale to his career. His recall was a political action by Keppel but, as far as Rodney was concerned, his name had been made and there was nothing more he could have achieved had he stayed, as the fruitless chases of Hood and Pigot proved. Taken all in all, he was the best British commander of the war despite the blemishes of St. Eustatius.

Hood had great tactical ability, as witness St. Kitts and his abortive plan to destroy the squadron of Martin in the Mediterranean in 1794. He believed in prior consultation and discussion with his captains, in contrast to Rodney's school of obedience. However, once the operation was under way he would not tolerate failure any more than Rodney. He was not let down at St. Kitts; each captain knew what to do and adjusted his behavior to make sure the operation was a success. In his first action off Martinique he was learning his business and made no serious mistakes but, from a position of inferior numbers and (on the orders of Rodney) wrong location, he was unable to stop the French getting their convoy through to Port Royal.

On the downside of Hood, his published correspondence for the period of the West Indies campaign[13] reveals a carping and querulous character, with little regard for any opinion but his own. He was a dutiful subordinate to Rodney on the surface, but in his private correspondence he was undermining Rodney's reputation by his criticisms of his superior's actions. Perhaps this side of his character was already known in the service, which may account for Keppel's comment to Rodney following the appointment of Hood: "I wish you joy of Sir Samuel Hood! It is impossible for me to say more than that."[14] Although Keppel and Samuel Hood had worked apparently harmoniously during the fitting out of the fleet in 1778, since the

Keppel/Palliser affair Keppel had held a grudge against the Hood family for Alexander's evidence in favor of Palliser.

If we must chose the most influential and able British naval commanders of the eighteenth century, excluding the period of the French Revolutionary Wars, then two names stand out as supreme, Lord Anson[15] and Lord Hawke[16]—the former for his skills as navigator and administrator and the latter for his fleet command abilities including two crushing victories and the difficult task of the blockade of Brest. The commanders of the American War have to take their place below these illustrious predecessors in the scale of achievements.

The judgment on Hood must take into account the failure at the Chesapeake. In his final years he became, as Nelson described him, "the best officer . . . Britain has to boast of." In the Mediterranean in 1793–94 he managed that complex command competently despite his age, although at Toulon he was guilty of overoptimism that the port could be saved. On balance, on the basis of the American War only and given the fact that his lack of seniority denied him opportunities of chief command, he must be considered as below the level of Rodney but above that of Howe. A critical opinion on Hood is given by Brian Tunstall in his work on signaling and tactics. After admitting that "Hood's position as a tactician and signaller is difficult to determine," he says: "It is doubtful . . . if he was really interested in advanced tactical ideas."[17]

In this book I have followed Hood's career and shown how he handled the various commands he was given. He was a very good frigate captain and performed competently when he was a commodore on the North American station. As commissioner at Portsmouth he was able and dedicated, the qualities that had got him the post. Finally as a flag officer he had the good fortune to serve on a station where he could expect to be involved in more action than might have been his lot elsewhere. I have given the full story of Hood's actions at a critical moment for his country in order that an assessment might be made on how culpable he was for the final failure and the results that arose from it.

HOOD'S EARLY CAREER

Samuel Hood came from a long-established Dorset family with their roots in South Perrott and Mosterton in the southwest of England. The family had farmed there in the time of Henry VIII. His father, also Samuel, was vicar of Butleigh, a village in Somerset near Glastonbury. It was here that Samuel Hood was born in December 1724, though some sources give his birthplace as Thornecombe, a nearby village.[1]

It was unusual for the firstborn son of the family to be sent into the navy, with the dangers attendant on such a career. For the eldest son of a clergyman, a career in the Church would likely have been in prospect. The eventual decision of both Samuel and his brother Alexander to go to sea has been explained by the fact that their father offered shelter to Captain Thomas Smith,[2] illegitimate son of Lord Lyttelton, when the latter's carriage broke down on the way to London. This story is unprovable, and the more plausible explanation is that the Hood brothers entered the service under the patronage of the Grenville family, the local lords of the manor.[3] They did, however, first go to sea with Smith in the *Romney* (50 guns).[4]

Alexander left home first, in January 1741, but it was only four months before Samuel followed him. The navy was the only profession for which neither money nor influence was required to enter. At that time the quarterdeck was open to all men of ability, even from the lower deck.[5]

The Hood boys were under the patronage of Captain Smith in the same manner as Nelson later benefited from the patronage of Captain Maurice Suckling. The navy that the two brothers joined in 1741 would have represented something of a culture shock for sons of a country parson, who had to get used to lack of privacy, a rougher diet, cramped conditions, and the constraints of being the newest-joined among the *Romney*'s "young gentlemen."

On the *Romney* they were better off than they would have been on a larger ship. Although nominally rated a ship of the line, the *Romney* was now considered too lightly armed to serve in the line of battle. In such a small ship the newcomers had a closer relationship with the officers and warrant officers who were to teach them their trade. Their quarters were more confined than on a larger ship, and they had to accommodate themselves to sharing with a number of boys with the same ambitions. By the standards of the time, Samuel Hood was relatively old at sixteen to enter the navy. If he had joined at the more common age of twelve or thirteen, he would have had the opportunity of being made master and commander, perhaps even post captain, before the end of the War of the Austrian Succession in 1748. This loss of early years was to prove critical when it came to the question of command of the British fleet on the fifth of September, 1781.

With the country at war and with a powerful patron, there was no limit to what the future promised. The connection with Smith brought the Hood boys into contact with the Pitt family. They both formed friendships with William Pitt the Elder and later with his son. It was the friendship of the younger Pitt that is said to have kept Alexander Hood, by then Lord Bridport, as commander in chief of the Channel Fleet when by age and ability he was no longer fitted for the post.

The *Romney*'s first duty was to escort trade to Newfoundland, where Smith had been appointed governor. Thus very early in his career Hood was to become acquainted with the coast of North America. In 1742 the *Romney* returned home and was sent to the Mediterranean under Captain Thomas Grenville,[6] a promising officer who was later killed at the first battle of Finisterre. When Hood was transferred to the *Sheerness* (24) in 1743, he met George Rodney for the first time. The ship operated around the coast of Britain and in the mouth of the Channel in a time of rising invasion fever, with the Jacobites expected to land with French support.

In June 1746 Samuel Hood was promoted to lieutenant and appointed to the *Winchelsea* (24), and it was in this ship that he first saw action. The *Winchelsea* pursued and took the French frigate *Subtile* (26) in the mouth of the Channel. During this engagement Hood suffered, as far as can be traced, the only wound in his whole career, when his hand was gashed by a splinter. In February 1748 he gained appointment as third lieutenant of the *Greenwich* (50), quickly followed by a transfer to the *Lion* (60). Smith used his influence to obtain this post for Hood with Rear Admiral Charles Watson,[7] who was going as governor to Newfoundland. Watson was impressed by Hood and became another of his patrons until his death in India in 1757. Hood returned to England with the end of the war and came ashore on 24 January 1749.

With the peace Hood married Susannah Linzee of Portsmouth in August

1749. Susannah's father, Edward Linzee, was several times mayor of Portsmouth and a prominent figure that the Admiralty had to reckon with in its desire to "manage" the borough. This would give Hood further leverage in the struggle to obtain appointments in the service.

Having to support a wife and family (his first son was born in 1753), Hood was glad to be appointed to the guard ship *Invincible* (74), a French prize whose design was much copied by the British.

Much as he may have appreciated duty on a Portsmouth guard ship, what he needed to advance his career was a promotion to master and commander. At one time he had a chance of going as a lieutenant to the East Indies with Sir Charles Watson, with the promise of a subsequent transfer into a vacancy as a commander, but in the end it did not come about. Thomas Smith had also been talked about for the command, but he told Hood that if he was appointed he would not take Hood with him. In saying this, Smith was probably aware that influence at the Admiralty was to be brought to bear to get Hood the next vital step on the ladder. Hood's hopes were raised by the appointment of George Grenville, the brother of Hood's late captain Thomas Grenville, as treasurer of the navy. Soon after, his commission as commander of the *Jamaica* (14) was issued.

There is some debate over whether Hood's appointments to the guard ships and then the *Jamaica* were attributable to his "influence" with the Grenvilles or to his marrying into the Linzee family who, as part of the powerful local authority in Portsmouth, had to be accommodated to keep them "friends" to the Admiralty.[8] The choice of Susannah Linzee as his wife was a good one for Hood, and though he may have entered into it looking for assistance in his professional advancement, it soon became a love match on both sides.

Hood had to make his own way to the ship, which was on the other side of the Atlantic. The *Jamaica* had been detached just before he arrived on the station, to take troops to Virginia. He finally boarded his new command on 1 September 1754.

Amid fears of a war with the French, various reinforcements were sent to the North American station, and many captains who later rose to be flag officers in the American War were gathered in Hampton Roads: Keppel,[9] Barrington,[10] Palliser,[11] Arbuthnot,[12] and Hood. Keppel was the senior officer of the squadron.

A British squadron under Boscawen[13] cruised off the coasts of Newfoundland hoping to intercept French reinforcements. Although fog hampered the operation and only two French ships were taken. Boscawen's ac-

tion succeeded in provoking a formal declaration of war.   The *Jamaica* too
was at the seat of the action. While stationed at Halifax, Hood—who had
been promoted to post captain on 27 July 1756, though the news had yet to
arrive from England—took part in a creditable action at Cape Breton Island
under the command of Commodore Charles Holmes.[14] Holmes's ships were
engaged in cruising off the French fortress of Louisbourg, which was under
siege by the British, to stop supplies or reinforcements getting in. On 27 July
a cluster of sails were sighted and were identified as two line-of-battle ships
and two frigates. The British were inferior in gun power, and the French,
under the command of Captain de Beaussier de l'Isle, had the windward
gauge. When the French bore down on the British, Hood diverted the attention of the two frigates and was able to escape from them, despite the lack
of wind, by rowing, something possible in a small ship like the *Jamaica*. The
ship suffered only minor damage to her masts and rigging.

After the action was over, Holmes called Hood to the quarterdeck of the
Grafton to thank him publicly. Being as yet unaware of the captain's commission already in existence, Holmes offered Hood the command of the
Grafton when the ship returned to Britain in the near future, and Hood was
home by 13 December 1756. Now a post captain, Hood was on the ladder to
flag rank in which longevity would bring him to the top.

When his biography was published in the *Naval Chronicle* in 1799, his
then secretary John McArthur remarked on how fortunate Hood had been
in the patrons who were his role models as he developed his career. Smith
and Watson were both excellent and conscientious officers who put the service and the country before anything else. It was Smith, it has been claimed,
who imparted to Hood his willingness to sacrifice prize money for the good
of the service.[15]

THE FRIGATE CAPTAIN

The appointment as post captain brought Samuel Hood to one of the most active and successful phases of his professional career. His return coincided with the court-martial of Admiral John Byng, about to take place at Portsmouth.

Admiral Smith was president of the court-martial. This appointment in itself gave rise to suspicions that the government was determined to get a conviction. Thomas Smith, with his close government ties, was considered unlikely to bring the necessary impartiality to the proceedings.

The court-martial may have been an unfortunate time for Byng, but for Hood, freshly arrived in the *Grafton*, it presented a golden opportunity. He had no desire to be "idle ashore" and wrote to the Admiralty offering to command any of the ships whose captains were involved in the trial. His connections still worked for him. Although Thomas Grenville had been killed in 1747, his brother Lord Temple was First Lord of the Admiralty in 1756–57 and Lord Privy Seal from 1758 to 1761. Alexander Hood was to marry Molly West, a distant relation of William Pitt, who was now secretary of state for war. All would be useful to the brothers in securing commands.

The trial of Byng began on 28 December 1756 and lasted a month, the verdict of guilty being given on 27 January 1757. After the trial Smith wrote to the Admiralty, enclosing the verdict of the court and a letter, signed by every member of the court, asking the Admiralty to intercede with the king for clemency. This appeal, like all others, was unsuccessful. Byng was to die, partly for his own professional failings but largely as a public example on whom the government could lay the blame for the loss of Minorca. Byng was executed on 14 March 1757 on the quarterdeck of the *Monarch*. This thoroughly shabby episode was redeemed only by the loyalty of Byng's friends and by the courage of Byng himself, who comported himself bravely through the weeks of appeals and met death calmly when it came.

Meanwhile, Hood had secured his first temporary command in place of an officer involved in the court-martial. He was appointed to the *Torbay* (74), Augustus Keppel's ship, then to the frigate *Tartar* (28), and finally to the *Antelope* (50) as a temporary replacement for the ship's permanent captain, Thomas Saumarez.[1] Hood's orders were to cruise in the mouth of the Channel and watch for French ships, either outward or homeward bound. He sailed on the thirtieth of April, the very day he took command.

On 14 May three sails were sighted, and again Hood's vessel took up the chase. As the British closed, they were able to identify the three ships as French men of war, which, with the *Antelope* approaching, hoisted French colors. Hood had not yet hoisted British colors, but the French can have been in no doubt about the nationality of the warship bearing down on them. At 1:30 p.m. the largest of the French ships hoisted a pennant and ensign and fired a gun to leeward, presumably as a signal to her companions. Shortly after, she fired another gun to leeward. The three French ships came round and bore down on the *Antelope*. As the French had apparently decided to begin the action, Hood hoisted British colors. Before the French came within gun range they altered course, bearing up before the wind with the *Antelope* in pursuit. The two smaller vessels then parted company with the larger one and steered to make their escape.

The *Antelope* gained on the larger ship, and by 4:00 p.m. Hood was within point-blank range. The *Antelope* had been under fire from stern chase guns for the last part of the pursuit. Hood's opponent was the frigate *Aquilon* (50), a close match for the *Antelope*. He ordered the gunners to hold their fire as both ships raced under full sail, with the British slowly closing. The combatants were heading towards the French coast, which would be dangerous if the action should prove of long duration with both ships on a lee shore.

At 4:20 p.m. Hood gave the order to fire. The French replied, and the exchange continued for just over an hour. By this time both ships were well into Audierne Bay and advancing deeper with every minute. If they continued on the same course for much longer, both would strike the rocks.

Hood put his ship about, and his seamanship saved the *Antelope*. The *Aquilon*, with less room to maneuver, was wrecked. Hood brought his ship to, then set sail and steered out of the bay. He wanted sea room in which to be able to inspect the damage and carry out repairs. These did not amount to much, for the French had been firing high in hopes of disabling the *Antelope*. Once the rigging was repaired, Hood took his ship back into the bay to see what he could do about the *Aquilon*. He found that the French ship had driven over the rocks in her flight and now lay in the water beyond. She had lost her mizzenmast, and it was obvious she was doomed. When last seen, she was firing distress signals.

The engagement had ended decisively in favor of the British. The *Antelope* had lost 3 killed and 11 wounded. The French losses were later reported as 30 killed and 25 wounded.

Hood also took a French privateer that had been with the *Aquilon*. He returned to Spithead on the first of June to undergo repairs, and on the fifth he handed the ship back to Saumarez and went ashore.

The successes of his cruise pleased the Admiralty, and he was appointed to the *Bideford* (20) and ordered to join Hawke with the Western Squadron off Brest. Hawke was to prevent the French fleet from leaving or supplies and reinforcements getting in. The frigates were to look into Brest to watch the movements of the French fleet and intercept the coastal vessels trying to reach the ports in the bay.

Hood's next command was the 32-gun *Vestal*, which he did not find in good condition for such a new ship. He told the Admiralty that she was "two months foul" and had thirty men sick on shore or on hospital Ships.

Hawke sailed from Portsmouth in March without any frigates or sloops, as none were in a condition to leave with him. At Plymouth he expected to pick up further ships, including the *Vestal*, but again he found none ready to join him. He left orders for these ships to follow as soon as possible and sailed for his station. The *Vestal* reached him before his decisive attack in the Basque Roads.

Hawke, having intelligence that a French expedition to Canada was about to sail, took his ships to the Basque Roads, where he found five of the line, together with seven frigates and a convoy of forty merchantmen containing about 3,000 troops. He decided on instant attack. As the British came down, the merchantmen began to cut their cables to get the ships closer to shore or even up the river Charente. The French warships made for Rochefort, but the tide was not suitable and the ships ended up stranded, unable to move until the tide changed.

The following morning revealed a chaotic scene. Hawke too had to wait until the tide turned before another attack could be considered. Once the water was deep enough, he sent his two smallest ships of the line with the best pilots to see just what could be done.

The French had tried to get their ships afloat again and warped closer inshore to protect them from attack. Everything that could be jettisoned was thrown overboard, guns and stores and even ballast, in order to reach safety in the Charente. Some of the warships, however, and many of the merchantmen were still open to attack, with the latter in particular lying on their sides with their bottoms exposed. Hawke had done enough to ensure that the French would not be sailing for North America before the British force had got safely away. By this time the state of the tide had forced Hawke to withdraw his force, effectively bringing the operation to a close, but the following day he destroyed the fortifications on the Ile d'Aix.

The attack on the Basque Roads had been facilitated by the combined operation carried out the previous year by Hawke and Sir John Morduant in charge of the troops. The objective had been an attack on Rochefort. This had misfired, but the fortifications on the Ile d'Aix had been destroyed by Howe in the *Magnanime*, leaving the roadstead open to the sort of attack that Hawke now carried out.

The success Hawke achieved was second only to his victory at Quiberon Bay. He had been willing to hazard the fleet for the purpose of destroying the French squadron. Hood might have noted that boldness was rewarded. The French setback completely disrupted their operations in Canada and eventually led to the total loss of French Canada.

The *Vestal* was back in Plymouth before much longer, and was still there to see in the year 1759, the annus mirabilis of the war in which the British seized the advantages offered by sea power and destroyed French colonial and naval power. Two sea battles went decisively in favor of the British, the threat of invasion was lifted, and French Canada was laid wide open to final conquest.

At the start of the year, invasion was an immediate problem. By this means the French thought to retrieve a situation that was turning out disastrous to them. They believed that the situation of the '45 could be replayed, a landing of French forces and cooperation with Jacobite sympathizers, and that this would be enough to bring Britain to the negotiating table. With French forces holding some of the British homeland, the British would cede their colonial conquests to achieve the withdrawal of the French.

The British were well aware of this threat and were manning every possible ship to deal with it. At the same time, they continued with their own offensive plans for the Far East and North America. Sir Charles Saunders[2] was to command the naval element for the offensive in North America in partnership with James Wolfe.

The whole of these offensive operations—indeed the whole future of the war—hung on the safety of the British mainland, and this in turn depended on the supremacy of the Channel Fleet. There was also a squadron in the Downs commanded by Thomas Smith, now carrying out his last duty at sea, and the newly promoted Rear Admiral Rodney was cruising with a squadron off Normandy with a particular brief to watch the ports on that coast for invasion preparations.

Hood was ordered to join the force under Rear Admiral Holmes, which was the advance guard for Saunders and Wolfe in North America. The force consisted of six line-of-battle ships and eight frigates including the *Vestal*. In addition, there were sixty-two transports to be escorted across the Atlantic.

The *Vestal* was sent to scout ahead of the main body, and on the morning of 21 February a strange sail was sighted. Hood signaled the sighting to Holmes but was unable to say whether the ship was French. Holmes ordered the *Vestal* to close with the stranger and make positive identification, but it was nearly midday before Hood was able to identify the ship as a French frigate.

The *Vestal* was by now some way ahead of the main body, and Holmes sent the *Trent*, another fast-sailing frigate, in support. The two frigates set off in pursuit, with the *Vestal* leading and proving the faster sailer. Before long the rest of the squadron were lost to sight. By 2:30 p.m. Hood was within pistol shot of his opponent and was able to see that the French ship was the *Bellone*, which also mounted 32 guns.

The action started soon afterwards and lasted for nearly four hours. Like the engagements with the *Aquilon* and the *Subtile*, this was a chase action. The *Vestal* suffered damage in her rigging, with the French firing high. By the end of the engagement the British ship had only her lower masts standing, the log recording that all the running rigging with the exception of the main braces had been shot away. The fire of the *Vestal* had been even more effective, and by 5:55 the French frigate was forced to strike. The main mast and mizzenmast had gone, and the fore-topmast went overboard soon after. The French had lost 40 men killed, the *Vestal* 5 killed and 22 wounded. The credit for the victory belongs entirely to Hood, for the *Trent* was still four miles off when the *Bellone* struck.

The damage to the *Vestal*'s rigging caused her own main and mizzen topmasts to fall when she was brought to after the action to secure her prize. Hood set parties of seamen to repair the damages to his ship, and he sent his first lieutenant to take possession of the *Bellone*.

The state of the rigging prevented the *Vestal* from continuing with Holmes's squadron, and Hood was ordered to return home with his prize, thereby losing the chance of being associated with the capture of Quebec. He had, however, fought another successful frigate action, which could only reinforce his reputation within the service. After repairs the *Bellone* was taken into the Royal Navy as the *Repulse*. And when Hood was next in London, Anson took him to a levee and introduced him to the king.

The commander of the French frigate is of note. He was the comte de Beauharnais, one of a well-established and aristocratic Martinique family. His son, a general, was later to marry a lady called Joséphine Tascher de la Pagerie, also of an old Martinique family. After her husband was executed during the French Revolutionary period of terror, she married Napoleon Bonaparte, who was to figure very prominently in the last stage of Hood's career.

Following repairs the *Vestal* was briefly with the Western Squadron. Hawke gave her the task of looking into the Biscay ports to see what movements the French were making.

The Admiralty recalled Hood from this duty and ordered him to join Rodney, who had been given command of a squadron of frigates and small vessels to attack the French invasion forces at the port of Havre. The reports of the preparations being made at Havre alarmed the government. The threat was taken seriously, and the invasion craft were to be destroyed. The size and composition of the British force was quickly decided.[3] The work of destruction was to be done by bomb vessels. Normal gunfire would not be effective in the circumstances, and a combined operation with troops landed to carry out the destruction was not practicable, given the lack of troops, transports, and time.

Rodney, although only five years older than Hood, had now gained flag rank while Hood was only halfway up the Captains List—a good example of what the right contacts allied with professional ability could do. Rodney's squadron for the task consisted of one 60-gun ship (*Achilles*, flag), four 50-gun ships, five frigates, one sloop, and six bomb vessels. A galaxy of naval talent was in the force, including Barrington, Hyde Parker,[4] George Darby,[5] Samuel Hood, and Thomas Graves.

The utmost secrecy was imposed regarding the destination of the squadron. The fact that a force was being assembled could not be hidden, but rumors were circulated to the effect that it was bound for Gibraltar. The Admiralty even wrote false orders to this effect. The deception seems to have succeeded, for the French at Havre took no extra precautions against an attack.

Preparations for the attack required that information on the Normandy coast be available. Officers in the force with experience of the area were asked to send their observations. Reliance would have to be placed on pilots to get the ships into position. To recruit pilots experienced in the navigation of the area would mean inquiring in the maritime community for such expertise—a fact that would make it difficult to believe the official story that the force was bound for Gibraltar!

The Admiralty ordered Rodney to send two frigates to blockade Havre while at the same time taking soundings of the inshore waters in which the bomb vessels would have to operate. The *Vestal* was one of these ships. The work was partly done out of gun range of the French shore defenses, and in the port there were no French ships big enough to interfere. The inshore work had to be done within range of the French guns, but an ingenious method was devised that rendered the French powerless to intervene. Seizing a Dutch merchant ship leaving the port, the British put a party of sailors on board and continued with their vital work uninterrupted. The French were reluctant to fire on a neutral. Eventually they got off some warning shots, but it was too late and the work was finished. Hood is tentatively credited with the conception of this ruse.[6]

The need for speed was great. It was known that the preparation of the invasion craft was well advanced and that some had already been tried out at sea with good results. A final delay was imposed on the expedition when the *Blast* found that some work done by the dockyard had been badly carried out and had to be redone. This completed, only the *Carcass* and the *Mortar* were missing, still en route from the Thames.

On 3 July 1759 Rodney anchored off Havre Roads. The larger ships were anchored furthest out, the frigates closer in, and the bomb vessels still closer. Havre was fortified in the classical manner of Vauban with ramparts, a moat, and outworks. The entrance to the inner harbor lay between two moles. For ships to sail in was too hazardous, hence the use of bomb vessels. The targets were not only the vessels in the harbor but the stores of wood, rope, and other items massed along the quays. So hectic had been the construction of the invasion craft that the builders were forced to construct them on the beaches outside the town, which made a good target for the British force.

The defenses of the town precluded an attack by land. The strong garrison was ample protection against a landing. The French, however, lacked long-range artillery to impede the British force in its preparations and during the attack. The British therefore had unobstructed use of the waters outside the harbor and could place the bomb vessels without interference by French fire.

The placing of these vessels was critical to the success of the attack. The advice of the artillery officers, serving as specialists with the fleet, was that they should be moored right up against a shoal known as the *banc de jambe*, which presented navigational and operational dangers. The pilots with the squadron were unwilling to risk stranding a ship on the shoal and thereby disrupting the operation. Rodney called a conference of the captains on board his flagship, the upshot of which was that Captains Hollwall (and his first lieutenant), Hood, and Phillips (captain of the *Juno*) all volunteered to place the bomb vessels where they were wanted.

The first bomb vessels, the *Basilisk* and the *Firedrake*, were in position by late evening of the third of July, and some ranging shots were fired. These fell short, and during the night the vessels were moved closer. By midnight the Portsmouth bomb vessels *Firedrake*, *Basilisk*, *Blast*, and *Furnace* were in position, the *Furnace* being nearest to the edge of the shoal. During the night the *Carcass* and the *Mortar* arrived. At daylight the British opened fire, with the two late arrivals taking up their assigned positions as the bombardment continued.

Rodney went on board the *Vestal* to get a better view of the proceedings and to see the effect of the French counterfire. The latter he noted as "pretty brisk," but as yet it had not caused any significant damage to the attacking vessels. Generally the French fire was ineffective, for the British mortars were beyond its range. French reports received by the Admiralty indicated that the bomb vessels were firing one shell every fifteen minutes, a considerable rate of fire for this type of weapon. The initial attack was directed at the vessels being built on the beach. Once these were disposed of, the target was switched to the warehouses, the harbor, and the town beyond.

As evening came on, the bomb vessels began to feel the effects of the prolonged bombardment. The vibration caused to the vessels and to the mortar mountings by continuous firing was taking its toll, and slowly the fire slackened. Each vessel had two mortars, so the fourth of July had commenced with twelve mortars firing, but at the end of the day only seven were still operable, and by midnight of 5-6 July the last of the bomb vessels fell silent. Opposition had been negligible. Considerable damage had been caused, and the invasion preparations had received a serious setback.[7]

Rodney rehoisted his flag on the *Achilles* and reported the success of the operation to the Admiralty. Hood was to take the letter to London.

The *Vestal* returned to operations in the Channel, but Hood had no part in the action at Quiberon Bay on 20 November in which Hawke removed any fear of invasion once and for all.

At this time Hood seems to have been suffering ill health and strain from his years of service. The doctors he consulted recommended a warmer climate. He wrote to the Admiralty asking for such a posting for the good of his health. He does not seem to have considered the other possibility: coming ashore for a period of sick leave at home to recover.

The Admiralty gave him orders to join the squadron of Vice Admiral Saunders, who was about to sail for the Mediterranean. Alexander Hood with the *Minerva* (32) was already attached to the squadron. Saunders and his force sailed in April 1760 before the *Vestal* was ready for sea, and it was not until 14 May that Hood followed.

Because Spain had remained neutral, the Mediterranean had not been the scene of any significant action since Byng's ill-fated engagement off Minorca in May 1756. The navy did not really feel the loss of Minorca, as there were no operations to conduct. In 1759 Boscawen had been given the command and had pursued a French force making its escape from Toulon and defeated it at Lagos Bay on 18 August 1759. After the victory there was no longer a need for a large force in the Mediterranean. The new commander, Brodrick, had now to include Cadiz in his responsibilities, for although the Spanish were not yet in the war, the remnants of the French squadron defeated at Lagos Bay were sheltering there. Only when Brodrick was driven off by a storm were the French able to get out and return to Toulon. This was the situation when Saunders arrived to take up the command.

Hood was given a commission in the Levant where there were important British trading interests to protect. He had the task of drawing charts of the various ports he visited. Such work was often carried out to build up a record for future use and to update existing information. The results of his work in the survey field are preserved among his papers in the National Maritime Museum.

Although both were serving in the Mediterranean, Samuel and Alexander did not get a chance to meet until early in 1763 when, by chance, they were both moored in Gibraltar Bay and Samuel invited his brother to dine in the *Vestal*. Apart from family and professional matters, the conversation might very well have included comments on the prospects for peace. The war had been successful for the British. The objectives of Pitt had been largely achieved, and France was looking for an honorable exit from the war.

The chances of peace were much increased by the fact that Pitt no longer held any position in the government. He had resigned over the question of a preemptive strike against Spain. The new king, George III, was keen to end the war and to enjoy the fruits of peace. Without Pitt the government, now headed by Lord Bute,[8] put out feelers to France. Negotiations took place, and the Peace of Paris was signed in February 1763. It was a good treaty for Britain, but many of the conquests were returned to the Bourbon powers, including those, like Manila, that had taken place after the signing of the pact. The French government felt that they had been humiliated and looked forward to the first opportunity to reverse the position. An active policy of reform of the French administration under the duc de Choiseul[9] prepared the country for resumption of the struggle.

Hood returned home soon after the meeting with Alexander when news of the Peace reached them. By April 1763 the ship had been paid off and he was ashore without employment.

THE COMMODORE

Hood was not immediately offered a further command after the war. He could not live comfortably off his own means and could not therefore contemplate for long a life on half-pay. He asked for an appointment to one of the guard ships at Portsmouth and was appointed to the *Thunderer* (74). As a frigate captain he had gained two victories without excessive casualties on his own side, demonstrating seamanship and determination. He had earned the good opinions of Hawke, Saunders, Holmes, Rodney, and Keppel. He was, however, still short of those precious years of seniority that would be so vital later in his career.

Promotion to flag rank was the goal of all post captains, though some achieved it only by being "yellowed"—that is, placed on the Retired List. There was to be only one promotion to flag rank in the period between the end of the Seven Years' War in 1763 and the beginning of the American War in 1775. This took place in 1770 and promoted to their flags the post captains of 1745–46. As Hood's seniority as a post captain dated only from 1756, it is obvious that, barring some special circumstance, he would have to wait a further ten years at least for his turn to come around.

At this period Lord Chatham was prime minister and had chosen Hawke as First Lord of the Admiralty. At Portsmouth Edward Linzee was chosen mayor again in 1766 and put pressure on the Admiralty to find a place for Hood.[1] Chatham suggested to Hawke that Hood, with the temporary rank of commodore, be made commissioner at Halifax. Hawke had no objection, and in April 1767 the appointment was agreed. With his naval patrons now all dead, the political contacts that Hood had with the Grenvilles and Lytteltons as well as the position of his father-in-law at Portsmouth were useful to his continuing employment.

This appointment would turn out to be the most difficult he had yet faced. Relations between Britain and its American colonies were strained at this time over the principle of "No taxation without representation." In Britain the dispute was seen from the opposite end of the spectrum, as a challenge by the colonists to the supremacy of Parliament and the constitution arising from the Glorious Revolution of 1688. In addition, the displeasure of the American merchant classes over the operation of the Navigation Act, which was costing them money, fermented an atmosphere of discontent. It is alleged that one of the later radicals, James Otis, took the path he did only because Governor Bernard did not appoint him to a lucrative position under the Crown.[2] The possibility of actual hostilities between the colonists and Britain was still unthinkable for most people on both sides. There was an element in the colonies, however, that saw the future differently and wanted complete independence from Britain.

Hood proceeded to Portsmouth on receipt of his orders and went on board the *Romney* on 9 April 1767. Among his retinue was his eldest son, Henry, aged fourteen.[3] This was to be Henry's one and only time at sea, At its conclusion he went ashore for good in 1770 and would later enter the army when his father purchased a commission as a cornet in the dragoons. Hood does not seem to have made any effort to persuade his son to remain in the service. A much younger recruit was his cousin, Alexander Hood,[4] who was only nine-and-a-half years old as he took his first steps in the service. To look after these two youngsters Samuel took his wife Susannah with him. As a commodore he had a residence on shore, and his wife would be his hostess for the social occasions that such a post entailed.

Also with Hood was John Linzee,[5] on whose behalf Hood had intervened with the Admiralty in trying to get his commission as lieutenant confirmed. Linzee's commission had been granted by Sir Piercy Brett during the war but not confirmed by a later board. Now that Brett was a Lord of the Admiralty, further application was likely to get a sympathetic reception, and in fact John's confirmation took little more than a year. Also serving as a lieutenant on board was Robert Linzee,[6] brother of John.

The *Romney* made a good passage, and on 5 July land was sighted at Cape Samborough to the northwest. Shortly afterwards the ship stood into Halifax harbor to be greeted with a salute of thirteen guns.[7]

British naval power in the area was at a low ebb and in fact remained so for the duration of Hood;s command. It has been pointed out[8] that the number of ships on the North American station had been steadily declining since the end of the war. In the period 1763–66 the navy had maintained 41 ships on the station, down from the wartime peak but still respectable. In the years of Hood's command the number of ships shrunk by 17 percent down to 34 ships. Apart from the flagship of the commodore, these were mostly ships of the smaller class—frigates, sloops, and schooners. These types of vessels were very useful, but there was never enough of them. The government's watchword was retrenchment, the pursuit of which had led to the present difficulties with the colonists.

The principal task of the navy was to work in conjunction with the civil authorities to enforce the laws passed by Parliament on trade and revenues. This particularly meant the suppression of smuggling, which was widespread and tacitly accepted by the American traders as the only way to make a profit. All seizures were to be shared between the Crown and the officers and crews of the vessels that made the capture. One-quarter of the Crown's share went to the commander of the ships and vessels on the North American station.

Previously the colonial officials had also been given a share of the prize. As they now felt some antagonism towards the navy for taking their share, the prosecution of apprehended smugglers grew. Before long the merchants began to offer bribes to naval officers to turn a blind eye to smuggling. Along the coastline of North America the navy became an object of hatred for those whose lives were affected by its anti-smuggling activities or those who saw it used towards the unjust imposition of an illegal tax.

Hood's first inspection of his command revealed that the standards maintained by the base were a good deal lower than he was prepared to tolerate. The dilapidation of some buildings was obvious, and he ordered a survey made of the "Wharfs and other Buildings in His Majesty's Careen Yard." Equally important to the efficient running of the yard, he needed to know the resources available for maintaining the ships of war stationed there and the sources of supply. He therefore ordered a further check of the stock of all masts held by the yard. He suspected, quite rightly, that many of them would be rotten and unfit for further service.

The situation was so serious, he informed the Admirality, that not a single plank of oak was held in the yard. This he ascribed to "the various accidents that have befallen the Saw Mills in this Province." The dockyard officers had been purchasing the oak in "driblets" to "the manifest disadvantage of the Crown." It is a damning commentary on the administration of the dockyard that, in a continent where large tracts were covered in forests, the storehouses should be short of timber.

Hawke, in his position as First Lord of the Admiralty, was to try to tackle the problem of timber reserves, but as with every natural product, there was no easy solution. The huge increase in naval construction for the last war had severely drained the available sources of supply. Now the growing size of merchantmen was also calling for the special timbers that had once been the sole province of naval construction. With oak the favored material for ship-building, the problem would only get worse until alternative sources of oak could be found. To rely on foreign supplies would involve a risk very similar to that taken by the Admiralty before 1914 when the decision was made to convert the battle fleet from burning home-produced coal to burning imported oil.

In the eighteenth century the naval dockyards were a byword for corruption and inefficiency both in Britain and abroad. The navy, especially in bases abroad, was at the mercy of local contractors who did not hesitate to supply poor-quality supplies, especially food, to the fleet and to ensure that profits remained high. In Halifax these men controlled the local timber supplies and dictated the prices the dockyard would pay. Previous naval commissioners had had to deal with these men, for it was difficult to arrange another source of supply. Samuel Hood faced the same obstacle, a monopoly on timber supplies by contractors operating a price ring that ensured high profits.[9]

When Hood turned his attention to the neglected state of the dockyard buildings, he found the ravages of weather compounded by a lack of money spent on repairs over the years. Instead of hiring labor on a casual basis to complete the work, he engaged six bricklayers and masons and three laborers to carry out the work and entered them on the dockyard books as full-time employees. Hood was thus able to keep a check on the time they spent on the upkeep of the dockyard buildings and ensure that the men gave value for money and that the work was carried out in a regular and efficient manner. The Admiralty did not, unfortunately, supply him with the funds to keep the men permanently on the public payroll. When the job was completed they had to be discharged, but at least the saving over the previous method of hiring contract labor had been demonstrated.

Hood was looking at his surroundings with the eyes of practiced realism. He was not new to this area of the world and would have been aware of the struggle that the province faced to survive. He had already pinpointed one major shortcoming, the poor state of communications, that hindered further development. What was needed was a source of regular income. Unlike the American colonies further down the coast, Nova Scotia was not economically advanced and did not have a sound trade base to provide it with the means of improvement. The province needed British government money, or private investment, to help develop its potential. The chances of the former in a time of retrenchment were small; only the funds necessary to maintain the naval and military forces in the area would be provided. British merchants and bankers with money to lend could be expected to choose the more obvious area for profit, the American colonies, rather than make a long-term investment in the future of Nova Scotia.[10]

The events in America were to largely occupy Hood's time on this station. He had the responsibility of maintaining the naval presence on the seaboard of the American colonies, and he was subject to calls for reinforcements which were a constant drain on his resources. The most hard pressed of the local British officials, and the most frequent callers for naval assistance, were the commissioners of customs, who went in fear of reprisals for their pressure on smuggling. Purely naval problems also loomed large in Hood's priorities. To run his command efficiently he had to have a repair and replacement policy. Wooden ships were frequently in need of repair, particularly those built in the emergency wartime building program, where unseasoned wood had been used. Many of the ships on the station were in urgent need of the services of a fully equipped dockyard. In earlier years these ships had often been sent to New York, killing two birds with one stone, as the ships could be available between repairs to assist in the anti-smuggling patrols the navy carried out. This policy was found to be flawed, and it was decided to order such ships back to Britain during the winter months. Weather conditions were so hostile then, with ice forming, that active operations were not possible. If the repairs proceeded smoothly, the ships could be back in service by spring.

On receipt of the order to return three ships to Britain, Hood informed the Admiralty that as soon as their services could be dispensed with he would send them home. In the meantime, for the good of the service and to assist the commissioners of customs at New York, he would direct the sloop at New York to be stationed at Sandy Hook, which, in a report to the Admiralty in December 1767, he called "by no means a bad roadstead for a frigate … the key to New York."[11] The commander of this sloop would have an armed sloop or a schooner under his orders. It was also arranged that another sloop, the *Hope*, would spend the winter at Boston and a third, the *Senegal* (14), at Rhode Island.

In accordance with normal procedure, Samuel Hood reported to the Admiralty the force available to him at Halifax—that is, the ships immediately under his command as opposed to those stationed at various points along the American seaboard. The list at this time shows the type of ships that his force comprised:[12]

Romney (50)
Mermaid (28)

Glasgow (20)
Viper (12)
Beaver (14)
Gaspee (schooner)
St. Lawrence (schooner)

The *Romney*, then, was the only ship of significant force on the station. Apart from the two frigates, the vessels were small ones needed for anti-smuggling work. The schooners were the smallest vessels under his command, and there was a pressing need for such craft. But the Admiralty, under pressure to reduce costs, refused to send additional vessels of this type to the station. Without them, the operations against smuggling could never be effective, and the navy was less successful after 1767 than before. Hood was forced to tackle the problem by purchasing vessels locally and bringing them into service.

The vessel allotted to the post at Sandy Hook was the *Viper*. Although serving further down the coast than her home base, the ship was still subject to the vagaries of the climate. While she was moored off Sandy Hook, a local pilot thought she would be at risk from the masses of floating ice in the area. The pilot recommended taking the ship into Long Island Sound for safety. This opinion was confirmed by a second local pilot. In reporting to the Admiralty, Hood noted that the first pilot had made himself very unpopular with the local people ("rendered himself exceedingly obnoxious at New York" was the way Hood put it) by using his talents to anchor the frigate *Garland* "in so many different places where the King's ships have never been before" that it acted as a severe curb on the activities of smugglers.

The city that was to give Hood the most problems during his time on the station was Boston. The governorship there was in the hands of Sir Francis Bernard.[13] Bernard was by no means a reactionary, and he was described as having scholarly tastes. He was not totally in sympathy with Townshend's ideas on taxation and did not approve of taxing the Americans until the provincial governments had been reformed. He even held the view, rejected by the government, that some American representation in Parliament was desirable so that the population might feel that they had a say in the overall management of their affairs.

The colonists were never on good terms with him, for his lack of tact and brusque manner continually grated on them. He was the mouthpiece of Parliament and, as often as not, he bore news of legislation of which they disapproved.

The winter of 1767–68 had passed in rather a restless fashion, with the commissioners of customs in some alarm for their personal safety. There had been disturbances in Boston "originating in caprice and designed for intimidation." Not only were the commissioners the public officials who would feel the brunt of public anger through their activities against smugglers, but the application of the new fiscal measures passed by Parliament were also their responsibility, Unfortunately, when they communicated to Bernard their fears for their safety, the governor had virtually no troops to call upon to protect them.

Governor Bernard was in a difficult position. He could not call in troops to Boston without the advice of the Council, and the Council were very reluctant to give such advice. They were local men who lived in the town, and they either did not dare or did not care to pass a measure that would earn them the hostility of their neighbors. They therefore refused all applications made by the governor to receive and billet troops in the town.

More in Hood's immediate province was the question of suppressing smuggling. Both the home government in London and the local administrators recognized the necessity of cracking down. The smugglers were substantial contributors to the local wealth, and smuggling was considered acceptable means of avoiding the new duties imposed by the British Parliament. It was even seen as a patriotic duty to engage in it or at least to turn a blind eye. The commissioners of customs, or revenue men, could not suppress it, and the calls for naval assistance became more frequent. Hood tried his best, with the limited means at his disposal, to meet the calls made upon him. Even with navy help, however, the efforts to put a stop to the trade were not successful. Smuggling was endemic along the whole North American coast, and the resources were not there to stop it. Hood even had a report from Lieutenant Mowat of the survey vessel *Canceaux* that in Canada smuggling was carried on by English ships from the Channel Islands.

The first ripples of the coming storm were felt by Hood when he received a request for a frigate and sloop to be stationed at Boston in aid of the civil power. A supporting letter to Hood from the commissioners of customs spoke of the "temper of the people of the Town" and "the safety of the officers" as requiring two or more ships to be employed at Boston.[14]

The position of the revenue officers is understandable. Their situation was made extremely uncomfortable by the hostility of the population. As they often went in danger of their lives, the presence of a naval vessel would give them some peace of mind as well as an escape route should things get too volatile. Hood was able to render some immediate assistance by ordering the sloop *Beaver* to return to Boston and support the power of the commissioners. The schooner *St. Lawrence* was also sent south to join the *Beaver*, and more naval support was promised if necessary.

Lord Hillsborough, the government minister responsible for the colonies, ordered that troops be sent to Boston to help control the situation. Sir Thomas Gage,[15] the military commander, asked Hood to make preparations to transport two regiments, the 14th and 29th, from Halifax to Boston. In addition to the infantry, Hood was asked to carry a company of artillery. General Gage then wrote to Bernard telling him that troops and artillery were sailing from Halifax. Accommodation for the force was to be split between Boston and Castle William, and quarters were to be found for them in the usual manner. Hood collected these troops from Louisbourg and sent them on in the *Launceston* to Boston. The appearance of the army at Boston could not fail to create a very uneasy situation.

Bernard informed the council of the request for the troops to be quartered in Boston. The council suggested that the troops, for the sake of the peace of the town, be quartered at Castle William. The governor repeated his request to the council and had the shock of seeing that body's reply printed in the local papers before he had received it! The substance was that they refused to have the troops quartered in Boston, but would pay for the fitting out of a barracks at Castle William.

General Gage was under the impression that revolt had actually broken out at Boston and had contingency plans should the "rebels" have succeeded in taking Castle William. When the troops landed, they did so under the cover of the guns of the ships in the harbor.

Bernard learned that two more regiments were being shipped from Ireland. He had grave doubts about the arrival of this force, thinking that it could only exacerbate the situation. As the troops were already on their way and could not be stopped, he decided to give some advance warning so that their coming would not be a complete surprise to the Bostonians. He ordered a rumor put about, and himself casually mentioned it in a conversation with a member of the council. Before long the rumor had spread throughout Boston. A society calling itself the Sons of Liberty met and passed an address, to be presented to the governor, protesting the troops' arrival.

A severe gale in April caused much damage in the Halifax Dockyard. Such a natural disaster could affect the availability of vessels for the many calls made upon Hood. The damage to the dockyard facilities would hold up the program of ships to be careened or repaired, which would upset the dispositions he had planned.

Fortunately, there seemed to be no serious loss or damage among the naval vessels. Most had ridden out the storm in the harbor. Those at sea had also managed to survive without loss. Naturally Hood felt some anxiety until he was able to confirm that all his vessels were accounted for.

About a month later the sloop *Beaver* arrived from Barbados. Hood immediately transferred his flag to her from the *Romney*, which was soon to go to Boston. The *Beaver* herself would not be long at Halifax, for she too was promised in reinforcement of the naval presence off the town.

Life was no easier for the custom officers in Boston. They struggled to carry out their allotted task of collecting the new dues, but had little success in imposing the will of Parliament. The taxes were meant to bring in a good-sized revenue to the Treasury, but so far they had brought little but trouble to both collectors and the government. The commissioners of customs grew more and more anxious and more desirous of the protection and aid of the navy.

On 10 June 1768 the collector and the comptroller of Boston seized a vessel that had been smuggling wine into the colony. With the aid of a naval contingent from the *Romney*, the vessel was secured. On the return of the two finance officers to land they were attacked by a mob and only just managed to escape with their lives. The mob then streamed through the streets to the Comptrollers House and did some damage to it and destroyed a boat belonging to the collector. The comptroller was a Mr. Hallowell, who had a son named Benjamin.[16] Father and son were soon to be included within that part of the American population known as Loyalists, who at the unsuccessful conclusion of the war would be forced to leave their homes and flee to Canada.

The commissioners told Hood that the situation had "became more critical and alarming every day." They appealed for the return of the *Beaver* to Boston as "we should have been very desirous of Captain Bellew's continuance in this harbor if he had not had your orders to return."[17]

On 13 June another meeting was convened by the Sons of Liberty with the express purpose of passing a motion that called for clearing the land of all customs men. The comptroller and the collector took the hint, and they and their families went aboard the *Romney* and from there were transported to Castle William.

The naval force at this time at Boston consisted of the *Romney*, the *St.*

Lawrence, the *Hope*, and the *Senegal*. The *Hope* had been in the port for some time, while the *Senegal* was a recent arrival. The appearance of the *Romney* seems to have had a calming effect on the people of Boston, but this soon wore off.

Hood had instructed Captain Corner of the *Romney* to station the ship where she could most aid the civil power. He was to prevent desertion (a common problem on the station) and to prevent clashes between sailors and Bostonians. All boats going from ship to shore were to contain two petty officers and were not to wait for the person put ashore but to return immediately to the ship.

So far Hood had not felt that his presence was needed at Boston. He remained fairly remote from the center of the tumult, though well informed of the progress of the crisis. He had supported the civil authorities by the dispatch of naval support from his meager resources.

Information continued to reach Hood of further disturbances in Boston. Those studying the situation, either at first hand on the western side of the Atlantic or in London reading dispatches, were left in no doubt that matters were in a serious way, with no sign of the colonists retreating from their stand against the new duties. Hood put it rather well in one of his letters to Alexander: "the ferment amongst the people is by no means subsided, it sometimes appears smothered, but then diligent search is making for fresh fuel to kindle the flame."

On October first the transports carrying the troops from Ireland arrived in Boston harbor. The thorny matter of where to billet the troops remained undecided. The council was still against billeting them in the town of Boston. A meeting was held to discuss the question, and a compromise was reached whereby some troops would be billeted in an empty factory in Boston and the rest at Castle William.

The following day the troops landed, while the ships of the navy covered the town with their guns. By the orders of Governor Bernard the empty factory had been taken possession of, but the council had filled the building with vagrants who proved difficult to evict. Prior to the arrival of the troops Bernard had heard a rumor that the Bostonians intended to storm Castle William, and he asked Captain Corner to put his marines there as security. Corner said that he would be glad to do so if he received a formal order from the governor, but Bernard said that he couldn't issue such an order without the consent of the council. As an alternative he suggested that Corner land his marines there for "refreshment."

Both Corner and Hood seem to have been unaware of the restraints that the Boston Charter imposed on Bernard. Hood wrote to Grenville that the town wanted a "Governor of spirit and dignity, and who preferred the honor of his King, and the interest of his Country to his own little views." He did not know or appreciate the tight democratic restraints under which Bernard had to operate.[18]

Hood decided to see for himself how things stood in Boston. He arrived on 15 November to find the situation very much as described. There was, however, one piece of good news awaiting him when he came to Boston: the arrival of the 60-gun ship *Rippon* at Hampton Roads, Virginia. On arrival, Hood found himself face to face with one of the major problems facing the navy in North America, the question of manning the ships. Even at the end of the previous war in 1763, Lord Colville had had trouble enlisting men and had asked the Admiralty for guidance. While he was moored in Boston he was losing forty to fifty men per month through desertion. In America the use of impressment was of doubtful legality, and in the present situation a resort to it would be inflammatory. The Americans were encouraging crews to desert, and no manner of incentive encouraged them to enlist.

Because of the general feeling of uneasiness, Hood ordered the *Rippon* to remain in Hampton Roads in case of trouble in Virginia. The example of the Bostonians might be catching, and a watch was necessary at all possible points. As winter was coming on again, no more ships than necessary should be deployed further north. The weather would put a stop to all operations from Halifax and Louisbourg. The following dispositions were therefore made by Hood for his ships over the winter months:

At Halifax: *Glasgow*
At Louisbourg: one schooner
At Boston: *Romney, Mermaid,* two sloops and two schooners
At Rhode Island: one sloop
At New York: *Deal Castle* and a schooner
At Hampton Roads: *Rippon*

By far the largest part of his command was now stationed on the American coast, where they would most be needed. The northern part of his command was left to the *Glasgow* and the schooner at Louisbourg.

Towards the end of 1768 the situation at Boston seemed to be relatively calm. Hood felt able to write a confident passage in his report to the Admiralty:

There does not appear the least probability of the peoples taking arms. I think it cannot happen. Indeed some few at the convention took pains to bring the ignorant lower class into that mind, and possibly might have succeeded had not the Troops arrived as they did; but those few are now alarmed and expect nothing less than a voyage to England against their inclinations.[19]

The government, seeking a solution, did finally decide to take the plunge in May 1769 and repeal the duties. It was judged necessary, however, to make a concession to those who believed in the right of Parliament to raise taxes, so they left one tax just to emphasize the principle that the right still existed. The tax that was left in place was the tax on tea. It must have seemed to the government that they had the best of both worlds, winning credit with the colonists for their moderation while still retaining the rights of Parliament to satisfy the feelings of its members.

Nothing, however, could be further from the truth. The tax on tea was sufficient for the discontented in America to fasten on and exploit as a continuing sign of the British will to levy unjust taxes on the population. For the government, the amount of money the new tax would bring in was small. As an irritant to the Americans, it was more trouble than it was worth. It denied the principle that the Americans could be taxed only by their own assemblies. For all the good, and the great deal of harm, that this tax was to do, it might as well have been repealed along with the rest. The government just could not bring itself to bite the bullet and accept the total repeal of the taxes—a temporary humiliation and one that would have made life very difficult with the king (and many others) but the only sure way to totally defuse the situation in America.

It was also decided to recall the governor. Bernard was to be made a baronet as a balm to ease the pain of his dismissal. This new honor was granted in 1769, and Bernard was informed of it and of his impending relief soon afterwards. Before he was recalled, he had to see through another meeting of the Boston Assembly.[20]

The Assembly met in May 1769 and sent a demand to Bernard calling for the withdrawal of the troops from the town and the ships of war from the harbor. Bernard rejected this demand on the grounds that they had not elected a speaker and thus he could not answer their message. The Assembly duly elected a speaker and resubmitted their complaint. Bernard's reply was that he had no authority over the armed forces of the Crown and therefore could not order their removal—a reply that, although patently true, nevertheless annoyed the Assembly. During this period Bernhard also received news of the repeal of the Townshend duties but of the continuance of the tax on tea.

From his knowledge of the situation, Hood had written to the Admiralty at the end of the previous year that it would be a very difficult task to get the colonial assemblies to acknowledge the power of the British Parliament. His considered opinion was, however, that the colonists were not likely to take their opposition to the lengths of resisting by armed force.

The tension between the navy and the local seagoing community is shown by the violent death of a British officer. The *Rose* (24) had stopped an American packet ship, the *Pitt*, to search for contraband. Lieutenant Panton[21] was sent by the captain of the *Rose* to board the *Pitt*. A seaman resisted his entry into the *Pitt* and, when Panton persisted, killed the unfortunate officer with a harpoon.

Meanwhile the *Liberty*, a locally purchased vessel, had been involved in preventive duties, a task that did not make her popular among the community. A crowd had been inflamed by tavern orators and the liberal application of drink, and the *Liberty* was stormed and set on fire. The masts and rigging were cut down, the sails slashed, and the guns thrown overboard. As a final step the ship was scuttled.

With the winter of 1768–69 drawing to a close Hood decided, rather than return to Halifax, to remain at Boston over the summer months while the situation looked so tense. He intended to leave the *Rose* and two other armed vessels for continuing assistance to the local authorities. To complete his naval dispositions, the *Beaver* was left at New York and the *Senegal* at Rhode Island. By the summer of 1769 Hood felt that the reason for the troops to be in Boston had now passed and that they should be withdrawn. He was strenuously opposed in this opinion by the Custom House commissioners, who still feared for their own safety.

Prior to his departure Bernard had been informed by General Gage that he intended to withdraw some troops from Boston and send them back to Halifax. Bernard thought the situation warranted that they stay. The question of whether the troops would go or stay was settled by Hutchinson, the deputy governor. He decided that they should return to Halifax, and they sailed with Hood, leaving Boston at about the same time as Governor Bernard.

In 1770, as he was coming to the end of his time as commissioner, Hood received news from Hutchinson of another milestone along the road to American independence, the so-called Boston Massacre.

The Boston Massacre, though well known and significantly serious at the time, was blown up out of proportion to serve the political purposes of the radical opposition. A party of British troops had been subjected to stone throwing and taunting by the mob. Shots were fired, whether deliberate or accidental is not known, and five of the crowd killed. The event was chosen by the radicals to show the ruthlessness and cruelty of the British government and their representatives in America.

The troops involved were arrested and were later put on trial for murder, much as would happen with the recent troubles in Northern Ireland. In fact there was very little choice, given the prevailing atmosphere in Boston. Popular sentiment was very much against the men, and it was expected that they would be found guilty. The men were fortunate in that they secured the support of one of the most ardent of the Boston radicals, John Adams,[22] who was later President of the United States. Adams came to the opinion that the event was being overplayed. There was so much exaggeration, he felt, that the men would be found guilty just for the sake of scoring a point off the British. He therefore offered to conduct the defense of the men, which he was able to do successfully. The incident widened further the breach between the two sides. This breach was not yet unbridgeable by men of good will and moderation, but such men were becoming harder to find.

While Samuel Hood was not directly involved in the incident, he did feel that the mob that taunted the British soldiers had not intended to sack the Custom House. He told James Bowdoin[23] that there "does not seem the least foundation" for this claim.

By 1770 Samuel Hood's time on the North American station was almost up. He had completed three years in which the situation with the colonies had slid slowly downhill on the inexorable road to the final breakdown. He had been starved of ships and faced with implementing a policy that called for positive action against a civilian population that gradually grew more hostile. He was impotent to affect the political situation. He could only support the civil power. Hood had not been as unpopular with the Bostonians as either Bernard and Gage. He was known to be a protégé of Pitt, and this ensured his receiving a warmer welcome than was given to other representatives of British power. Hood had had a long time to think over the situation at Boston and the difficulties of British rule generally. At the beginning of his time on the station he was of the opinion that only harsh measures would serve to quell the troubles. By the end of 1768 he began to change his view. As we have seen, he still believed that the troubles would not end in violence, but in this he was mistaken. Hood wanted to heal the rift between Britain and the colonies. One of the last orders he received from the Admiralty was to transfer his naval headquarters from Halifax to Boston. He had no time to act on this before he departed—or perhaps he just preferred to leave the matter pending for his successor.

He worked at improving relations between the authorities and Bostonians by small acts to appease angry feelings. He came to know and like one of the radicals, James Bowdoin, with whom he continued to correspond even when he had left Boston and returned home to the village of Catherington, near Portsmouth, where he had settled since his marriage. He also met and gained the respect and friendship of John Adams, a gift that was rarely given, especially to representatives of the British government.

The new commodore arrived in Halifax on 10 October 1770. The chosen officer was another senior post captain, James Gambier.[24] Shortly after, having made the handover of his command official, Hood was ready to sail. The *Romney* left Halifax on 14 October and was back in Portsmouth on 9 November. So ended Hood's second period on the American station. It had not been an easy appointment, but he had been powerless to control events and could only react to them. When he next operated on the same coast, he would have the power to alter events but would not use it.

THE COMMISSIONER

On Hood's return from North America there was a dispute with Spain over the Falkland Islands, and at one time it looked like it might result in a war. The crisis had been provoked by the belief in France and Spain that Britain had lost the will and power to enforce her interests at sea. The Spanish, acting with the encouragement of France, had ejected a small party of British settlers from the islands. The driving force behind the idea was the duc de Choiseul, who wanted an alliance with Spain to attack Britain and gain revenge for the defeats of the Seven Years' War.

The British had long believed that the French wished to reverse the verdict of the previous war. To counter this, but without going to the final resort of full hostilities, British governments of all complexions had used the threat of naval power. The British had not been able to establish any alliance with a Continental power to counter France and draw some of its resources away from the anticipated French naval expansion.

On its own, even with its enlarged navy, the French government could not provide a sufficient naval force to offset the British superiority at sea, and Bourbon France relied on Bourbon Spain to join forces in the Family Compact. In the case of the Falklands, Spain had actively pressed their case, but when it came to the point of supporting Spain, in the end the French government, with the exception of Choiseul, was not keen on the idea of war with Britain.

The ineffective governments of previous years had been replaced by one led by Lord North, who in the face of crisis mobilized the navy. Pushed to the brink of war, France backed down, Choiseul was sacked, and pressure was put on Spain to withdraw its claims to the Falklands. The threat of British naval power had been enough to bring a satisfactory end to the crisis. Still, the government had to maintain increased naval expenditure in the face of continuing Bourbon hostility. Throughout the next few years the strength of the navy matched the combined fleets of France and Spain. In the last few years of his reign, Louis XV turned to more domestic concerns and tended to neglect his navy, so French naval strength fell.

In the period leading up to the American War there were various clashes of interest between Britain and France. The most important of these was the British reaction to the buildup of French naval forces at Ile de France (present-day Mauritius). The British position in India was delicate at that time due to the bad government of the East India Company and the practice of some Indian states to play off the Western powers against each other. The French had the opportunity to do serious damage to British interests, and in 1771 the Admiralty proposed a force of three ships of the line and one 50-gun ship, commanded by Sir Robert Harland, to go to the area. The French were told that this force was in reply to their own expansion. The crisis rumbled on until the French began to withdraw their additional sea and land forces in 1773.

In the aftermath, one development was of particular benefit to the navy. Sir Edward Hawke retired from the post of First Lord of the Admiralty and was replaced by Lord Sandwich. Sandwich was by far the better person to fill the post and became, with Lord Anson, one of the two most effective First Lords the navy has ever had.

As the tension dissipated, so did the opportunity of a new active command for Hood. He was appointed instead to the *Royal William*,[1] a guard ship at Portsmouth, one of a series of such assignments over the next few years. Hood spent just under two years in the *Royal William* before being moved to the *Marlborough* (74). Among the midshipmen of whom he had charge was the Hon. James Pitt, the youngest son of Lord Chatham. While Samuel Hood was denied an active command, his young cousin and protégé Alexander Hood joined Captain Cook in his second voyage round the world. Alexander had been serving in the yacht *Katherine* with his namesake, Samuel's brother, who had pushed for their cousin to be given this chance. The elder Alexander Hood's wife, Molly, had written to Lady Chatham on Christmas Day 1771 to give her the news and to enthuse that "it must lead him to the greatest knowledge in his profession."[2]

In May 1775 while Hood was still in the *Marlborough* the first sparks of the American War burst into flame at Lexington. In Britain there was no doubt that the majority of Parliamentary and public opinion was behind the government in asserting the right of Parliament to tax the Americans. The progress of the crisis sharpened divisions and reduced the members of Parliament who were supporting the American cause to the Pitt-Rockingham factions and the more vociferous radicals like John Wilkes.

The first clash between the army and colonists would quickly escalate to a full-scale war. Chatham had warned of a rift with the colonists, for he saw that this would give the French their opportunity to intervene and avenge their defeat in the previous war. For Hood the war was to make his name, and he was to be the key participant in an action on which the whole outcome of the war in America depended. This first movement of active revolt reignited the dormant desire of the French to take advantage of British embarrassment. The new king, Louis XVI, did not desire war but agreed to naval preparations continuing. Later this would be increased to encompass all aid to the Americans short of war.

The British decision to impose a blockade on the coast of North America made a clash with the French likely. Consequently, the British kept a keen eye on French ports by means of their intelligence network. Any reported increase in activity would give them advance warning that the French intended, or contemplated, intervening in the war. The French were waiting for an indication that the colonists could sustain a war with Britain. The news of Bunker Hill (or Breed's Hill, as it should more correctly be called) convinced the French that the British could never recover the colonies by force of arms. The British belief was that the revolt could never survive if it was starved of European support. In this respect the attitude of France was crucial.

The new active phase of the war meant little to Hood in professional terms. There was no immediate opportunity of service on the other side of the Atlantic, though as commander of the *Marlborough* he was well placed in the event that the fleet should be expanded.

On the fateful date of 4 July 1776, while Hood was having breakfast in his house at Catherington, he heard the news that there had been an explosion on board the *Marlborough*. Fifteen men had died or were soon to die of injuries, and fifty more were injured and in hospital. He advised Lady Chatham on 10 July of the safety of her son, as he feared that the letter the young Pitt had sent might have gone astray.[3] A subsequent enquiry established that the cause had been powder illegally concealed about the ship, which the Gunner and his yeoman were hoping to sell for personal profit. The damage was such that the ship had to be put out of immediate service. Hood and the remaining crew were transferred to the *Courageux* (74). The explosion on the other side of the Atlantic that day was fueled by the Declaration of Independence.

By the end of 1776 Hood was expecting to be relieved of command of the *Courageux*, but his term was extended. He made several cruises in the Channel, both to raise men from the incoming trade fleets and to look for American merchant ships trying to make their way into French ports. With the French operating on a policy of assistance to the Americans without declaring war, British ships could not seize French ships without provoking a diplomatic incident that might lead to immediate hostilities.

Intelligence fueled the fears of the British government that the French and Spanish were conspiring against them. To counter the alliance of the Bourbon powers, Britain had only the support of Portugal, which was itself involved in a dispute with Spain. The Portuguese informed Britain that Spain had taken out a large loan at Amsterdam and that this could only be meant for the support of the Americans. It was suggested that Britain confront France and Spain and ask whether the armaments they were preparing were designed for use against Britain. Any delay in replying should trigger a naval blockade of Brest and Cadiz. This suggestion was too strong for Britain and raised fears that it would instigate a European war. The Portuguese were told that Britain had assurances that the armaments preparing in French and Spanish ports were not hostile to Britain. Yet in the light of subsequent history, the Portuguese proposal had much to recommend it. A preemptive strike in 1776 might very well have altered the course of the conflict.

In Britain the Admiralty would need any extra men it could get to prepare the fleet for service in the Channel upon the anticipated entry of France into the war. Hood told his brother that he expected Keppel to be appointed to the Channel command. Keppel was the natural choice. With Sir Charles Saunders now dead and Howe absent in America, he was the most experienced commander available. Keppel's political connections with the Whigs were a difficulty Lord Sandwich had to accept. Sandwich had been rash enough to boast in Parliament that "Our Navy is more than a match for that of the whole House of Bourbon"—words that would come back to haunt him when the Franco-Spanish armada was cruising in the Channel with a numerically superior force in 1779–80.

With the news of Saratoga reaching Britain in late 1777, it was generally expected that the French declaration would not now be long delayed. In fact a treaty was signed between France and the American rebels on 6 February 1778 binding both parties not to make a separate peace. The French had been preparing for war since 1776 not only by supplying the Americans but also by building up their navy. The British had a good intelligence service and soon learned of French intentions. The British Cabinet realized that sooner or later they would face a direct threat in home waters far more serious than anything the Americans could present. With the surrender at Saratoga time was running out for the British to prepare to meet the challenge. Sandwich husbanded his resources so that only smaller ships went over to Howe in the American command, while the bigger ships were retained for use in home waters. But he was unable to persuade his colleagues to order an early mobilization of the fleet, and when war came the navy still lacked a decisive superiority at home.

It was urgent for the British to fit out the Channel Fleet as swiftly as possible. Since the present commissioner at Portsmouth, James Gambier, was recognized in the Admiralty as totally incompetent, Sandwich offered the job to Hood. As a sop Gambier was made second in command to Howe, who, when Gambier arrived at New York, promptly removed him from operational command by making him dockyard commissioner there. By appointing Hood, Sandwich gained two vital points. He first of all got a man of ability and drive for the job; secondly, he was appointing Edward Linzee's son-in-law, which would do well for Admiralty influence in the borough.

Hood accepted the appointment on the understanding that eventually he would go back to the "military side" of his profession. He left the *Courageux* on 10 February and set off for London to see the Navy Board, who were responsible for the administration of the dockyards, to receive his patent for the post and his formal instructions. He had earlier written to Sandwich asking to have Alexander succeed him as captain of the *Courageux* when he gave up the command of the *Katherine*.

From a note he wrote to Lady Chatham,[4] it seems that Hood was in poor health at this time, feeling the effects of strain and long service. He may have hoped for a more active position, but he doubted if he was up to it. The offer of the dockyard post may therefore have come as a relief.

The French ambassador formally notified the British government on 13 March 1778 of the alliance with the Americans. This was followed by a reciprocal withdrawing of ambassadors, though formal hostilities were not yet officially declared. Further deterioration in the situation led to increased activity to fit out and man the fleet. Keppel was no longer in good health, and immediately before assuming his command he had been taking the waters at Aix-la-Chapelle. He was a Whig by inclination and was opposed to the American War but had no objection to serving against the French. His appointment had been made on 18 March, and he arrived at Portsmouth on the twenty-fourth to take command of a force of twenty sail of the line.

Because of the political complications there were doubts on both sides as to the wisdom of the appointment. Keppel was told by his friends that his reputation would not be safe under Lord Sandwich—that he would not be given the force he needed to do the job, and that he would then take the blame for any failure. On the government side there was uneasiness that the command was being entrusted to such a strong Whig figure and political opponent. Both sides tried to make the best of it, but judging by the conditions that Keppel put on his command about numbers of ships in his fleet, it seems he was looking over his shoulder to make sure he was not stabbed in the back. In point of fact, Keppel and Sandwich looked at the new situation from similar viewpoints. Both wished to strengthen the Channel Fleet and not send ships abroad in reaction to French moves until Keppel was satisfied that he had equality with the French.

Fitting out the Channel Fleet was not the only call on Hood's time and the dockyard resources. He had found it difficult to get all the supplies he wanted for Keppel's fleet, but he was also faced with fitting out a squadron under Admiral Byron for North America. Manning the ships was the great stumbling block, for there were never enough seamen for all services. Sandwich told Parliament that there were thirty-five sail of the line ready for immediate service and seven more almost ready, to be allotted to both Keppel and Byron. Keppel was to have an initial force of twenty of the line, with others to follow as they became available. The force for the Mediterranean was gradually whittled down until it ceased to exist. The natural tendency to overinsure in home waters was a necessary feature of Admiralty policy at this time.

There were obvious advantages to having a strong squadron in the Mediterranean, but with the dangerous situation in the Channel, especially after Spain joined the war in 1779, the government strained to make the home base as secure as possible by trying to match the numbers of the Combined Fleet. Some officers later thought it tactically better to have a fleet of only about twenty ships, all coppered, which could be handled more easily than a vast armada and could operate as a "fleet in being." This idea was articulated by the talented Richard Kempenfeldt, Captain of the Fleet to Sir Charles Hardy after Keppel resigned from the command. In the situation that existed in 1778 with only France hostile in home waters, the need for a Mediterranean fleet was less pressing. There was no need to observe the motions of the Spanish fleet and prevent their junction with the French. It was now a question of being strong where it mattered, and that was in the Channel. By the time Spain did enter the war the following year, the Spanish policy was based on invasion of the British homeland. Their strength was therefore concentrated in the Channel, and the Admiralty had to maintain the strength of the Western Squadron to counter the Franco-Spanish fleet as well as a fleet in the West Indies, so no force remained available for the

Mediterranean. One strong advocate for a squadron based at Gibraltar in the early months of 1778 was Lord George Germain, who found the unobstructed departure of d'Estaing galling and who enlarged to his colleagues on the damage which the Toulon squadron could do to British interests in North America and the West Indies.[5]

The detachment made by both sides for fleets to operate in North America and the West Indies could be said to have squandered opportunities for either British or French fleets to achieve a decisive advantage in the Channel. The ships detached with d'Estaing did not achieve their objectives in either North America or the West Indies. As d'Estaing sailed before Byron, the British could have taken advantage of this detachment from French strength and retained the ships detailed to go with Byron in the Channel until operations for that year were over. This is what both Sandwich and Keppel wished to do, but they were overruled by the cabinet.[6]

The entry of France into the war led to a rethink of British strategy. Lord Sandwich saw the new situation in stark terms. The war in America should be relegated to the second priority. The first was to secure Britain from invasion by a superior Franco-Spanish fleet (for Spain was confidently expected to join France in the war), and Sandwich sent a memorandum to Lord North on this subject.[7]

The cabinet had settled on a policy of reactive reinforcement. In previous wars the navy had sought supremacy in the European seas, as Sandwich now did. In this war, perhaps influenced by the importance of the sugar islands in the West Indies and the value of both the West and East Indian trade, they decided to send reinforcements to follow French or Spanish naval forces. Most important of all, they wished to maintain supremacy in the Leeward Islands and on the North American station. This explained the priority given to fitting out Byron's squadron and the haste to get it to North America. Sandwich, Keppel, and Palliser fought a rearguard action to stop Byron sailing until the final destination of d'Estaing was known, and finally succeeded in getting the king to support their contention that the security of the British mainland should not be risked until the French movements were certain.[8]

The two stations were regarded as one interconnecting station for operational purposes. The admiral commanding the Leeward Island station could reinforce the North American Squadron when operations were ended in his area by the hurricane season. There was one change to this procedure at the end of the campaigning season for 1779: the government decided that the British naval forces would not withdraw from the West Indies, which would give them an overwhelming superiority at the start of the 1780 season, especially if early reinforcements arrived from Britain.

* * *

If the combined forces of Keppel and Byron had fought the battle off Ushant, the numerical advantage would have been with the British. It has been suggested that, knowing of such a disadvantage, the French might not have sailed at all, and a British blockade of Brest could have seriously impeded any French attempt to send forces across the Atlantic to the Americas. A concentration in the Channel and on the task of knocking France out before she could exert any influence in America would have changed the course of the war. If the French fleet had been defeated or blockaded in 1778, Spain would never have entered the war in 1779.[9] Unfortunately for final British victory, the king and the government could not bring themselves to temporarily abandon America while France was dealt with. Byron sailed across the Atlantic and achieved as little as d'Estaing, when his presence in the Channel might have been decisive.

To give heart to those fitting out the fleet, George III paid a visit to Portsmouth accompanied by Sandwich and was received by Hood at the Commissioners House along with several other high-ranking naval and military officers. Hood and the king seem to have got on well, and it was probably at this meeting that the King formed the favorable opinion of Hood that he generally held until Hood's dismissal from the Mediterranean command in 1795.

The King had many conversations with those present and asked Hood where he thought France's Toulon Squadron would go, as there was no British fleet to watch it. Hood told him he believed that the French would cross the Atlantic rather than come north to join the Brest Fleet and that Byron should take his fleet to New York rather than Halifax, as it was easier to go north from New York at that time of the year than to go south from Halifax. The French, under the comte d'Estaing, did in fact steer for New York where, on arrival, they outnumbered the squadron of Lord Howe. Howe managed to foil his opponent by mooring his ships in a defensive position inside Sandy Hook and commanding the entrance to the harbor.

Before the King left Portsmouth he distributed honors among those present, including a baronetcy for Hood, probably a douceur for his accepting the dockyard post and perhaps to persuade him not to press for a more active command. Before the king left, he told Hood that he was sending his third son, Prince William, into the navy. William was to go to sea with

Captain Robert Digby,[10] a member of a family already established in royal service.

Hood and the dockyard workers toiled away at the task of getting Keppel's fleet to sea, and he finally sailed on 13 June, a creditable achievement. It was still a fleet that had never worked together, and a common mode of signals and instructions had to be issued to each ship. Keppel was under orders to take or destroy the Toulon Squadron should he come across it, to watch for the Brest Fleet, and to safeguard the coasts of Britain and Ireland. An engagement with two French frigates off the Lizard saw the first hostilities between the British and French. From one of the captured frigates Keppel learned that the French strength was twenty-seven of the line, and he felt justified in putting back for reinforcements. Sandwich came down from London to speak to Keppel and try to persuade him to sail with the three extra ships that were immediately available, but Keppel declined, and it was 11 July before he sailed again with twenty-nine ships of the line. The French had left Brest the day before with thirty. With Byron's squadron the British might have had the decisive superiority Sandwich wanted, but that chance had been lost.[11]

The two fleets sighted each other on 23 July, sixty-six miles west of Ushant. The British had now increased their numbers to thirty of the line, but no action took place that day. The following day the French had the windward gauge, which meant that Keppel was now between them and their base but the French had the choice as to whether they wished to force an action.

After some maneuvering, in which the prewar tactical practice of the French showed to advantage, the two fleets passed each other on opposite tacks, cannonading as they went. Neither was in a well-formed line, and no ships were lost on either side. At the end of the action the rear division under Sir Hugh Palliser, which had been the part of the British fleet most closely engaged, was some distance from the main body. Signals for Palliser to close on the center were not obeyed owing to the serious damage to masts and rigging that the division had suffered. This situation formed the basis of the controversy that was to cause the officer corps of the navy much trauma. Palliser was a Tory and a member of the Board of Admiralty, and although Keppel's report to the Admiralty made no criticism of his action in not closing, it was not long before a newspaper article appeared in which he was faulted, with his actions ascribed to the fact that he was a Tory and therefore an opponent of Keppel.

Having been involved with the fitting out of the fleet, Hood was disappointed at the negative result of the action. And he was naturally concerned about the safety of his brother, who was commanding the *Robust* (74), and his young cousin Samuel,[12] also on board. His fears were not allayed until he had seen a copy of the *Gazette* with the news of the action and the list of casualties.

The trouble between Keppel and Palliser escalated. Keppel refused to publish a letter refuting the criticisms in the previous article, and Palliser, driven by professional pride, took the unusual step of demanding a court-martial on Keppel. This was a risky course, as an acquittal of Keppel would imply that he himself was guilty. It would have been safer to ask for a court-martial on his own actions, which would give him a better chance to state his case. Such a court-martial had already been demanded by the Rockingham Whigs in Parliament, which raised the dispute to political status.

The court-martial on Keppel commenced on the *Britannia* in January 1779 but was soon transferred to a building ashore because of Keppel's poor health. The procedings were heavily weighted in favor of Keppel, with the courtroom filled with his supporters, and it soon became obvious that he would be acquitted. For the Hood family, however, the affair had serious repercussions. Samuel, as Commissioner, was responsible for the welfare of the members of the court, including providing them with a meal during the day, but Alexander was a witness. It was soon noticed that the entry for the day of the battle had been altered in the *Robust*'s logbook, and Alexander was asked the reason. He explained that he had added more detail than he had been able to do on the day, so that it would reflect a truer entry for the court. The members of the court accepted his explanation, but he was damned in public opinion as part of an Admiralty plot to get rid of Keppel.

The court-martial dragged on until early February and a "not guilty" verdict was reached. Palliser complained to Sandwich of the violent prejudice the court had shown for Keppel. The London mob, on hearing the result, vented their fury on Palliser, whose house was ransacked, and on all associated with him, including the Admiralty, members of the government, and Alexander Hood in his house in Harley Street.

Following the verdict for Keppel, momentum began to build up against Palliser. A memorial for presentation to the king was prepared and signed by several high-ranking officers demanding that Palliser be stripped of all honors and employments. Before the memorial could be presented, Sandwich met Palliser and suggested that it would be better if he voluntarily resigned his honors so that when he faced his court-martial he would not bear this stigma of having had his honors stripped from him.

The second trial opened on 12 April and found Palliser not guilty of the charges brought against him but administered a mild censure for not informing the commander in chief of his inability to bring his squadron down to join the rest of the fleet. Following the verdict Palliser asked for the restitution of his honors, but the political climate of the time did not permit Sandwich to do this. Palliser therefore retired to his estate in Yorkshire, though he was appointed governor of Greenwich Hospital in 1780, a post he held until his death in 1796, when he was succeeded by Hood. Sandwich also found Palliser a seat as Member of Parliament for Huntingdon, a borough he had in his control.

The controversy over the log of the *Robust* had made Alexander Hood something of an embarrassment to the Admiralty. He was retained in command, but he was disturbed that the next promotion to flag officer would stop just short of him. He appealed to Sandwich to include him in the promotion, as his omission would be considered a mark of censure. If this was not possible, he asked that he be given some other mark of favor, such as the colonelcy of the Marines, which would indicate that no stain remained against his name. He was disappointed in both expectations, as the flag promotion ended just six places above him and the vacancy in the Marines also went elsewhere.

After consultation with Samuel, Alexander went to see Sandwich and was offered the command of the *Robust* in North America. He would not be a commodore but a senior post captain. Alexander rejected this posting, which he viewed as a move by the Admiralty to get him out of England. Such an implication of censure of his past conduct he was not prepared to accept. With his ranking on the list of post captains, he would have expected a senior position on the station where he served. Samuel Hood was in complete agreement. He appealed to Sandwich to reconsider, but Sandwich would do no more, hinting that it was not only his own opinion that had to be considered. No offer of employment in home waters arose, and Alexander resigned the command of the *Robust* and accepted the command of the yacht *Katherine*, a largely shorebound appointment.

Following the resignation of Keppel, a new commander had to be found for the Channel Fleet. Of the suitable officers on the active list, only two fitted the criteria for the post. One was Keppel, now politically unacceptable, unlikely to accept another request to serve, and too ill to take up the post anyway. The obvious alternative was Lord Howe, who was professionally the most suitable man for the post. But Howe, who with his brother Sir William had now returned from their commands in America, proved unwilling to serve as First Lord in a government reshuffle suggested by the king. Lord Dartmouth was to retire as secretary for the Northern Department and Sandwich was to take that post, with Howe coming in at the Admiralty. However, Sir William, with the weight of the surrender at Saratoga attached to his reputation, was engaged in a dispute with Lord George Germain, who had overall responsibility for affairs in America and whom Sir William blamed for the disastrous outcome of Saratoga. Lord Howe was active in support of his brother, and while he indicated his willingness to serve as First Lord of the Admiralty, he unfortunately attached to his acceptance certain conditions that the government could not completely meet. Howe demanded promotion for both himself and his brother, a financial inducement for himself in the form a sinecure as Treasurer of the Navy, and the dismissal of Germain from the government. If all the other conditions could have been swallowed, the dismissal of a cabinet minister at the request of a naval officer was constitutionally unacceptable. The offer to Howe was therefore withdrawn. Given his known terms, it was not considered possible to offer him the command of the Channel Fleet, and his talents were lost to the service until 1782. In his own circles Howe let it be known that the reason he had declined the command was political and that he mistrusted the Admiralty under Sandwich.

The contrast with Samuel Hood's attitude could not have been more obvious. Hood had stated many times that he would never be a "party man" and ally himself with any faction. Like the Duke of Wellington thirty years later, he was first and foremost a public servant willing to serve where required.

The government was saved from embarrassment by the offer of Sir Charles Hardy, the Governor of Greenwich Hospital and a very respected officer, to serve. The government accepted, hoping that such a senior figure would help heal the divisions in the fleet. For a Captain of the Fleet to Hardy, three names were apparently under consideration, Samuel and Alexander Hood and Richard Kempenfeldt. As Alexander was temporarily unacceptable following the incident with the log of the *Robust* and Samuel was considered more valuable at Portsmouth as commissioner, Kempenfeldt became the natural selection.

Hood was faced with the task of reequipping the Home Fleet for the campaign of 1779. In addition he needed to find the resources to prepare the squadron of Vice Admiral Arbuthnot, who was to escort troops to North America and assume command on that station in the place of Lord Howe.

On 16 June the Spanish joined the war. This restored the odds in favor of the Allies. If Spain had not come in, there would have been about ninety British ships available for service in 1779 as against sixty-six French. The Spanish had a disposable force of some fifty ships, which would more than offset the previously assumed British superiority. The Spanish government had no common interest with the French in helping the American rebels. They brought to the war their own special interests, Minorca and Gibraltar being their chief objectives in European waters. They had further interests across the Atlantic, which were later expanded to include the conquest of Jamaica. Without the Spanish the French could not have continued the war at sea with any prospect of success. The Spanish government therefore were the driving force in the campaign of 1779, with the objective of making a landing in Britain and capturing Portsmouth. The French had not been keen on a second summer's operations in the Channel, but they had to bow to Spanish desires.[13]

Of the three fleets, the French under d'Orvilliers sailed first and made for the rendezvous they had arranged with the Spanish. Hardy sailed next, under orders to look into Brest and, if the French were still there, to block them in. If they had sailed, he was to try and ascertain where they had gone. After some delay the Spanish contingent joined with the French, and eventually the combined force totaled thirty-eight sail of the line with more from Cadiz still expected. The final Allied preponderance would be sixty-six ships to thirty-nine British.

The delay in assembling the whole force meant that the French were using up their provisions and their sick lists were lengthening.[14] The endurance of all large fleets was bounded by the need to provision and to keep crews healthy. In the following war the British managed a tight blockade of Brest, as they had done under Hawke, and it needed a considerable feat of organization to resupply the blockading force and thereby keep the crews healthy. The French and Spanish arrangements were not up to this task, and the price was paid in high mortality rates.

At Portsmouth Hood waited with the rest of the nation for news of the two fleets. Despite the difference in numbers, he was always sanguine about good news from the Channel to hearten the country. He pressed his brother to offer his services in the present emergency, but Alexander was still rankled by the attitude of the Admiralty to his promotion. Samuel finished his letter with the remark "God grant a day may come in the month of July 1779 to obliterate the recollection of the 27th July 1778."[15]

The two fleets spent some time maneuvering in the Channel, with Hardy determined to draw the Combined Fleet further up the Channel to unfamiliar waters. In the event, the season petered out with no contact between the two sides. At one time Hardy had determined to engage, but he later reconsidered and retired to Portsmouth. The campaign could be looked on as a success for Hardy.[16] Trade had been protected, the coast had not been invaded, and the fleet had not suffered any disaster. For an elderly sick man it was a considerable achievement, and it was his last, for he died before the next year's operations. The campaign cost the French fleet 8,000 dead from disease. The British and Spanish did not suffer casualties on such a scale, with better provisioning and hygiene making the difference. The campaigns of 1778 and 1779 had ended far more favorably for the British than they had a right to expect.

Once again Hood was facing the task of refitting the Channel Fleet. The shortages of various spares were as acute as ever. Sandwich came down to Portsmouth to see Hardy, do what he could to assist the refitting, and assess the mood of the fleet. The latter he found fairly buoyant, and Hardy expressed his willingness to go to sea again once the refitting had been completed.

Hood also had the task of refitting eight ships coming back across the Atlantic from Byron's squadron after an unsuccessful engagement off Grenada. Byron was soon to be replaced in the command of that area by Rodney. The latter had recently returned from Paris, where he had gone to hide from his creditors. Unfortunately he also had creditors in France and was allowed to leave only when the duc de Biron paid his debts for him, a gesture of unique chivalry that gave Britain the chance to get out of the war on fair terms. Rodney was, and remains, a controversial character. He did not hesitate to bend the rules and to practice outright dishonesty to advance his ends. He was not universally popular in the navy, but in the situation that existed the government needed an aggressive fighting admiral, and this description fitted Rodney.

Following his appointment Rodney came down to Portsmouth to supervise the fitting out of his fleet. His outward passage to his new station was to include the relief of Gibraltar, for which he would take a detachment of ships from the Home Fleet. Rodney sailed at the end of December 1779 and within a week had taken a Spanish convoy and escort. On 16 January he met and defeated the squadron of Lángara near Cape St. Vincent. The attack was well executed by night and in worsening weather with the fleets running into shoal water. It was the first clear-cut victory of the war and boded well for Rodney's command in the Leeward Islands.

While Rodney was making the most of his opportunities, Hood was feeling the strain of a never-ending task. The work was heavy enough to keep him fully occupied, for there always seemed to be squadrons to be fitted out for service. He must have envied Thomas Graves, who had been given his flag with a seniority date of 19 March 1779 and was now to go to North America as second in command to Arbuthnot. Graves had served with the Channel Fleet during the 1779 campaign and was being sent to North America in response to intelligence that de Ternay had left Brest with six ships of the line and 6,000 troops.

Hood knew well that Graves had a year's seniority over him as a post captain, and he could have calculated how long he would have to wait for his own flag, should it be offered. He was well into middle age and was missing the stimulation of an operational command. From his position, the situation of Graves must have seemed enviable. In a letter to Alexander he complained that the pressure of the work was unrelenting. The moment he thought himself clear, a fresh lot of work came in. A continuing problem was the manning of the ships he had to fit out. He had a lot of sympathy for the seaman in his present situation:

> No sooner is the complement of a ship completed than such men as are not liked, are sent to Hospital; and a demand made for more; and the poor devils of seamen are so turned from Ship to Ship, without the smallest consideration to them, that there is not a possibility of doing them justice respecting their wages. It often happens that they are lent (and of course borne as Supernumeraries for Victuals only) for many months, and at the end of that time are ordered to be put on the ship's books, as part of her complement, from their going on board probably not ten days before six months wages become due, which excludes them from a farthing of wages till the subsequent payment.[17]

Such were the feelings of the seamen that, when the signal was given for Graves's squadron to sail, the crews refused to weigh anchor. After some persuasion the men returned to obedience and the squadron sailed as ordered. Hood drew the lesson that a good many of the officers were neglect-ful of the care of the men under their command, a fact Hood considered "astonishing." These comments show Hood as sensitive to the necessity of treating the seamen fairly and mindful that they should not be deprived of their pay without good reason.

In March 1780 Hood again pressed his case for active service as a flag officer, recounting his "painfull feelings" at seeing his inferiors "brought forward to distinguished commands" while he languished at Portsmouth. He told Sandwich of his desire to hoist his flag and serve in the "military line" again.[18] The reply from Sandwich was quick in coming and was totally unsatisfactory. There was no possibility of his being given a flag officer post, and he was much more valuable where he was.[19] This reply brought the re-sponse from Hood that he was "pained to the quick" at his failure to obtain "justice" from Sandwich. Surely, he said, in time of war "old officers" who have served well and have had royal approbation must be considered for active posts. He would wait and at the next promotion he would lay claim to his flag and hope that he might find someone "more favorable to my views and pretensions" than Sandwich had proved to be![20] The following day he wrote yet again, laying out his full list of complaints against the Admiralty and Lord Sandwich in particular. He complained of his failing to get the colonelcy of marines:

> I beg leave to enlarge upon the grounds of my pretensions to your Lordships favour, not only as an officer who has done his duty well, but as a private man. So long ago my Lord, as Captain Digby gott the Marines I was a candidate also, with as fair pretensions as any Captain ever sollicited but Mr Digby was my senior, and I could not complain; I was from the same motive silent when Captain Rowley was hon-oured with a similar mark of your Lordships favour. Since which three captains my juniors have been appointed to Marine Divisions, though your Lordship then well knew it was my greatest pride and wish to have one. I have now served my Lord forty years, within a month, and in all that time I have never once been told I did wrong, but I have been honour'd with very many flattering testimonies of approbation from the Board at which your Lordship now presides.[21]

He then enlarged on his being refused a commodore's position and the favor he had done the Admiralty by accepting the Portsmouth commis-sionership:

I accepted the office I now fill, from a desire of giving accommodation to Government and to your Lordship (which I expressly said at the time) not conceiving it possible I should be forced to experience the very severe mortification of seeing junior officers brought forward to distinguished employments, when I was within four of the top of the list of Captains. This my Lord is laying me by, and sorely afflicts me. Your Lordship has doubtless examples to plead in favour of establishing Commodores, but no period of time can be produced wherein five were employed to the injury of their *seniors*, with, I will be bold to say, full as just pretensions (if good & gallant services can give pretensions) as either one of them; and with respect to myself, I will yield to no man, as an officer, that has served well and faithfully, and as a private man, I have not only most readily obeyed your Lordships wishes, but have studied to anticipate them to the utmost of my power. . . . With regard to your Lordships objections to my being second-in-command at Jamaica, I beg leave to observe that I mentioned that station because one Flag Officer was there only, and it is impossible your Lordship can think me so ignorant of the Service as to suppose that was I to be sent out in that character, that I *must* continue so; no my Lord, was it necessary to employ more Admirals in that part of the world I should be unworthy of your Lordships notice, was I to become third or fourth, or even fifth or sixth and to utter a murmur, should the King's Service require that number of officers senior to me.[22]

The inference to be drawn from the correspondence is that Sandwich did not consider Samuel Hood suitable for a promotion. Was his professional competence in question? He had not been offered an active post since the French joined the war in 1778. Why then did Sandwich make the offer he did six months later? It may be that political "interest" required Hood to stay where he was. He was not even give the solace of being told that the next promotion would include him and that at that point a more active post would be offered. The reply to this last letter was again in the negative and must have been a crushing blow to Hood. He had no option but to wait and see what the next promotion to flag officer might bring.

He told Alexander that despite the shattering of his hopes he could not dream of joining the opposition faction in the navy: "I have but one road to pursue, which is to give support to the King's Government." He told his brother that if Sandwich ever sought his opinion as to who should be promoted to a flag, Samuel would certainly name him, but after all that had passed, he doubted whether he would be asked![23]

Having a line of contact with the King, Hood wrote to George III telling him of his desire to move to a more active post. The King replied that he understood Hood's wishes and would use his best endeavors to get him a position when the opportunity arose. The reply seemed to offer Hood a gleam of hope in an otherwise dark prospect.

It was the West Indies that provided Hood with the opportunity to act again "in the military line" of his profession. Rodney had fought two actions there in April and May that, though marked by considerable tactical ability, were rendered indecisive by the failings of the signal system and the fact that Rodney did not take his subordinates into his confidence. He expected from them immediate and unquestioning obedience to his orders, not "initiative." Rodney was now in dispute with his junior flag officers, Hyde Parker and Joshua Rowley. Both had left—Parker under such acrimonious conditions that on arrival in England he was prevented only by the cajoleries of Sandwich from bringing charges against Rodney. There were therefore openings for two flag officers to support Rodney. Given his known temperament, filling them was not going to be easy.

Sandwich had given the problem some thought and told Rodney frankly, "I know not what to do to find a good second in command for you." He said he would give the matter serious consideration and would endeavor "to pitch on a person who, I think will be likely to second you properly and with proper subordination."[24] The post was first offered in July 1780 to Sir George Darby, who was serving as second in command of the Channel Fleet under Geary. Darby was told that, given the state of Rodney's health, he could soon expect to take over the supreme command. Darby nevertheless declined, and on the retirement of Geary through ill health succeeded him as the commander of the Channel Fleet. The following month the post was offered to Sir Francis Drake, junior to Hood, who also declined. This was a puzzling move by the Admiralty. As noted, Drake was junior not only to Samuel Hood as post captain but also to Sir Chaloner Ogle and Alexander Hood. Alexander may still have borne enough of the stigma of the Keppel-Palliser affair to make his appointment a political impossibility. Ogle, like Hood, also represented an unknown quantity, and his career was not to be distinguished by any particular command or action, so he may well already have been written off as not up to the demands of an active command.

The mystery remains why, in a straight contest between Francis Drake and Hood, the former was preferred. Hood had the connection with the

Linzees and his links with the Pitt and Grenville families, and in addition he was known and admired by George III. This amount of "interest" far outweighed anything Drake could command. The fact that Drake was chosen over Hood in the first instance allows of only two interpretations: first, Sandwich really did believe that Hood was doing far more vital service as commissioner at Portsmouth than he could in an active command or, second, Drake was considered better flag officer material. I favor the first: Hood was too valuable at Portsmouth to consider his change to other duties. Only when Drake declined did Sandwich decide that, in the interests of securing a proper second to Rodney, the offer should go to Hood.

The selection of Hood may also have been made easier because he had served under Rodney earlier in his career and might be considered to have some sort of personal relationship with him, though there is no indication that Rodney asked for him. It is true that Hood did not in fact quarrel openly with Rodney and to all intents and purposes appeared the ideal second, yet his letters home in 1781–82 were continually critical of the actions and motives of his chief. If Sandwich did not know of this aspect of Hood's character, it was unfortunate. Hood was a man who could serve happily only in first place. He was not an ideal second, for he thought too highly of his own abilities not to be critical of others. He has recently been called "able but disloyal."[25] This is probably a rather harsh judgment, as he never actively campaigned for Rodney to be dismissed, but it is true that his words of denigration would have become known and done damage to Rodney's reputation.

On 14 September the cabinet approved Hood's appointment and decided he would take five ships of the line to Rodney as reinforcements. He would be included in the next flag promotion and offered the post of second in command to Rodney forthwith. It is not known what influence, if any, the King may have had in the choice. Some must be suspected since Hood had been decisively turned down earlier.

Sandwich wrote to Hood on 15 September giving him the news that he was promoted and was to proceed on active service.[26] If Sandwich had any expectation of Hood's reply, given the bout of pleading earlier in the year, the letter he did receive must have come as something of a shock. Hood replied to the First Lord on 16 September:

I have the very obliging letter your Lordship did me the honor to write me yesterday. The very flattering offer of my Flag, and going to the West Indies, I should have accepted with great joy and thankfulness months ago, but now those bodily infirmities with which I have been afflicted for near twenty years, are of late become so very heavy and severe, that I have no spirits left, & can scarce keep myself upon my legs and should only be the shadow of a flag officer, for that reason I think it a duty I own to the best of Kings, and to my Country as well as to your Lordship, to decline the honor you have the goodness to offer me, and must content myself, with doing my duty as a zealous and faithful servant to my most gracious Sovereign in the office of Commissioner for the short time I have to live.[27]

To finish his letter of refusal, Samuel suggested that the post be offered to his brother, who would fill it in a very satisfactory manner. There is some possibility that Hood replied in this vein solely to maneuver the government into offering the post to Alexander. After all, he had been actively concerned with his brother's apparent "disgrace" with the Admiralty and had pressed Sandwich to offer him some suitable post.

Hood's reply must have been more surprising to Sandwich than those he had received from the Keppelite faction who refused to serve. Taken in the context of the letters Hood had been writing six months before, full of injured pride and a determination to secure his flag and an active post, it is hard to explain how such a change could have come over him unless we accept the letter as a ploy to seek advantage for Alexander.

For himself it is impossible to believe that, faced finally with the opportunity to serve in the "military line," he was suddenly filled with self-doubt and felt it better to stay in the safe position of Commissioner. The use of health grounds for declining is not easy to reconcile. His correspondence makes no mention of any particular ailment over the few months prior to the offer of the post with Rodney.

Hood had a whole weekend to think over the action he had taken. More likely he used the time to contact Alexander and to ascertain his wishes. It must have struck him that when the King heard of his action he would suffer a loss in the King's esteem, but this was a price he was willing to pay if Alexander could be restored to the confidence of the Admiralty. If there was one thing Hood believed in, however, it was professional pride and honor, and apart from the reaction of the King, the opinion of his fellow officers was important to him. He had talked to his brother of serving the King, and now he was invited to do so in the kind of active situation he had been seeking. With his brother's reaffirmed decision not to serve, Samuel was free to accept the offer on his own part. The result was that he wrote to Sandwich again on 18 September in a much more cheerful and optimistic tone:

> Feeling myself so much better than I was on Saturday, when I received the honor of your Lordship's letter of the 15th, and flattering myself that a warm climate will tend more towards removing my complaints than any assistance I can gett at home, I hope and trust I am not too late in signifying my very great readiness to accept my flag and to go to the West Indies, at your Lordship's pleasure.[28]

Having apparently accomplished a complete about-face, he could only hope that Sandwich had not offered the post elsewhere. It was a period of high anxiety while he waited to hear whether his "repentance" had been successful, and he felt it necessary to write to Sandwich again on 20 September:

> I have the very great satisfaction to say, that I find myself so much better within these few days, as to flatter myself, with being as stout and well as I usually am in a very short time, which leads me to repeat my very great readiness & wish of going to the West Indies with my Flag, and if it is your Lordship's pleasure so to dispose of me, I shall quit the Dockyard with pleasure and take the liberty of naming to your Lordship, Captain John Inglefield of the LIVELY sloop to be my Captain.
>
> and if my hasty reply to [Sandwich's letter of the 15th] should have led your Lordship to make the offer to any other officer I have only to blame myself for it.[29]

Comparisons of this letter with the one in which he talked of the short time he had to live are remarkable. His belated acceptance of the post was accepted, and his name was duly published in a list of flag officers with a seniority date of 26 September 1780. Other promotees included his brother Alexander, his future companion in arms Francis Drake, and Richard Kempenfeldt.

Now that the promotion had been agreed and the post accepted, Sandwich had to inform Rodney. In outlining his choice Sandwich said that it had been "difficult" to find officers willing or able to serve under Rodney. Some were politically objectionable, others infirm, and others not considered capable of performing the job. He said he had had to make a special promotion and that Hood was to have his flag and to bring out the next convoy and reinforcements.[30]

Rodney's reaction was mixed. He thanked Sandwich for sending "so good a man"—not a totally ringing endorsement.[31] When Hood arrived in the West Indies he received a more friendly letter from Rodney: "I know of no one whatever that I should have wished in preference to my Old Friend Sir Samuel Hood."[32] In private conversation he is reported to have said, "They might as well have sent me an old apple woman!"[33] Both sides would have had their reservations and been wary of the reputation of the other. Rodney did receive a letter from Keppel wishing him "joy of Sir Samuel Hood. It is impossible for me to say more than that."[34]

It has to be admitted that the selection of Hood for the command was something of a gamble. He had never fought in a fleet action and never handled any number of battleships. His reputation in the navy was as a frigate captain with victories in the previous war to his credit. He was now going to a different type of war without, seemingly, the tactical experience to satisfactorily fill the post.

Within a month Hood had hoisted his flag on the *Barfleur* (98) at Spithead. He came on board on 21 October to find that the force under his command now consisted of eight sail of the line: *Gibraltar* (80), *Invincible* (74), *Princessa* (74), *Monarch* (74), *Prince William* (64), *Belliqueux* (64), *Panther* (60), and his flagship. In addition there were four frigates and 120 merchant ships to escort. He wrote to Lady Chatham on 21 October that he hoped to sail with the first fair wind after 31 October but doubted if the convoy would be ready by that date.[35] The two Hood cousins were to go with him, and young Samuel was already on the *Barfleur*. The squadron sailed on 10 November.

Hood had heard from the Admiralty that a French squadron, believed to be in superior force, was also heading for the West Indies. Hood's first care was for the convoy and not to engage an enemy squadron, so he steered well to the north. By taking this course he hoped not only to avoid meeting the French but also to meet the homeward-bound East India convoy, which could then be warned of the presence of the French. Despite a stormy passage, Hood and the convoy came to anchor in Carlisle Bay, Barbados, on the morning of 7 January 1781. Not all the convoy were present. Some had been seen to depart as they neared their destination. These ships were later found at St. Eustatius.

At the time of Hood's arrival at Barbados, Rodney and the rest of the fleet were at St. Lucia. All the Leeward Islands as well as others in the West Indies had suffered from the great storm of October 1780. Barbados was particularly badly hit, and Rodney wrote that "the most beautiful island in the world has the appearance of a country laid waste by fire and sword."[36]

On the twelfth of January further sails were sighted making for Barbados and were subsequently identified as Sir George Rodney with seven sail of the line. The junction of Rodney's ships with those in Barbados raised his strength to twenty-one sail of the line. The partnership of Rodney and Hood would soon be tested as the French, once their reinforcements under de Grasse arrived, would be ready for the next round in the campaign.

The Other Side of the Channel

For the government of France, this was a time of preparing for conflict. The king, Louis XVI, had succeeded to the throne in 1774 at the age of nineteen. The diplomatic situation between Britain and France was delicate. While French representatives in Britain stressed their country's desire for untroubled relations, many French ministers felt that Britain's power was too great following her successes in the Seven Years' War and should be downgraded. The American War afforded a chance to do this, and it was understood in these circles that support for the Americans short of war would sooner or later lead to all-out war.

Ever since the Peace of Paris in 1763 the King and the governing elite had felt strongly that the humiliation inflicted on France had to be avenged. This feeling can be compared to that in Germany following the Treaty of Versailles. Under the government of Louis XV, intensive planning went on for the time when revenge could be taken. As conceived by the duc de Choiseul and the comte de Broglie,[1] a key element of this revenge was an invasion of Britain. The planners, mainly de Broglie and his agents, put together what is still regarded as the most detailed and competent invasion plan the French government ever produced. In its final version it entailed six separate operations to distract the British defenses, and the participation of Spain. The French were to mount attacks on Scotland, Minorca, and British possessions in the Indian Ocean. The Spanish were to attack Gibraltar, Jamaica, and Ireland. When British defenses had been sufficiently weakened by detachments to meet these threats, an army of 60,000 men was to be landed at four points along the coasts of Kent and Sussex and combine to march on London.[2]

This is not the plan, however, that would have come into operation if the Falkland Islands dispute had ended in hostilities. By that time the French realized that a major naval battle in the Channel was an essential preliminary to any invasion. Naval superiority would be achieved by a force of fifty French and Spanish ships of the line massed in the Channel prepared to fight and defeat the British fleet. But when it came to the point, Choiseul was unable to persuade the king and his colleagues to back the Spanish, and after the dispute was ended by negotiation, Choiseul resigned.

Partly this outcome was dictated by the weak state of French finances. War with Britain and a successful invasion would require a strong fleet—stronger than France in the 1760s could afford to build. In 1767 a British intelligence source said that the French needed to avoid war for at least ten years. Quite by chance this timescale brings us to the French intervention on behalf of the Americans.

The main ministers about the King held varying views. At this time the comte de Maurepas[3] was one of the most influential. De Maurepas had no official post but was adviser to the King, a similar position to that held by the Prime Minister in Britain. He had been French navy minister until dismissed in 1749.

The finance minister, Anne-Robert-Jacques Turgot,[4] who had also once held the post of navy minister, was well aware of the difficulties of the French financial position. Turgot was undoubtedly a man of genius and vision but was accused of arrogance. His enemies undermined his position with the king, and despite his best efforts he was unable to stop France entering into the war.

The most important minister of all was the comte de Vergennes,[5] the foreign minister. An accomplished diplomat, urbane and charming, he was dedicated to the "balance of power" in Europe. He had been a strong opponent of Choiseul and his virulent anti-British policy. Vergennes was not anti-British—in fact, he favored a rapprochement—but he concurred that the Peace of Paris of 1763 had left Britain too powerful. He wished not to destroy Britain but to reduce British power. Like many of his contemporaries, both French and British, he saw British control of America as the main ingredient in maintaining British power and prosperity. The loss of America would serve to reduce this power, and in the postwar period France would have a chance to increase her share of the American market and thereby increase her wealth while Britain suffered a loss of economic power and hence of influence in diplomatic matters. In the event, the exact opposite happened, and France inherited a crippling financial burden from the war with no compensating trade boom to offset it. Only Turgot had forecast the likely economic effect if France entered the war, and his opposition had not sufficed to stop the inevitable move to conflict. The British too had vastly increased their debt because of the war, but the British financial system was better able to cope with it, and the first flowering of the Industrial Revolution would transform the British trade position to one of increasing strength. Neither Turgot nor Vergennes lived to see the catastrophe of the French Revolution which swept away the Bourbon monarchy and the world in which they had lived and operated.

Vergennes believed that the loss of America by Britain would damage British trade, remove the power of Americans to assist Britain in her colonial conflicts, and lead to a reduction of naval strength. These French beliefs were influenced by the American delegates in France, who exaggerated how vital the trade with the Americas was to Britain's prosperity.

If France was to intervene in the American War, one precondition was necessary. Britain had to be denied any Continental allies that might come in on her side and conduct European land operations, thereby diverting French effort from naval operations. If the war could be presented as a means of restoring the balance of power in Europe rather than an aggressive war to destroy British power, then this end would be achieved. In 1775 the French sent a representative to meet the Americans. Their discussions had concentrated on what the Americans expected from France. The Americans said they wanted arms in exchange for goods, technical help, and goodwill.

The French financial weakness meant that war with Britain had to be deferred. In this period of restraint, it was argued, the Americans should be supplied with arms and other support in order to prolong the war and give the Bourbon powers time to prepare their own forces. The line had to be drawn very finely, so that the French support for the Americans was not enough to force the British into a declaration of war on their own account. On the British side, while there was a full awareness of French activities, the government likewise had no desire to come to an actual break with France. In these circumstances both sides made some pretense of normal diplomatic relations. As relations between Britain and France became more strained, so the French increased their naval expenditure.

The position of Vergennes was that war with Britain would certainly come. However, he knew that the King did not yet accept the inevitability of war or the support of the Americans, so he had to disguise his opinion. He certainly did not want Britain to seize the initiative and launch a preemptive attack on France or her colonies.

Eventually Louis was persuaded that aid to the Americans was in the French interest, and supplies began to flow across the Atlantic. Turgot as finance minister knew precisely where the path that Vergennes was treading would lead. He was not pro-British, but he was against war with Britain for financial reasons. Finally, having been unsuccessful in stopping the drift to war, he resigned from the government on 12 May 1776. His departure was the signal for increased funds to be allocated to the navy, which Louis XVI readily agreed to.

In conjunction with the discussions with the Americans, France was also talking to the Spanish. Both the Bourbon powers had been humiliated in the peace of 1763 and it was their common goal to lessen the power of Britain. Spain had a dispute with Portugal, who was an ally of Britain, but had been told not to expect French support. However, the French expected that when they went to war with Britain they would have Spanish naval support, which would offset the projected British naval superiority.

The French navy had been virtually destroyed in the Seven Years' War and had since then been on a slow path to recovery. Choiseul had taken over the post of navy minister in 1761 to begin preparing the French navy for the next war. He put in hand a shipbuilding programme and reformed the dockyards and the administrative system. Choiseul held this post until he was forced to resign by the Falklands crisis of 1770. The failure of the French and Spanish to enforce their will at that time led to the unpopularity and downgrading of the navy in the last years of the reign of Louis XV.

With the accession of the new king and the influence of Vergennes, the goal of a war aimed at reducing British power and avenging the humiliation of 1763 again came to the fore. The French government received regular intelligence from its representatives in Britain on the state of the British naval forces. In the year of the accession of Louis XVI the British strength was reported as 147 sail of the line, of which 72 were in service or ready for service. The French navy had only 64 sail of the line, of which about half were ready for sea. Choiseul's administrative reforms had not answered the purpose of increasing efficiency, and the the system was in chaos.

Louis XVI had an interest in naval matters. His first navy minister, Turgot, was replaced in 1781 by Sartine,[6] who became one of the most capable men France had ever had in that post. Sartine put through a series of reforms that energized the system and got work going again, and the numbers of ships ready for service began to increase. In 1775 Sartine began a process similar to that which Anson had introduced for the British navy. The sail of the line were to be classed: ships containing 80 guns or more, ships of 74 guns, ships of 64 guns, and 50-gun ships. Thrusting as Sartine was, he had to work within strict financial limits. Turgot was struggling to stabilize the budget, and retrenchment was the order of the day. This financial restriction severely affected the supply of timber. As in Britain, domestic sources could no longer supply all that the navy wanted, and purchases had to be made abroad. However, as Britain entered into war with the colonies, additional funds were released in order that the state of preparedness of the navy could be improved.

The French kept up their intelligence sources in Britain. Their main fear was that Britain would reach a settlement with the Americans and launch a surprise attack on France as had happened in 1755. They believed that Lord North would be replaced by Lord Chatham, who was more likely to reach a settlement with the colonies and was strongly anti-French. The French ambassador in Britain strongly urged Vergennes to enter into negotiations with Britain to solve the outstanding difficulties between the two countries.

In 1777, the last full year of peace, French naval preparedness gradually improved. There were British ships in the Bay of Biscay searching for American privateers and American trade with Europe, and these were often involved in nonviolent clashes with French ships. The American privateers used French ports both as a base and to return their prizes, which was a violation of the Treaty of Utrecht of 1713. The British government protested these actions by the American privateers and received bland reassurances from the French government that steps would be taken to control their activities. In the background Vergennes told Spain that by the end of 1777 the French fleet would be ready for war. Then came the news of the British defeat at Saratoga, which served as a signal to the French government that the British were not going to conquer the Americans easily and that the time for intervention was drawing near.

The French were meeting American representatives to agree a formal alliance. This was signed on 17 December 1777 and its terms included that American independence would be part of any peace treaty. The pact allowed France to enter the war when the time was right. France wanted the Spanish to come in at the same time, but finally agreed to proceed alone, as Spanish preparations were not as far advanced. The French at that time held a position of naval parity with Britain, but this was precarious, as there was sufficient timber available in the reserve stocks to build only nine sail of the line, three each at Brest, Toulon, and Rochefort. Unless France was successful in defeating the British in one campaign, they would be in a position of inferiority by the following year because of the better British building rate and the ships from reserve brought forward for service. The Spanish alliance would bring fifty sail of the line into the equation, which would give the Allies the necessary superiority over the British.

In January 1778 Louis XVI gave approval for the preparation of twelve sail of the line at Brest and ten at Toulon for immediate service. These preliminary preparations were necessary because news of the French alliance would be known in America by May and Vergennes would have to tell the British government before that time.

When Vergennes heard of the dispatch of the British Reconciliation Commission, consisting of the two Howe brothers, he was afraid that the Americans would agree terms with the commission and desert the alliance with France. He need not have worried, as the commission was not empowered to offer independence, which was the only position the Americans would accept. The appointment of the Howes made sense, for they were both considered talented in their respective fields. Both were very sympathetic to the American cause, though neither had spoken in Parliament on American affairs, so it is impossible at this remove to judge where they stood on the issue. They were believed likely to be acceptable to the American negotiators, partly because their elder brother had been killed in America during the Seven Years' War and had been popular with the Americans. However, the mindset in London was not really set on reconciliation. They still looked on a military suppression of the rebellion as the most likely scenario and the Howe brothers were instructed accordingly. The terms they were given were more on the lines of what would be offered a defeated America rather than one that was buoyed up by the news of Saratoga and the alliance with France, which alliance the Americans ratified on 4 May 1778.

On 18 March the French ambassador in London told the British government the news of the treaty signed with the Americans. He remarked that the "United States were in full possession of the independence proclaimed by the declaration of the 4th July 1776." The British immediately withdrew their ambassador from Paris, and both sides prepared for war. Neither side wanted to strike the first blow, though, and the two navies were instructed to avoid acts of hostility.

Within a month of these actions d'Estaing had sailed from Toulon with twelve ships of the line and five frigates destined for the American coast. The Admiralty did not received news of this force until a frigate from Gibraltar that had followed d'Estaing into the Atlantic reported back. The British had known about the preparations of the Toulon Squadron and had weighed the option of intercepting it but decided that this action would negate the Anglo-Dutch Alliance, which came into force only if Britain was attacked and did not bind the Dutch to come in if Britain was the aggressor.

Both sides had frigates cruising in the Channel watching for movements by the other side. It was these frigates that triggered the declaration of war by France. The French were aware of the fitting out of Byron's squadron and were unwilling to attack the British while Byron and Keppel stayed united, as together they had a force of more than thirty sail of the line. D'Orvilliers[7] wanted to know the movements of Byron, and it was his surveillance frigates that fought the first engagement of the war. On 13 June Byron sailed with thirteen sail of the line bound for New York. On 17 June two French frigates were sighted. Byron, wishing to conceal his movements as long as possible, sent two of his own frigates to ask the French captains to speak with him. The commander of the *Belle Poule* (36) refused, and an engagement between her and the *Arethusa* (32) followed. The engagement started at 6:30 p.m. and continued until 11:30 p.m. before both ships discontinued the action. The *Belle Poule* had lost 45 killed and 57 wounded and the *Arethusa* 8 killed and 36 wounded. The French ship made for the French coast and the *Arethusa* was unable to follow. This action was considered by the French to mark the beginning of the war. It is noteworthy that, judging from the difference in the casualty figures and the fact that the *Arethusa* was disabled, the French were again pursuing their strategy of firing to disable their opponents' rigging—a tactic that, unless it was followed up by an attack on the disabled opponent, was unlikely to show the decisive victory at sea the French hoped for.

THE FLAG OFFICER

Prior to Hood's arrival Rodney had returned from North America wanting to undertake some action against the French islands. There were only four French sail of the line in the area, at Martinique, and Rodney agreed with General Vaughan[1] to make an attempt on St. Vincent. Although the fleet was at St. Lucia by 9 December 1780, there was a delay in embarking the troops and the expedition didn't sail until the fourteenth. The delay had enabled the French to learn of the expedition and to reinforce their garrison. When the British arrived off the island, they found it had escaped damage in the hurricane and the garrison was well manned. Vaughan carried out a reconnaissance in force but, seeing no possibility of carrying the fortifications except by a regular siege, the British departed. This was the situation that prevailed when Samuel Hood arrived at Barbados with his reinforcements.

Now that Hood was in a theatre of active operations, he had a chance to demonstrate his abilities. He was, however, in second place in the chain of command, whereas his previous posts as commissioner at Portsmouth and as Commodore in North America had given him a taste of power and a certain freedom of action. Notwithstanding his later reputation, his promotion from Portsmouth to be Rear Admiral and second to Rodney must have surprised his contemporaries. In all his later career Hood never achieved what Howe, Rodney, Jervis, and Nelson achieved, a victory in a major engagement. His position in naval history is dependent on his brief tenure of supreme command in the Leeward Islands in 1781–82, his writings, and his Mediterranean command. In the Leeward Islands he demonstrated tactical ability; in the Mediterranean he showed himself, even at an advanced age, to be fully up to the demands of the political and naval facets of command. His writings show a keen mind often laboring under severe frustration and do not, to a modern reader, enhance his character.

In the middle of January Hood suggested to Rodney that he cruise at sea for a while. He had been feeling unwell and hoped that some sea time would restore him to health. He also hoped to intercept any French reinforcements coming from Europe for the new campaigning season.

Rodney was anxious not to lose contact with Hood completely, and he ordered him to cruise to windward of Martinique but on no account to get involved with a superior force. If the French were superior, he was to fall back on Rodney at St. Lucia. While on his cruise, Hood was also to arrange protection for the trade going to Jamaica. Rodney's orders gave Hood permission to stretch as far north as Marie Galante "and every eight or ten days to make Point Salines on the Island of Martinique." As soon as other ships were ready they would be sent out to join him. Hood sailed on 22 January 1781 with eight sail of the line and the frigates *Sybille* and *Swallow*. Two other frigates were also placed under his command, the *Boreas* and the *Hyaena*. These were the ships detailed to escort the merchantmen to Jamaica.

Under Rodney the advances in tactics and signaling that were so much discussed in the Channel Fleet had made little impression. Hood was the first flag officer to arrive who would have been familiar with current thinking on these matters. But he was not, as we have seen, practiced in the handling of ships in fleets or squadrons. A practical seaman with an inquiring nature, he must have been reasonably conversant with the ideas of his contemporaries, particularly Kempenfeldt. On his new station he would have been constrained by Rodney's own ideas. He would have sailed on his present mission with Rodney's code of signals and Fighting Instructions. Rodney was the determining force in the West Indies and the most successful British admiral of the war, but his fleets depended on obedience to signals and not on any freedom for individual initiative allowed by the admiral.

After the indecisive action off Ushant in 1778, all the fighting had been done across the Atlantic. In fact there was to be no fleet action in European waters until Howe's action off Cape Spartel in 1782. The fighting was being done in the West Indies, and later in the East Indies also. This was the result of the government policy in seeking superiority in distant seas rather than securing the home base. In the respective commanders in the West and East Indies, Rodney and Sir Edward Hughes, Britain had two men who adapted and used the existing instructions to fight their campaigns, and it has to be said that they did it successfully.[2]

While Hood was away, Rodney received dispatches telling him that war had been declared on the Dutch and he was to undertake attacks on Dutch ships and possessions, with particular mention of St. Eustatius as an object for early conquest.[3] This island was serving as a major center of trade in the region, especially with the American colonies. Even British merchants were later found to be keeping goods there and in some cases trading with the enemy. The British government believed that British merchants connived in shipping to the enemy not only commercial goods but naval stores including arms and ammunition.

The cabinet had heard a report from Sandwich in 1779, based on his conversation with Rear Admiral Barrington, estimating that two-thirds of the goods shipped across the Atlantic would end up at St. Eustatius and from there go on to support the French fleet at Martinique. This island, Rodney considered, was the prize whose capture would bring the greatest discomfort to the enemy. Even worse in Rodney's eyes, the island seemed much less inclined to oblige the British than it did the French and Americans. Rodney had long regarded St. Eustatius as a source of strength to the enemy through its trading activities.

If such a blow could be got in early, Rodney might very well catch the Dutch commanders in the area ignorant of the declaration and be able to pick up some easy captures. He consulted with General Vaughan about a combined operation. When Hood's squadron returned from its cruise, the troops were embarked and the expedition sailed on 30 January.

In an attempt to preserve the secrecy of the mission, Rodney took the fleet to Martinique and paraded it off Fort Royal (present-day Fort-de-France) and Saint-Pierre. He then left Rear Admiral Sir Francis Drake with six ships of the line to watch the four French in Fort Royal. (The French were still expecting their reinforcement from Europe under de Grasse.) Hood was also detached and went ahead with the *Barfleur, Alfred, Alcide, Invincible,* and *Monarch,* and the frigate *Sybille.* He had orders to block the entrance to St. Eustatius by stationing himself between Montserrat and Nevis. From this position he could stop all ships approaching and leaving. These ships, whose masters would more than likely be unaware of the declaration of war, would be taken by surprise and made easy captures.

On 3 February the British arrived off St. Eustatius and summoned the Dutch governor to surrender. The island had virtually no defenses, and the governor, who had just been assured that war with Britain was unlikely, had no alternative but to comply.[4] Later in the day Hood anchored in the harbor, having met very little in the way of incoming trade on his cruise.

When Hood dropped anchor, he was greeted with reports of riches almost beyond belief. The warehouses along the waterfront extended for a mile and a quarter and were filled to capacity with goods of all sorts, valued at more than £3 million—the equivalent of £300 million today, and a huge amount by any standards.

In addition to the stores of merchandise there were more than 150 merchant ships at anchor in the harbor. Some were British and may have been identifiable to Hood as ships from the convoy he had escorted over the Atlantic. Also in the port were the Dutch frigate *Mars* (38) and six small American warships. All of these were taken as prizes by Rodney, manned with British crews, and commissioned into the Royal Navy.

Rodney, with his sense of grievance against the island, fell on the spoils that now came his way. He believed, as did many others, that the island was a vital source of supply to the rebellious colonies and that its capture would be a serious blow to the rebel cause. Taking into account also the friendly and accommodating attitude of the Dutch in the West Indies towards the Americans, he needed no further incentive to adopt the stand that all goods on the island were forfeit to the Crown. No distinction was made between the types of property seized, much of it belonging to British merchants.

It is true that a certain element in the British mercantile community were happy to continue trading with the former colonies as they had always done and took no notice of the declaration of war between the colonies and Great Britain. It is also true that Parliament in 1780 had legitimized trade in some American exports because of their importance to the British sugar islands and to Britain herself. This all tended to complicate the situation and made Rodney's seizure of all the goods on the island less tenable. Rodney also had a chance to study documentation found on the island which showed that de Guichen had been supplied with stores after his action with Rodney on 17 April 1780. The provision of these supplies and additional workers had enabled de Guichen to proceed without having to detach any of his ships to Saint Domingue for repair.

The whole episode reveals Rodney at his worst and shows why so many people felt so unsure about appointing him to command at all. Apart from seizing the goods stored on the island, Rodney adopted some questionable methods, including even selling to enemy, to dispose of them. Eventually the goods were loaded on a convoy and sent home. This convoy fell victim to a French squadron cruising in the Western Approaches. When he eventually arrived home, Rodney's legal position was weak, and he was sued in the courts and lost. The papers seized at St. Eustatius and forwarded to the British government had mysteriously disappeared, and a vital element of his defense was gone. His life in retirement, up to his death, was bedeviled by his inability to pay the damages awarded against him.

In these circumstances it is not surprising that Rodney was accused, not least by Hood, of letting the riches of St. Eustatius affect his judgment. Overwhelmed by the prospect of being relieved of further financial want, he was unable to tear himself away from the details of the seizure and devote himself to the strategical and tactical problems of his command. It is said that the only thought he gave to the French was the possibility of their mounting an expedition to retake St. Eustatius. Vaughan, in his dispatch home, was cheerfully optimistic and said he believed that the capture of St. Eustatius would "completely crush the American Rebellion" and "greatly distress if not entirely ruin the French Islands."

On 5 February Hood was sent with a small squadron (*Barfleur, Alfred, Invincible,* and *Terrible*) to cruise to leeward and watch for French ships reported to be heading for Martinique. The order from Rodney contains a phrase that has become memorable for perfectly encapsulating Rodney's philosophy of complete and utter obedience to orders:

> My Captain [Young[5]] has presumed to think for me instead of obeying. I have desired him never to do so again, but obey the Messages sent him.[6]

The force under Hood cruised off St. Eustatius and picked up one merchant ship from a convoy that had sailed from there on 1 February. Rodney had heard of this convoy and had ordered Captain Reynolds[7] in pursuit. Overtaking it, Reynolds had forced its escort, a 60-gun ship, to surrender and brought the convoy back to St. Eustatius. The ship that Hood had stopped was a straggler. In this early period after the seizure, other merchant vessels were sighted and taken and sent into St. Eustatius.

In addition to the seizure of St. Eustatius, Rodney had planned other strokes against Dutch possessions in the area. He sent a small force to capture the nearby islands of St. Martin and Saba and planned expeditions to take Curaçao and Surinam. He promised Hood a force of five of the line and some frigates together with troops to attack Curaçao. Both Rodney and Vaughan had initially been keen on this venture, and in fact Vaughan had asked Hood to raise the matter with Rodney. According to Hood, Rodney and Vaughan lost interest when they saw the magnitude of the prize they had in their hands at St. Eustatius. As the government had ordered its capture as soon as hostilities against the Dutch were declared, they too probably understood the financial ramifications of the capture, and it is hard not to agree that a civil commissioner should have been sent out to deal with the matter of the seized property, freeing Rodney and Vaughan to resume their normal operational duties.

Hood returned to port on 12 February expecting to find arrangements in hand for the expedition to Curaçao, only to be told it had been cancelled because a French squadron had been seen in mid-Atlantic apparently making for the Leeward Islands. The news had been brought by Captain John Linzee of the *Santa Monica* who, while escorting some merchant vessels, had seen a force that he counted as nine or ten two-deck ships, presumably French, engaged on a similar task. Linzee had sent word ahead of their position and course. On receipt of this report Rodney immediately cancelled the operation against Curaçao in order to keep his force united.

The case is made by supporters of Rodney that he was influenced only by the thought that he might have to engage a superior French force. If he had sent ships from his own fleet on a long chase to leeward, it would be difficult to recover them. He was thinking strategically first of retaining his new conquest, which might be in danger from a French superiority, and then of a possible fleet action, for which he would need his maximum force. He was not, as Hood wrote to friends at home, entangled in the "lares of St. Eustatius." The news of the French ships, which were thought to be the Brest Fleet, proved to be a false alarm, but by that time the Curaçao plans had been irreversibly shelved.

It was obvious, however, that French reinforcements would be arriving soon. If Rodney received advance warning of the number and course of the French ships, he would be able to intercept them. Had St. Eustatius not been seized, Rodney would have taken his whole fleet to sea and cruised in the area most likely to intercept a fleet bound for Martinique. There were now pressing reasons for him to stay at St. Eustatius, quite apart from the increasing number of British merchants involved, for the financial implications of the capture were enormous, and all involved knew that they must protect the potential fortune in their hands from recapture by the French.

The letters of Hood give the appearance of a man uninterested in financial gain where the good of the country was involved. Hood knew, as well as anyone, the financial implications for himself. Unlike his brother, who was relatively well off and not known as generous in the distribution of his wealth, Samuel always suffered from a degree of financial insecurity. As previous correspondence has shown, he was not above seeking sinecures or the repayment of expenses he believed due him. In this he was not unique among eighteenth-century naval officers. But despite everything, he did have a professional ethic that placed national benefit above personal fortune.

With Rodney at St. Eustatius, Hood was to command the squadron sent to intercept the French convoy and escort. He was given ten sail of the line and ordered to join Drake, who was off Fort Royal with a further six sail. The combined force was then to cruise to windward of Martinique, along the approach considered most likely to be used by any force coming from Europe.

It would have been far better, of course, if Rodney could have been at sea with the whole fleet to await the arrival of the French. The seizure and looting of St. Eustatius thus was unfortunate for Rodney in two respects: it not only ruined him financially and cast a shadow on his professional reputation but it vitally affected the British cause by allowing de Grasse to slip into Martinique without having to engage in a fleet action.

Hood sailed on 13 February, and among those glad to see him get away was Walter Young. Young was a newly appointed post captain, but he had definite ideas on the management of the fleet and Rodney. He was virtually serving as Rodney's chief of staff and was in the best position to appreciate the strengths and weaknesses of his admiral's character. Rodney in turn appreciated his subordinate and the work he did. When Young died later in the year, he was genuinely sorry to lose him.

After the failure of the earlier attempt on St. Vincent, on 22 September, 1780 Young wrote to Middleton, a regular recipient of his letters: "at times [things] will get a little *outree*, but in this I am obliged to you great men at home who have so poisoned my admiral that he really, and *ipso facto* thinks and believes himself to be the very man you have represented him. God help us. How much mistaken you and he are." This was typical of Young's refrain to Middleton and also would become familiar with Hood in his correspondence. The criticism of his chief came from a very junior captain and must be looked on in that light.

With the departure of Hood, Young took the credit in his letter to Middleton for having got him sent out: "I am exceeding happy in having got Sir Samuel Hood to windward with ten sail of the line and frigates" where, Young said, he was expected to intercept a French force reputed to be eight or ten sail of the line—information evidently based on Linzee's report.

Having formed a junction with Drake, Hood issued his ships his order of sailing and battle:[8] *Triumph* (74), *Prince William* (64), *Gibraltar* (80), *Invincible* (74), *Barfleur* (98, flag), *Terrible* (74), *Princessa* (70), *Alcide* (74), *Intrepid* (64), *Resolution* (74), *Montagu* (74), *Russell* (74, Rear Admiral Drake),

Centaur (74), *Ajax* (74), *Vigilant* (74), *Alfred* (74), and the frigates *Thetis* (32), *Sybille* (28), *Convert* (36), *Hyaena* (24), *Boreas* (28), *Venus* (38), and *Cyclops* (28).

Hood reported regularly to Rodney on the condition of the ships under his command. The *Triumph* and the *Vigilant* were in such a bad way that they had to go to St. Lucia for repairs. The remainder were not much better, and he told Rodney that he would have to "carry the whole in in ten days at most." The ships had almost all seen a good deal of service and would be leaky and unsound, much as Rodney was to find his own flagship, the *Sandwich*.

While at sea Hood received regular letters from Rodney saying he hoped to join him as soon as matters at St. Eustatius had been arranged. His biggest problem at the moment was the British merchants who had stored goods there. These merchants claimed that they used St. Eustatius for storage because it was a neutral territory, safe from American and French privateers. Rodney believed that they used St. Eustatius as a base for trading with the enemy, and he despised them as a form of traitor. The more he dug into the affairs of the British merchants, the more incensed he became. He wrote to Hood on 25 February:

> It is impossible for you to conceive the trouble I have in putting matters to rights here and hastening this very rich convoy to Great Britain, every possible delay is given by those People who have the assurance to call themselves British Merchants though they had forfeited that name when they demeaned themselves and their Country by making themselves Dutch Burghers and as such it is my duty to treat them.
>
> The merchants of a neighbouring Island are equally guilty and have the impudence to lay their claims to part of the stores seized at St. Eustatius, and greatly threaten to arrest General Vaughan and myself for refusing their claim if we ever put our feet on shore at St. Christophers.[9]

While Hood and his ships waited and hoped, the French ships sighted by Linzee had headed further north. Rodney forwarded to Hood some intelligence stating that the French fleet and convoy had arrived at Martinique. On first receipt of this intelligence Hood doubted its authenticity, and on 10 March he wrote a letter to Rodney that shows to advantage his powers of reasoning:

On turning in my thoughts again and again the very interesting and important subject of your letter, I could not bring myself to believe the information that had been brought you respecting the arrival of the Enemy's convoy at Martinique.

I reasoned thus, had it taken a northern circuit between Martinique and Guadeloupe the ships bound to the latter Island would not have *passed it* and gone to Martinique to return back the next day, for the person from whom you got the intelligence says that it was brought *from* Martinique to Guadeloupe, this demonstrated that it was next to impossible the convoy went to the northward of Dominique [Dominica], and that it went to the southward round Point Salines was still more unlikely, for the *Prince William* left me the 27th of last month to reconnoitre the enemy at Fort Royal, and on the 28th (the *very day* the *convoy is reported* to *have arrived*) at Noon Captain Douglas was within five miles of the Men of War in the Bay, and was very positive no more than four ships of the line and three frigates were there, and as the *Prince William* came round Point Salines on her return to me, so large a convoy must have been seen, had it taken that route and on *that* day. From these circumstances I could not bring myself to give credit to the enemy's arrival at Martinique, and concluded it was a tricking rascally report of the St. Kitts gentry to take you from St. Eustatius, or else the French to take me from my station.[10]

There was nothing fanciful about the reasoning in this letter. It was the stated opinion of someone who had weighed all the known facts and had come to the opinion that, though an event was reported as having happened, it could not in fact have happened. To double-check his reasoning, Hood brought to off Point Salines and sent the *Thetis* to look into Fort Royal. While he waited for the return of the *Thetis*, twenty-one sail were sighted from the *Cyclops*. Hood signaled his squadron to form in line of battle and went down to investigate. The return of the *Thetis* confirmed that the French fleet had not arrived at Fort Royal. This must have been welcome information to Hood. He was also convinced that the sails sighted by the *Cyclops* were in fact a convoy of merchant ships bound from Jamaica to England. He therefore returned to his cruising station north of Dominica.

Rodney had also concluded that the intelligence was false, and he wrote immediately to Hood telling him to ignore it. (The false information was spread, Rodney believed, by the merchants of St. Kitts to draw the British forces away from St. Eustatius, since Rodney had taken the extreme step of arresting some of the merchants for "treasonable correspondence" and had sent them to England under guard in the charge of Sir Chaloner Ogle with a cover letter to Lord George Germain explaining the whole matter.) Rodney was pleased therefore to receive Hood's letter confirming that his subordinate had not left his station and been drawn to leeward, which would have left the route to Fort Royal open. He wrote a complimentary note to Hood on his reasoning and said that he too had given little credence to the information and now believed that it was a trick to get him to leave his station.[11]

Although Rodney had no thought of leaving St. Eustatius in the present situation, he was worried that the French reinforcements would get into Fort Royal without being intercepted. He therefore ordered Hood to abandon his cruise to windward and take his squadron close in to Fort Royal, which was on the leeward side of Martinique, to blockade the port and prevent the junction of the two French forces. He told Hood that this change of station would make it impossible for de Grasse to escape an action, as the French "always come down between Dominique and Martinique" and an advance frigate would give timely warning of their approach. Rodney also feared that the French might intercept the convoy he was sending home from St. Eustatius, which would have been a political and financial disaster. Rodney's critics believe that this reason, rather than any other, prompted him to alter Hood's cruising ground. From a remark in his letter to Hood it was plain that Rodney felt very tired and ill at this time, and he told Hood that he had asked for permission to go home with the convoy.

Rodney knew the chosen cruising area well. Apart from his present command, he had served there in the previous war as naval commander of the expedition that captured Martinique, and he was more recently commander in chief at Jamaica. His experience of the station was therefore far more extensive than Hood's, and he stood firm against the latter's pleas to be allowed to return to his old station to windward. Rodney was sure that with frigates properly placed there would be no trouble in bringing to action any French squadron arriving from Europe. But if he really believed that close in to Fort Royal was the best station to intercept French ships coming from Europe, why did he station Hood to windward in the first instance?

Hood received the order to change stations with dismay. The move to leeward would, he thought, give him less room for maneuver should the French be sighted. It would be difficult to mount a close formal blockade of Fort Royal, as the winds were variable and fluky, and he did not have the smaller vessels he needed for inshore work. He was to keep as close in to the port as wind conditions would allow, but he was not able to stop small vessels from entering the port, and his own vessels were fired on by French shore batteries when working close in.

Hood continued to be concerned with the condition of his ships. Rodney had borne this in mind in choosing the station off Fort Royal. Ships in need of provisions or repair could be sent to St. Lucia. In Rodney's later opinion, Hood had "grossly neglected" the facilities offered by St. Lucia and his fleet suffered accordingly. But in fact, on accepting the order to change stations, Hood told Rodney that he would have to take the *Barfleur* and five line-of-battle ships (*Alcide*, *Invincible*, *Resolution*, *Russell*, and *Prince William*) plus the frigate *Sybille* into St. Lucia to repair weather damage and to take on stores, water, and provisions. He placed the remainder of the squadron (*Gibraltar*, *Intrepid*, *Ajax*, *Centaur*, *Alfred*, and *Montagu*) under Drake, who would assume the command off Fort Royal until rejoined by Hood.

According to Mahan,[12] Rodney was aware from French sources that a large French reinforcement was on the way. This intelligence put the number at twenty-four sail of the line, and Rodney admitted in a letter to Admiral Parker at Jamaica that "I have scarcely sufficient number line of battleships to blockade the island of Martinique, or to engage the enemy's fleet . . . if their number should be so large as reported."[13] The Admiralty too had told him of an armament fitting out in Brest and gave its number as twenty-five sail of the line, but professed themselves ignorant of certain knowledge of its destination, though they guessed that it was likely to be North America and the West Indies. Given this information, Rodney should have been at sea with Hood where the vital action would take place. Rodney told the Admiralty that all of his ships except the *Sandwich*, which was not fit to cruise, were close in to Fort Royal but he had yet to see any sign of the anticipated French reinforcement.[14]

At St. Lucia the work on Hood's ships was soon completed, and he was able to sail again early on the morning of the twenty-eighth. Two hours later he sighted Drake, and by 10:15 the two squadrons were reunited off Fort Royal.

At about the same time, de Grasse had sailed from Brest with twenty-six ships of the line and a large convoy of merchantmen. The whole armament left Brest without being observed by any British ship, though it was lucky in not being seen by Admiral Darby, who was taking a relief convoy to Gibraltar. Darby had sailed from Spithead with twenty-eight of the line, having under his protection not only the Gibraltar convoy but also the East and

West Indies and North American convoys. He picked up some victuallers from Cork, and this diversion meant that he missed an encounter with de Grasse. While the Admiralty knew that de Grasse was to take a squadron to the West Indies, they had no watch on Brest to track his departure. More information on the sailing would have enabled Darby to be in a position to intercept the French squadron. An engagement between Darby and de Grasse in the mouth of the Channel would have altered the whole strategic outlook for 1781. Rodney would have been warned of the likely arrival of a French force and its condition. This must have brought him from St. Eustatius to join Hood and Drake. As it was, de Grasse got clean away and arrived in the West Indies, detaching Suffren with five sail of the line for the East Indies on the way.

Meanwhile Hood remained at his new station, still bothered by the change. He hoped, and told Rodney so, that the commander in chief would soon arrive with the remainder of the fleet and see for himself what Hood considered the falseness of their present position. Rodney, however, did not move. He had the affairs in St. Eustatius to concern him and the preparation of the convoy for home.

In early April Hood wrote to Rodney that he was eager to act "immediately under your flag" as he did not feel at all comfortable in the present position of the fleet. He stressed that he could not intercept French ships going to Martinique unless the French commander actually courted a battle, a most unlikely course. If the French did not want a battle, only a slight skirmish would result, which "may operate as a Defeat to the British Squadron, though not a ship is lost, and the enemy suffer most." Rodney was unmoved by the appeals of his subordinate:

> 'Tis with concern that I cannot possibly concur with you relative to the Fleet under your command, cruizing to windward of Martinique at this critical moment, I am well acquainted with the distressed condition of the inhabitants of that island, and of the infinite importance it is to the state, that their distress should be multiplyed, by a close blockade, which I must by all means desire you will persist in, and station your Squadron of line of battle ships and Frigates in such a manner as you may think most proper to answer so desireable an end.
>
> I cannot by any means approve of leaving the Bay of Fort Royal, and the ships therein (even for a day) unblockaded . . . I look upon the Blockading of the island of Martinique to be of infinite importance, and will hasten to you as many of the small Frigates, as can possibly

be spared from other services, the better to enable you to perform so essential a service.[15]

Rodney was preparing the spoils of St. Eustatius for dispatch home. The late arrival of the French fleet had convinced him that they had gone to some other area,[16] and his immediate concern was the four French ships in Fort Royal. A convoy under Commodore William Hotham was about to leave, and the escort would be no match for the French battleships if they should leave Fort Royal and intercept Hotham. The seizure of St. Eustatius was now known in London, and the proceedings of Rodney and Vaughan had been closely followed. The commercial interests involved with the British goods at the island had begun to protest the seizure of their property. They were able to bring pressure to bear on the government which Rodney was unable to counter. Sandwich, with his knowledge of the admiral, was bound to be influenced by the idea that Rodney was motivated purely by profit, given his known tendency to live beyond his means.

*   *   *

Ships and men were wearing out in the constant patrol off Fort Royal, and Hood told Rodney that he had two thousand men suffering from scurvy.[17] On 28 April, Hood and his squadron were off Point Salines when at 12:30 p.m. the frigate *Amazon* was observed signaling the approach of a hostile fleet. Some thirty minutes later the frigate was able to give details of the position and numbers, confirming that the approaching fleet was superior in strength to the British. The French reinforcements under de Grasse had finally arrived and the campaigning season in the Leeward Islands had now well and truly begun.

While the French reinforcements were far from unexpected, they had escaped from the Channel without being seen by any British forces, so there was certainly an element of surprise. There were reported to be twenty sail of the line, which gave de Grasse a superiority of three ships over the force Hood commanded. If they made a junction with the four ships in Fort Royal, then the British inferiority would be seven ships of the line. The French had under their protection a total of 150 merchant ships, the safety of which de Grasse made his first priority.

The whole force was coming round the southwest tip of the island and heading towards Fort Royal. As his squadron was situated, Hood was between de Grasse and Fort Royal, but he was to leeward of the French, so the options lay with de Grasse. Hood's fleet in order of battle and sailing was *Alfred* (74), *Belliqueux* (64), *Alcide* (74), *Invincible* (74), *Monarch* (74),

Barfleur (98), *Terrible* (74), *Princessa* (70), *Ajax* (74), *Resolution* (74), *Montagu* (74), *Gibraltar* (80), *Centaur* (74), *Russell* (74), *Torbay* (74), *Intrepid* (64), and *Shrewsbury* (74), together with the frigates *Amazon* and *Lizard* and the sloop *Pocahontas*. The British totaled 1,264 guns and included one 98-gun ship, one of 80 guns, and twelve of 74 guns. In addition to the ships under Hood's immediate command, the *Prince William* (64) was to join his squadron the following day. Although Hood was disadvantaged by being to leeward, the British ships, being coppered, should have had a sailing advantage over the French. In fact, as we have seen, many of the British ships were long overdue for refit and repair, while the French ships were fresh from the Brest dockyard.

In a situation of numerical inferiority and with a need to gain the weather gauge, speed of sailing was a vital element. The French had one ship of 110 guns, three of 80 guns, and sixteen of 74 guns, with a strength of twenty sail of the line and 1,534 guns. Waiting to join them were the further four sail of the line in Fort Royal, one 74-gun ship and three 64-gun ships.

With the two fleets in close proximity, de Grasse would have seen the strength of his position. He could prevent the British from closing with him while he carried out his mission to deliver the convoy under his protection to Fort Royal.

It was obviously too late for any operations that day, so de Grasse came to anchor and sent a boat ashore to acquaint them of his arrival and to concert action for the next day. He wanted the four ships in the bay to come out to join him.

Hood, being at an initial disadvantage, faced a different set of problems. Before the close of day on the twenty-eighth he formed his fleet in line and kept them cruising in close order in line of battle. First and foremost Hood had the task of getting to windward of the French and thereby gaining the initiative.

At 6 p.m. the British fleet was five or six miles off Diamond Rock at northeast a quarter north. The Diamond was a prominent pillar of rock off Fort Royal, which the younger Samuel Hood would seize during the Napoleonic Wars and use as part of the British blockade of Martinique. The order was given at 6:25 p.m. for the fleet to tack together, and it came round to the north and stood across Fort Royal Bay. This course seems to have been maintained until about 4:30 a.m., when the signal was made to bring to, "the signal for the line still flying." Some ships seem to have had difficulty at this point, being caught in the calm close to shore. Hood records that seven ships were three or four miles distant to leeward: *Torbay, Alcide,*

Ajax, Invincible, Belliqueux, Monarch, and *Terrible.* The ships caught the land breeze at 7:30 a.m. and made sail to close the center, as did the *Alfred,* which had also got slightly out of station. At 7:50 Hood made the signal for the van to fill, and at 8:30 for the rear to close the center.

The evidence about the events of the night is uncertain. Rodney accused Hood of lying to for the night as the French did, instead of making every effort to work to windward in order to be able to engage the French in the morning. As can be seen from Hood's journal,[18] the British did make efforts to achieve this but had to desist when it became obvious to Hood that nearly half of his fleet had got separated from the rest.

The French were sighted just after 8:30 a.m. De Grasse had got under way early on the morning of the twenty-ninth and taken his fleet and convoy around the southern point of the island, heading to round Diamond Point and Diamond Rock prior to entry to Fort Royal. It was as the ships were rounding the southern point of the island that they were seen by the British. The position of Hood relative to the French fleet on the morning of 29 April is not perfectly clear, but events indicate that he may have been to windward of the French when the two fleets sighted each other.

All the time they were in contact with the British fleet, de Grasse kept the merchant convoy to leeward and by that means got them safely to Fort Royal. While the French stood to the northward across Fort Royal Bay, the British were standing to the southward across the mouth of the Bay. In this situation an action of some sort was likely at any moment, and Hood ordered that the signal to prepare for battle be flown. The time was just after 9 a.m.

Hood reported in his journal that the French entered Fort Royal Bay sailing in line abreast. The British were in line ahead. By 11 a.m. de Grasse had been joined by the four French ships already Fort Royal Bay. Hood was unable to interfere with the junction. With the arrival of the *Prince William* to reinforce Hood, and with the four French ships joining de Grasse, the numerical inferiority of the British was now eighteen ships to twenty-four. At about this time some of the French ships are reported to have opened fire, but the range was too long and the British did not reply.

Hood signaled for the British ships to tighten the distance between themselves and to maintain the line of battle in close order. At this stage, finding French shot reaching their line, several British ships in the van began to return the French fire, but throughout the day the action was never fought closer than what Hood called "long shot."

Hood was now well into Fort Royal Bay and was sailing on a northerly course, parallel to the French. At 11:20 a.m. he signaled for the fleet to tack together, and the British came onto a southerly course. What had been the van ships were now the rear and vice versa. De Grasse, having got his convoy into Fort Royal, came onto the same course and made to close the gap between the two fleets slightly. The action became general from about 11:25 a.m. Hood kept his fleet close together and signaled twice for the van to close the center.

It is uncertain whether the British still had the windward position. Hood states in his journal that he was *unable* to close the French fleet and had to accept action at the range de Grasse chose. This would indicate that the French were to windward and able to dictate terms, but it could also mean that Hood recognized the inferiority of his force and was unwilling to engage at close quarters against such odds. Each side had something to gain by inflicting a decisive defeat on its opponent. For the British, it would have removed the threat of French interference from their operations in both the West Indies and North America. If Hood had crippled the French fleet off Martinique, it would not have been waiting for him and Graves at the Chesapeake four months later. For the French, a heavy defeat of the British fleet at this stage would probably have brought down the North government and ended the war. An active British fleet would always have a restraining influence on French operations.

The two van squadrons were most actively engaged at this point, though at such a range the firing was rather ineffectual. That it was not entirely so on the French part is seen by the damage inflicted on various British ships at this and other times during the day's fighting.

Soon after noon Hood recognized the need for closer action and signaled his fleet to shorten sail and heave to. By just after 12:30 p.m. the French were alongside the British, though at a distance, and the whole lines engaged each other for the first time that day. The French had the advantage of the windward gauge and did not close. This was Hood's grand gesture, offering battle to a superior enemy, and it was not an offer he repeated in the following days of the engagement. Long range though it was, some of the British ships took serious damage which necessitated them going for repair after the action. This does not indicate that de Grasse was "throwing away" powder and shot, as Hood claimed in a letter home.

There was a certain amount of risk in what Hood was doing. If de Grasse had taken his fleet to a close-quarters engagement, the preponderance of force he enjoyed would have afforded him a good chance of seriously damaging, if not defeating, Hood's squadron. In offering battle on these terms,

Hood must have been confident of the superiority of his fleet, particularly in gunnery. The most valuable asset the British had was the coppering of their ships, which gave them greater speed and maneuverability than their opponents. By slowing his squadron to allow the French to engage, Hood was discarding this advantage.

By 12:30 p.m. the action had become general all along the line, though the cannonading was still carried out at long range. Hood remarked that "most shots of both lines [were] falling short." The French began to draw ahead, with both fleets steering to the southward. Hood signaled for his van to make more sail.

Both fleets were nearing the channel between St. Lucia and Martinique. Once they entered, they would be exposed to fresher breezes from the land, which would tend to take the leading ships further away from the center and rear divisions until these too caught the breeze. The general effect was to stretch the line and create gaps between divisions. Hood made the signal for close order to try and maintain his formation as much as possible.

By now only the vans of the two fleets were still engaging. Hood noted that only one in ten of the shots fired by the British ships was reaching the French line. Since the damage caused was not worth the expenditure of powder and shot, he gave the order to cease fire. The center and rear of the British fleet did cease fire, but the van was left engaged and, led by the *Shrewsbury*, firing continued until just after 3 p.m. At one point the four leading British ships were engaged with eight of the leading French ships.

In this final part of the action the *Centaur, Russell, Intrepid*, and *Shrewsbury* suffered the most serious damage and casualties, as the center and rear British ships were not able to support the van. The *Russell* was the worst off, making a lot of water which the pumps could not control. Captain Sutherland informed Drake of his ship's condition and sent a message via the packet *Antelope* to Hood in the *Barfleur*. The crew had to work hard at keeping her afloat, and that night Hood ordered Sutherland to return to St. Eustatius. Some captains in the French fleet faulted de Bougainville for not pursuing and attacking these four British ships more vigorously.

The first day's fighting had cost the British 40 killed and 133 wounded. The most serious casualties among British ships were on the *Centaur*, which had 12 killed including her captain, John Nott, and 30 wounded. These totals are from Hood's journal, but Laird Clowes gives total British casualties of 39 killed and 162 wounded.[19] The French losses are variously given as 18 killed and 56 wounded (as given by Chevalier) and 119 killed and 150 wounded (quoting Beatson).

The day had seen de Grasse get his convoy safely into Fort Royal, but apart from that he handled his fleet cautiously. Given, however, that the safe arrival of the convoy was his first priority, this can be reckoned a major success for de Grasse, and Hood's failure to stop it a strategic defeat for the British. Hood can be credited with playing his hand well. He had to rely on the superior speed of his ships and trust to the competence of his captains. On the first day he tried to weather the French and, failing that, to have them come down to him. He was unsuccessful in both efforts, but he patently believed that a well-handled British fleet of coppered ships was capable of outmaneuvering, and if necessary outrunning, a French fleet.

The French had by now worked further to windward of the British, and Hood estimated that by 7 p.m. they were three miles from the British line. The French had not detached any seriously damaged ships to Fort Royal, and their numbers were still recorded as twenty-four of the line and three frigates.

The lights of the French were visible for most of the night, but about 1 a.m. on the thirtieth it began to rain, and by 2 a.m. not only had the watchers on the *Barfleur* lost sight of the French lights, but the bad visibility also made them lose sight of their own van squadron. Daylight, however, revealed both. The French were four or five miles to windward, the British fleet was somewhat scattered. Hood gave the signal for the van and rear divisions to close on the center and form line of battle. At about 8 a.m. the British thought that the French were going to attack their rear, but the movement came to nothing. The French were now about two miles to windward.

De Grasse had a better tactical position than on the previous day. His convoy was safe in Fort Royal and he still had twenty-four ships under his command. Hood with the loss of the *Russell* was down to seventeen, and others had suffered damage in the engagement of the previous day and were having difficulty in staying in the line. This time Hood did not try to tempt the French to come down to him, and he was unable to gain the windward position. He was aware of the condition of his ships as well as their numerical inferiority. It would not be a sensible decision, and contrary to his orders from Rodney, to hazard an engagement when he was in such a poor position.

The two fleets sailed in sight of each other but not close enough to engage. With the faster-sailing squadron, there might have been an opportunity for Hood to cut off part of the French squadron should de Grasse allow his line to become too separated. He made another effort to get to windward of the French by signaling a "general chase" just after noon. This signal flew for four hours as the British tried to gain the weather gauge. When this proved unsuccessful, it was hauled down and that for "line ahead" flown again.

Hood had been more circumspect this day, as he wrote he "judged it improper to dare the enemy to battle any longer." The French judged the day successful. They had pursued Hood, though too cautiously, and he had fenced with them and endeavored to keep his distance.

The night of 30 April–1 May passed quietly with no sign of the French fleet from the *Barfleur*. Serious leaking in two more British ships was causing concern. When the French were sighted at 5 a.m. they were counted as twenty-six sail rather than the twenty-seven (including three frigates) counted the previous day. There was a brief engagement between the *Torbay* and one of the French ships, but it came to nothing.

Hood signaled for his fleet to bring to at 8 a.m. to give the rear a chance to close with the van and center. He was soon under sail again and in line of battle. At 11:30 de Grasse and his fleet were seen "hauled close on a wind to the N" and by noon they were about eight or nine miles distant.

At 12:30 p.m. Hood ordered the signal for line of battle to be replaced with one to bring to on the starboard tack, effectively ending the action. The French continued standing to the northward on their way to Fort Royal. Hood recorded that he lost sight of the French fleet at 6:30 p.m.

The opinion of his contemporaries on the action is of interest. Sir Peter Parker, commander in chief at Jamaica, wrote to Sandwich:

> It is unlucky that Sir Samuel Hood was so much inferior to the enemy. I do not know the particulars of the action, but I can venture to affirm that he has, and ever will, conduct himself as becomes a brave and experienced officer, and to this opinion all the officers of the Navy who are acquainted with him must assent.[20]

This is a very generous tribute, but to Sandwich it must have seemed a slight "overegging of the pudding"! The government was keen for success, naval success above all, and all there was to report was another indecisive action. Sandwich may very well have taken into account the failure of the Channel Fleet (or the Admiralty) to warn Rodney and Hood that the French reinforcements were on their way, but to a hard-pressed government it would have been a welcome bonus to have a report of success against the French.

Hood wrote to all his usual correspondents on the action. To Henry Shales:

> I have had a long shot action with a French Squadron under the command of the Count de Grasse, consisting of twenty three sail of the line to my 18. My utmost endeavours were ineffectual to gett nearer, I therefore invited him to come to me, by putting His Majesty's Squadron under their Topsails, and though I am conscious of no one ommission and of having done everything that was in my power, which I am very sure will be readily acknowledged by Rear Admiral Drake and every Captain and officer I had the honor to command, yet my mind is not altogether at ease, fearing the fate of St. Lucia before I can get there. . . . I never once lost sight of getting to windward and tried every method, but it was impossible, and though the French Admiral had so great a superiority and his choice of distance, he has not, I thank God, no one advantage to boast.[21]

De Grasse had of course one great "advantage to boast" and that was the safe delivery of the convoy under his charge to Fort Royal without loss. In addition, though receiving damage, he had, while carrying out his primary mission, inflicted serious damage on some ships of the British squadron. These two factors gave him the best of the engagement. Hood had tried mightily with the force at his disposal but had not been successful either in intercepting and destroying the convoy or in defeating the French fleet. At the end of the two days the French were still seemingly as strong as when they started, while the British had several ships under the necessity of immediate repair. It was a strategic victory for de Grasse, and it is rightly called an "overwhelming French convoy success."[22]

Hood also wrote to Sir Charles Middleton on 4 May:

> . . . and though I am conscious of no ommission and of having done everything that was in my power for the support and honour of the British Flag, which I flatter myself will be readily acknowledged by Rear Admiral Drake and every Captain and Officer under my command, yet my mind is not quite at ease, fearing an attack may be made upon St. Lucia before I can get there. . . . I own to you I am not a little proud of my conduct while in sight of the enemy's Fleet, whatever may be thought of it in England.[23]

He wrote in a similar vein to his brother a month or so later, letters that illustrate very well how pleased Hood was with his performance, but with an underlying worry about the French being likely to strike against St. Lucia. If Hood had been able to engage and damage the French fleet at close quarters, there would have been no reason to fear a French attack on that island. As it stood, the French still had numerical superiority and appeared able to take the initiative whenever they wished.

Having protested to Rodney before the engagement over the close blockade of Fort Royal, Hood wrote on 21 May to his friend George Jackson, Second Secretary at the admiralty and onetime Judge Advocate of the Fleet, "never was a squadron so unmeaningly stationed as the one under my command." Hood told Jackson that the blockade of Fort Royal for so few weeks served no purpose unless it was intended to mount an attack on the island.

Rodney was not satisfied with Hood's actions prior to and during the engagement. In his opinion Hood had "grossly neglected" the availability of St. Lucia to replenish and repair his ships while the blockade was in progress. He further considered that Hood had wasted the night of 28–29 April by lying to instead of trying to work to windward. In fact, documentary evidence from the logs of the ships makes it quite clear that the British fleet was active during the whole night trying to achieve that aim. French intelligence sources later told de Grasse that Rodney was "extremely angry" with Hood when he heard that the latter "bore away from the French Fleet." On the opposite side, Hood was glad to make use of some comments of M. de Plessis, future governor of St. Vincent, who was with de Grasse during the action and said that "Admiral Hood had led his fleet like an angel."[24]

The condition of Hood's fleet after the action did not allow him great freedom of movement. The ships, excepting those that had come out with him in January, were in a poor state, having been on the station some time. Hood was also very short of men, with battle casualties aggravating an already acute situation. In addition, some of his damaged ships had to be got into port as soon as possible. Unable to maintain his position off Fort Royal, he withdrew in the direction of St. Eustatius. The *Intrepid*, *Centaur*, and *Torbay* were too badly damaged to continue with the fleet and were sent into St. Eustatius for repair. Hood with the rest worked their way to the northward to regain St. Eustatius, the currents making St. Lucia impossible for any crippled ship to reach.

The arrival of the badly damaged *Russell* at St. Eustatius was the first indication to Rodney that the French reinforcements from Europe were now in the area, and in sobering numbers. The news was enough of a spur to get the admiral to sea with his two remaining ships, the *Triumph* and the worn and leaky *Sandwich*, on 4 May. He steered for St. Lucia, expecting Hood to make for there after his action with de Grasse. Both admirals recognized the importance of the island as the only port in British hands that could conveniently be used to counter the French force at Fort Royal.

While passing near St. Kitts, Rodney heard gunfire. He altered course for the island and anchored. It seemed the garrison had sighted a large ship approaching. This later proved to be the *Centaur* returning to St. Lucia, following the death of Captain Nott, to repair battle damage. In addition to the *Centaur* the garrison had also seen a large fleet standing to the northward, which caused them some alarm, but officers from the *Centaur* were able to assure Rodney that the sighting was Hood's fleet.

Rodney received a letter from Hood via the *Centaur* containing an account of the events of 28– 30 April. The *Centaur* was soon joined by the *Intrepid* and the *Torbay*, both of which Rodney took under his command. Certain essential repairs were made to the damaged ships before they were ready for sea again. Rodney then sailed from St. Kitts to join Hood with the intention of frustrating the feared attack on St. Lucia.

The two admirals joined forces on 11 May between St. Kitts and Antigua, and on the twelfth the combined force went to Antigua for further repairs and provisioning. After some repairs, Rodney left with twenty sail on 14 May. The British were right to be concerned about St. Lucia, as a captured French document gave a very accurate summary of the actions and motives of the British commander at this time:

The enemy [the British] propose to relieve St. Lucia cost what it will. General Vaughan is in the SANDWICH, but they have not taken any troops from St. Eustatius or St. Christophers. They reckon about 800 men fit to land on board the Squadron. As well as we can judge of things Admiral Rodney's plan is to venture an action, but he did not exactly know our Naval force here. He was much afraid that we might attack St. Lucia when he sailed from St. Christophers. . . . There remains at St. Eustatius only the 15th Regiment. They have sent to St. Christophers the first battalion of the Royals, which makes that garrison 12 hundred men strong. The last news from England of March 16th made Rodney very easy. He was told our Squadron consisted of only ten ships of the line. He was told of eight who were to come after the Gibraltar expedition which must be over by this time. The naval force of the English in these waters consists at present only of twenty ships of the line and the *Panther* of sixty guns. They have strengthened their garrison at St. Lucia. General Vaughan told the person from whom I got this intelligence, that, that Garrison consists of fifteen hundred men, twelve hundred of whom are good troops. That is not the general opinion here, it is thought there are not eight hundred and Rodney's intended plan seems to prove it. I hasten to send you this account which I received from a vessel that came from St. Christophers last Friday. . . .

PS There is a general uneasiness among the English on account of their Garrison at St. Lucia. I judge it is founded on the number and quality of their Troops. . . . I beg you will excuse all mistakes in this it is written in such an hurry, it cannot be correct, but it contains what is true and what you may depend on.[25]

This intelligence report was originally addressed to the marquis de Bouillé, but the agent was unable to make delivery and so sent it to M. de Plessis at St. Vincent instead. It is a reasonable summary of the British position and an indictment of the lack of security that seemed to prevail, particularly concerning General Vaughan, in disclosing the number of troops to be taken on service.

At Barbados, another island Rodney perceived to be under threat, he received more news of the French. Together with an attack on St. Lucia, a secondary attack had also been made on Tobago. The French force attacking Tobago was small, only two sail of the line and 900 troops. Rodney dispatched Drake with six sail of the line to save Tobago and defeat the French detachment. Drake, however, was delayed in getting to sea by a shortage of provisions.

Hood learned from Edmund Affleck, First Captain to Rodney, of the decision to split the fleet, with Drake to go to Tobago and the rest to St. Lucia under Rodney. Reports reached the British that twenty sail of the line were off St. Lucia but not yet attacking. Hood thought that this was a decoy and that the main French force was on its way to Tobago. In fact Hood was wrong: de Grasse had brought virtually his whole force to attack St. Lucia with only a detachment at Tobago. He even anchored in Gros Islet Bay before being driven out. The saving of St. Lucia was entirely due to the fortunate arrival of three frigates that put enough men ashore to man the defensive batteries.[26] Only then did de Grasse take his ships to Tobago to join the detachment attacking that island. He had feared that the British might have descended on Tobago in strength and destroyed his detachment.

Hood told Rodney that if Tobago fell, the French would next attack Barbados, "where little resistance could be made." Hood proposed that the fleet go to Tobago "clearing the way" as it went. He suggested splitting into three divisions, one going to windward, another to leeward, and the final one steering for the center of the island. He judged that if de Grasse found that the British had not been drawn to leeward, he would have to fall back on Tobago to protect the detachment he had there. If he did, he would find Rodney with the united British force waiting for him. If de Grasse did not attempt Tobago, the British forces would still be able to get to St. Lucia, thereby securing both places.

Sending Drake to Tobago with only a small force might well have worked if Drake had been able to get away promptly and if the French had been occupied by their attack at St. Lucia. Drake could have attacked the detachment with his superior force while Rodney with the main force went to St. Lucia in sufficient strength to make the French abandon their attack. However, the French repulse at St. Lucia shifted the balance of their attack to Tobago, collecting further troops from Martinique on the way. De Grasse arrived at Tobago to unite his whole force and was glad to find that the British had not been sighted.

Drake sailed on 28 May and sighted Tobago on the thirtieth. He counted a French force of twenty sail of the line and, obeying instructions, withdrew and fell back on Rodney at Barbados. Drake had the windward position, so he was able to get his fleet out of danger without too much trouble. As Hood put in a letter to Shales, "Mr Drake very wisely retreated as fast as he could."[27] A frigate was sent ahead by Drake to warn Rodney that the main French force was off Tobago.

Drake arrived at Barbados on the evening of 2 June, and Rodney got to sea the following morning. He said he was determined to give battle to de Grasse, but if this was his intention, his lack of urgency foiled it. He could have sailed with greater certainty when he received news on 30 May that the French were to windward of St. Lucia, or he could have sailed when Drake's frigate brought the news that the French were at Tobago. Instead he waited until Drake was sighted before giving orders to prepare for sea.

The British were off Tobago by the afternoon of 4 June when a body of fourteen sail were sighted to the southwest, followed by thirty more coming from the direction of Great Courland Bay. It could only be de Grasse, and it could only be understood that Tobago had fallen. In fact the island had surrendered soon after Drake was seen to turn back, a decision helped by the threat of de Bouillé to burn the plantations until the garrison surrendered.

The British counted the French force as twenty-four of the line against the their own force of twenty. For some reason, in writing to Henry Shales, Hood gave the British strength as twenty-four of the line also.[28]

When he sighted the French, Rodney had the windward position and would be able to force an action. The French were in an irregular formation, as they had only just raised anchor and were coming out of Great Courland Bay. This situation, at 4 p.m. on the fifth of June, reflects the one that faced Graves at the Chesapeake three months later to the day.

By 6 p.m. the distance between the two fleets was estimated as nine or ten miles, with the French still not formed into a regular line. There seemed to be every chance that the British could attack the French before darkness made further action impossible. Rodney had his line well formed and had only to give the signal. Yet he resisted the temptation to attack and kept his line formed parallel to the French. In his dispatch he wrote: "the situation was such as rendered it impossible to attack them with a probability of success, as it was in their power to entangle His Majesty's Fleet in the Grenadines."[29] He stressed the strength of the currents in the Grenada Channel which would have carried the British ships far to leeward, exposing the rest of the British possessions to danger. Rodney also had to bear in mind the safety of Barbados. This island had suffered severely in the hurricane of October 1780 and its defenses were not fully restored. Rodney had also expected Tobago to hold out longer. To this end he had sent some guns the previous year, but they were never utilized and still lay where they were landed. The general surrender upon the French threat to burn the plantations must have lowered Rodney's opinion of the British West Indian commercial sector still further following the discoveries at St. Eustatius and the trouble with the St. Kitts "gentry."

These were good reasons for not attacking. The British had to protect their position in the area. The loss of Barbados and, worse still, St. Lucia would have been a disaster. Tobago was lost, but it was not so much a serious blow as a humiliation. The island could be recovered by the decisive defeat of the French fleet. However, this could occur only if both sides were willing to engage in a trial of strength, and there was no reason to believe that de Grasse would be so willing. For Rodney, occupying the windward gauge would be useful only if de Grasse cared to wait for the British to come down to him. Rodney guessed, probably rightly, that a fleet action was not necessary for the French and that their tactics would be to draw the British further to leeward.

The British could probably have won a battle with de Grasse, but would it have been decisive enough to end the French threat in the area? The power of the French fleet had already been proven by the damage its gunnery had inflicted on Hood off Martinique. If the British fleet received further serious damage, its future operations would be hampered, as any prospect of reinforcements from home were slight.

The opinion of Hood on the loss of Tobago is set out in a letter to his brother Alexander on 9 June:

> Had Sir George Rodney fortunately gone to Tobago with his whole force on the 27th (the day after the account came of 9 sail of the enemy being off that Island) he would not only have saved the island but must have taken every ship and soldier there, nay had he sailed on the 28th with Mr Drake the Islands would most probably have been saved, as it did not surrender till after the retreat of our ships from De Grasse's whole force. This is a very unlucky business, and if the force of this country is not kept together, I tremble at what may happen.[30]

Against this opinion Rodney maintained in his dispatch that the whole fleet was not in a position to proceed earlier than it did owing to the necessity to refit and reprovision.

During the night of 5–6 June the British stood further out to sea. Rodney ordered lights shown prominently on the British ships so that the French could see and follow them with a view to a fleet action the following morning. It was not part of de Grasse's plan to fight an action, and while Rodney shaped course away from land, de Grasse, having achieved his objective of the capture of Tobago, steered for Fort Royal. When daylight came the British found that they were alone.

As the French could have gone nowhere but Fort Royal, Rodney felt concern for the safety of St. Lucia and Barbados. He detached part of the fleet, including the ships carrying General Vaughan and his troops, to return to St. Lucia. With the rest he went to Barbados.

De Grasse was back at Fort Royal by 18 June, while Rodney had anchored at Carlisle Bay a few days earlier. The French had every reason to feel pleased with the campaign so far. They had secured the safe arrival of their reinforcements from Europe and had captured Tobago. They had been unsuccessful at St. Lucia, but they had a numerical advantage and held the strategic initiative. The British, on the other hand, had been reacting to French moves ever since the unheralded arrival of de Grasse off Martinique in April. They had seized St. Eustatius before the arrival of de Grasse, but this now became only one more island to defend. The British needed to bring on a fleet action. The French did not.

By the time the fleet arrived at Barbados, Rodney must have given some thought to his own personal position as well as the strategic position. He had received permission to come home during the winter months and leave the command to Hood. He felt inclined to this course, but as he wrote to his wife, how could he return home and leave Hood facing a superior fleet that he might have to engage at any time?

There seems to be no doubt that at this time Rodney was severely depressed by the course of events in the West Indies as well as by his own health. On the days when he felt worse than usual and his physical infirmities were bearing down on him, he told Hood that he would certainly be going home. Later he would change his mind and say that he was determined to serve on. Such a state of affairs was galling to Hood, who showed no sympathetic consideration for his chief:

> It is quite impossible from the unsteadiness of the Commander-in-Chief to know what he means three days together. . . . if he quits this command he will get to England at a time that many mouths may be opened against him on the topic of Tobago, and his not fighting the French Fleet off that Island after the public declaration he made to every one of his determined resolution to do it, and again if he stays much longer, his laurels may be subject to wither.[31]

The tone of the letters written by Hood at this time indicate a man rapidly losing patience with his position. He was irritated by Rodney's indecision and by his actions over Tobago. And if those causes had not existed, he would have been at odds with his chief over the question of patronage. Rodney had decided not to confirm one of Hood's appointments. Following the death of Captain Nott of the *Centaur*, Hood had posted Edward Smith[32] to its command, a promotion from the sloop *Pocahontas* that Rodney approved. In place of Smith in the *Pocahontas* Hood promoted John Burr,[33] his own first lieutenant. This appointment Rodney did not approve, instead appointing the Hon. Alexander Cochrane.[34] In answer to Hood's protest, Rodney said that he had his own obligations to meet, after which he would be glad to oblige Hood. Relations with Rodney were therefore difficult on several fronts.

The combination of Hood and Rodney had not broken down, like that with Hyde Parker, but it was under strain. Hood was basically kind and generous to his family and friends, and understanding to his juniors. He had, however, a high opinion of his own abilities and was not slow to carp and criticize in his relations with his superiors. It is doubtful if Hood ever spoke to Rodney as strongly as he wrote to his friends and acquaintances, but a sick man with a strong will and a view of strict subordination was not likely to sit easily with a self-opinionated man with a short temper. Working together with tact and understanding on both sides, they might have achieved much, but Rodney was not the man to accept such a position and Hood was not the man to offer it. As Dorothy Hood says, oil for troubled waters was not among the qualities of Samuel Hood.[35]

Up to this point, to outward appearances, the partnership had held together and showed signs of mutual accord. There were certainly no open splits as had occurred with Rowley, Hyde Parker, and Arbuthnot, though the recipients of Hood's letters would have known the true situation. The first open disagreement between the two men, over the goods seized at St. Eustatius, came soon after the fleet anchored at Barbados. Hood recounted the incident in a letter to Alexander on 22 June:

> I treat him with great respect, and keep rather at a distance from him, which appears to me to be the best mode. He has never flown out before me, but once and that was on anchoring in this bay, when he assembled the Captains to communicate the King's intentions respecting His Majesty's relinquishing to his Land and Sea Forces His rights in the effects taken at St. Eustatius, and told them, that if they will meet on board the *Barfleur* next morning, I would make known to them propositions with regard to the distribution, which propositions he put into my hands, without saying a word about them. They were handed to the several Captains, who said that as they bore no signature nor had any writing annexed explanatory of them to show from whence, or from whom they came, they thought I should mention it to the Admiral. After they were withdrawn and no one remained but Admiral Drake and me, I said to Sir George that I believed it would be satisfactory to the Captains that the letter which accompanied the propositions was shewn. He answered they were not sent to him, but to General Vaughan, and that the Admiralty had not said a word to him upon the subject. I then replied, don't you think it right Sir George, that I should be able to answer certain questions that will naturally be asked upon the subject. He said yes, by all means, rung his bell, and asked if General Vaughan was gone on shore. Word was brought that he was, he then desired Lt. Col. Ferguson might walk down. When he came some words in a whisper passed between them,

and the Colonel withdrew. Upon which Sir George sat down and took up a pen as if to write, and flew out in the most extraordinary manner you can imagine. Swearing and making use of language that a Boat-swains Mate would have been punished for, and saying he would not be ill treated by any Admiral. Upon which after his going on for some minutes I said if you mean what you have said to me, I beg to tell you that you shall never find me wanting in respect to you, and that I will never with a shadow of justice put in your power to say, I have used you ill; he then took up his hat, said good afternoon Gentlemen and went out of the ship, throwing his hat in every ones face as he passed along the deck, and muttered till he got in his Boat, that by God he would not be used by any Admiral whatever. Everyone thought he was mad. When he went on board next day, he expressed contrition to Affleck, as Affleck told me. I said I was glad of it, but would take care to put it in his power as seldom as possible, to behave to me in so unofficer like as well as ungentleman like a manner, and I never went to him for ten days, and then it was to carry a report of a Court Martial. He received me with great politeness, and began to apologise for what I have related, when I immediately stopped him, and said if he was convinced of any improper behaviour towards me, was all I wanted, and desired he would not say a word more. Since which he has been all humility.[36]

As the incident shows, Rodney was under a great deal of physical and mental strain. The question of St. Eustatius was more worrying to him than anything else, for he was by now aware of the increasing criticism at home. Now, however, the matter of what to do with the fleet over the winter had to be settled. Intelligence of French movements or at least clues as to their intentions were needed to make the great decision. Unfortunately, although the information was available, the British misinterpreted it with fatal consequences!

THE CHESAPEAKE

THE FORCES GATHER

While the British fleet refitted at Barbados, de Grasse and the French fleet arrived at Fort Royal on 18 June and began to prepare their ships for sea again. The time was coming when the trade convoys of both sides would have to be escorted to Europe. De Grasse ordered all the trade ships to collect at Fort Royal and took the convoy as far as Cap François (present-day Cap Haitien), where he arrived on 16 July to find the frigate *Concorde* from Boston with dispatches for him.[1]

The letters were from the comte de Rochambeau,[2] commander of the French forces in North America. De Grasse had written to tell Rochambeau that after the end of the campaigning season (about the end of June) he would be at Saint-Domingue (Santo Domingo, or Hispaniola) preparatory to bringing his fleet north, and he asked Rochambeau to send pilots for the North American coastline. Now Rochambeau had sent the *Concorde* bearing a reply and twenty-five pilots. The British soon knew of their arrival and numbers and, it is often observed, should have inferred the intention of de Grasse to take his whole force north. In fact, this action by de Grasse would be contrary to his instructions, which asked that he use some of his force, twelve or fourteen of the line, to cooperate with the Spaniards. This was still his intention until he heard from Rochambeau.

The letters informed him of the military situation in North America, including the invasion of Virginia by Lord Cornwallis[3] and the plans of Washington and the Franco-American army to attack New York, with an alternative plan to take the offensive against Cornwallis in Virginia. Washington had recognized that superiority at sea was a prerequisite to the success of either plan. Rochambeau urgently pressed de Grasse to bring his fleet north, either to the Chesapeake or to New York, leaving the choice to him. In either event the admiral was to bring with him as many troops as could be spared. Rochambeau also wanted de Grasse to bring 1.2 million livres to pay the troops in North America, where he was experiencing great difficulty in getting enough specie. Rochambeau stressed the desperate straits to which the American and French commanders were reduced:

> I must not conceal from you, Monsieur, that the Americans are at the end of their resources, that Washington will not have half of the troops he is reckoned to have, and that I believe, though he is silent on that, that at present he does not have six thousand men; that M. de Lafayette[4] does not have a thousand regulars with militia to defend Virginia, and nearly as many on the march to join him; that General Greene[5] has pushed a small force far in advance of Camden, where he was repulsed, and that I do not know how and when he will rejoin M. de Lafayette; that it is therefore of the greatest consequence that you will take on board as many troops as possible; that four or five thousand men will not be too many, whether you aid us to destroy the works at Portsmouth, Virginia, near Hampton Roads, where up to now they have always kept fifteen hundred men while the others operate in the country, and all their flotillas with which they have tormented the poor Marquis de Lafayette on the rivers in a very evil manner.[6]

When he read of the situation in Virginia and the critical position of the Americans, de Grasse decided that the proposed joint operations with the Spanish could wait until the following year. In reply to Rochambeau he said that he had consulted with the governor of Saint-Domingue and that 3,000 infantry and a small force of artillery and cavalry could be got together. More important, he could bring along with the artillery several siege pieces. He would hope to embark this force and be ready to proceed by 3 August.

The money requested by the French and American commanders was more difficult, and de Grasse found it could not be supplied from French resources. The French plantation owners, the most likely source of funding, were not willing to advance such a sum without some form of security. De Grasse offered his estate in France, as did another French commander, but he was not able to complete the deal. He would have to get it from the Spaniards in Havana, which he did. The Spaniards, showing more zeal for the common cause than their French counterparts, fully subscribed the loan in a few hours. One Swedish officer serving in the French fleet believed that it was a quid pro quo gesture because the Spaniards felt guilty about their seven idle line-of-battle ships in the harbor.

De Grasse did, however, set certain parameters with regard to himself and the forces he would bring with him and pointed out that he was exceeding his instructions and acting without the prior knowledge of either the French or Spanish ministers:

> As neither myself, nor the troops commanded by the Marquis de St. Simon, can remain on the continent after the 15th of October, I shall be greatly obliged to you if you will employ me promptly and effectually within that time, whether against the maritime or land forces of the enemy. It will not be possible for me to leave the troops with you beyond that period; first, because part of them are under the orders of the Spanish generals, . . . and, secondly, because the other part are destined to the garrison of St. Domingo, and cannot be spared from that duty by M. de Lillancourt. The entire expedition, in regard to these troops, has been concerted only in consequence of your request, without even the previous knowledge of the ministers of France and Spain. I have thought myself authorized to assume this responsibility for the common cause; but I should not dare so far to change the plans they have adopted, as to remove so considerable a body of troops.
>
> You clearly perceive the necessity of making the best use of the time, that will remain for action. I hope the frigate, which takes this letter, will have such dispatch, that everything may be got in readiness by the time of my arrival, and that we may proceed immediately to fulfil the designs in view, the success of which I ardently desire.[7]

Rochambeau had told de Grasse that he considered the most important object was to achieve a naval superiority at the mouth of the Chesapeake, though he also offered for consideration Washington's alternative plan of an attack on New York. It did not take de Grasse long to decide that a concentration at the Chesapeake was the right action, from which, as he told Rochambeau, "the advantage you propose may be most certainly attained." The *Concorde* took de Grasse's reply of 28 July to Newport to advise the Franco-American command of his decision.

The urgent financial pleas of Rochambeau were indicative of severe financial strain, the Achilles' heel of the Franco-Spanish war effort. Naval war with Britain had led the Allies into a serious financial crisis. The Bourbon monarchies' tax collection systems were not as efficient as Britain's, and a far lower percentage of the tax collected ended up in the treasury. This created a chronic shortage of money not only to pay the existing forces but to continue to fit out ships and provide troops for the future for both governments. It was the recognition of superior British financial power that forced the French and Spanish governments to negotiate reasonable peace terms when the time came in 1783, for the British had the means of credit to take out loans at much more favorable interest rates. The warning of Turgot, the finance minister of Louis XVI before the war, that it would prove ruinous to the country was proving true. The French had created their finest fleet since the days of Colbert, but it had been very expensive to build and maintain and was increasingly difficult to man. Despite all the efforts and the number of ships that the French and Spanish had managed to put to sea, they had been unable to inflict any decisive blow against the British.

In the current situation the troops were relatively easy to collect. The period during which they would be absent was the hurricane season, when the weather precluded any campaigning. Both navies withdrew their major vessels during these months, so combined operations would be impossible for either side.

Having now obtained the troops and the money, de Grasse was free to proceed to North America. The Spanish had agreed to stand guard in the area over both the French possessions and their own while de Grasse was away, so he could go north with an easy conscience. In one decision that eased his worries over possible French trade losses, he cancelled the sailing of the convoy to Europe. This convoy was to be escorted by ten ships of the line that needed to go home for essential repairs. It was a decision he would probably not have taken for any other reason than to achieve the numerical superiority that he considered essential in North America. It is doubtful if Rodney, no matter how hard pressed, would have been willing to take the same step. Rodney recognized, like de Grasse, that naval superiority on the American coast was vital. But, critically, he did not think the French would go with their whole force and that trade would be abandoned for political and strategic reasons. At this crucial time de Grasse proved himself the better strategist in concentrating all his available resources on the really important point.

With the French troops accommodated on board the line-of-battle ships and their heavy equipment loaded on fifteen transports, de Grasse was ready to sail. His force had in fact been reduced by one ship, which had been lost by fire at Cap François, and a frigate by a similar cause. He had concentrated his force at Havana, and on 17 August he sailed north. Some Spanish pilots were taken to navigate for him during the first couple of days of tricky sailing through the Bahama Channel, which route de Grasse had selected because it minimized the chance of detection by the British. This is believed to be the first occasion on which a significant French fleet made this passage. The Spanish pilots returned to Cuba on 19 August and the fleet made its way north through the channel between Florida and the Bahamas. When joined by the *Hector* and the *Bourgogne* a few days later, de Grasse's force consisted of twenty-eight sail of the line. On exiting the Bahama Channel the fleet passed through the Straits of Florida. On their voyage north they captured some small British vessels including one that carried Lord Rawdon,[8] an Irish aristocrat who had commanded British forces at Savannah and Charleston and who was on his way home for health reasons.

The French movements did not go unnoticed by the British. The frigate *Nymphe* had sighted de Grasse leaving Fort Royal with a force of twenty-six sail of the line, six frigates, and 200 merchant vessels. The destination of this force was estimated, accurately, as Santo Domingo. When Rodney was told, he assumed that the French trade would soon be going to Europe, but he did send a warning to both Sir Peter Parker at Jamaica and Thomas Graves at New York that a French detachment was certain to be coming north and might have intentions that would affect their stations.

Rodney had ordered Hood to take his squadron (*Barfleur, Alfred, Resolution, Invincible, Alcide, Monarch,* and *Centaur*) to Antigua to provision, which would lessen the strain on Barbados. When Hood arrived in Antigua on 12 July, Rodney had not yet made up his mind whether he would take the fleet north. His health had been obviously poor for many months, and he felt that he was not up to the journey or to the more rigorous climate when he got there. He told Hood to be prepared to command the squadron detached to go north in the event that Rodney himself finally decided to go home. This was looking increasingly likely. The intense pressure on Rodney, especially since the capture of St. Eustatius, had been aggravated by the death of his flag captain Walter Young in May. Although Young had been critical of Rodney in his letters home to Middleton, he had been a positive support to his chief and had been appreciated by Rodney.

Lord Robert Manners wrote to his brother from Antigua that they expected to leave for Montserrat soon to complete their provisions and then to join Rodney at St. Eustatius "where we shall learn our destination during the hurricane season." Rodney he expected to go home immediately. His lowness of spirits was reflected in this letter: "things do not seem to ne in the most flourishing situation in this country, nor indeed anywhere." He wished to hear some good news, for he was tired of hearing of "nothing but misfortunes."[9]

With the certain knowledge that a French force would be coming north, both Graves and Parker were told that its likely destination was the Chesapeake, and Graves was to have his frigates cruising off the bay so he could affect a speedy junction of all the British forces. Graves was also well aware from intelligence that the French were to send "a considerable force" to North America to act in concert with de Barras, and in a letter of 2 July he said that the fate of America "must depend upon the early intelligence and detachment which may be sent by you."[10]

While Hood was at Antigua he heard the news of de Grasse's fleet sailing from Fort Royal. Owing to the state of his own ships, he was in no position to take immediate action, and he told Alexander of his frustration:

> From a strange fatality that seems to have attended the operations of His Majesty's Fleet in these seas for some time past not four ships in the whole are in a fitt state to go any distance, with a view of meeting the enemy, being totally destitute of spare masts, yards, sails and every other species of stores.[11]

When Rodney reviewed the intelligence, it seems to have convinced him that the French would be sending only fourteen sail of the line to North America and that de Grasse with the remainder would be escorting the trade to Europe. He therefore directed Hood to escort the Jamaica trade as far to leeward as Cape Tiberoon, the southwest point of Santo Domingo, and then to proceed to North America with his squadron and Drake's. It is known that Hood was in general agreement with Rodney's assessment of French intentions. He thought it likely that only the coppered ships of the French fleet, which he estimated as twelve sail of the line, would be sent to North America by de Grasse.[12]

On receipt of his orders Hood sailed from Antigua to Montserrat, arriving on the morning of 26 July, and then proceeded on 28 July to St. Kitts, where he was briefly reunited with Rodney in Basseterre Roads. Rodney had four sail of the line under his command apart from his new flagship. The *Sandwich* had proved unfit to cross the Atlantic, and Rodney had transferred his flag to the *Gibraltar*, one of his prizes from the Moonlight Battle. This ship had been Drake's flagship, but she was now in need of home dockyard attention, though still considered capable of an Atlantic voyage. Drake moved to the *Princessa*, while Rodney brought to the *Gibraltar* a retinue including his Physician of the Fleet, Dr. Gilbert Blane, and the children of Benedict Arnold.[13]

At Basseterre Roads, Hood visited Rodney and was told that a French squadron under La Motte Picquet of six sail of the line and escorting a large convoy had arrived in Fort Royal. Rodney retained two of Hood's squadron and Hood sailed immediately with the rest for St. Eustatius. He got there on 29 July to find Drake with his squadron under orders to sail for St. Lucia. The *Torbay*, *Sandwich*, and *Prince William* were assigned to look after the Jamaica convoy. Rodney asked Parker, with whom he did not enjoy the best of relations because of his high-handed attitude over the use of Jamaican facilities for refitting his ships, to send the two 74-gun ships on to North America when their convoy duty was completed and to repair the *Sandwich*. When eventually sent on by Parker, these ships were too late for the engagement of the fifth of September and could only participate in the unsuccessful relief attempt.

The Jamaica convoy sailed from St. Eustatius on 31 July under the command of Captain John Gidoin of the *Torbay*. Rodney had ordered Gidoin to escort the trade as far as Jamaica but not to go into Kingston harbor, instead proceeding northward in support of Hood. For whatever reason, Gidoin disobeyed these orders and did enter the harbor. Here he was detained by Sir Peter Parker, who feared a Franco-Spanish attack on Jamaica. Parker used the *Torbay* and *Prince William* as escorts for a convoy to England. They were to detach themselves when they reached a suitable point and go to North America.

These various duties had reduced Hood's squadron to nine sail of the line, far short of the fourteen he had been promised to match the supposed French reinforcement. Rodney arrived at St. Eustatius from St. Kitts still in two minds as to whether he should go home for his health or go to North America and assume the command there.

On the day that Drake and his squadron sailed for St. Lucia, 31 July, Rodney asked Hood to call on him in the *Gibraltar*. He told Hood that he had decided to sail with the trade homeward bound for England. In the hope that time at sea would improve his health, he would defer the final decision for a few days. If he felt physically incapable of carrying on, he would dispatch a frigate to Hood, but if he felt better he would come himself.

From this point Hood was, in effect, in command of the ships that were to go to North America. He was given command of all the ships in the Leeward Islands and the task of assembling them for the trip north. Rodney was to take the *Gibraltar*, *Triumph*, and *Panther* home, as they were all in serious need of repair. He would also retain the frigate *Pegasus*, which he would use to send word to New York that he was not personally coming north after all.

Rodney was quite satisfied that the force he proposed to send to North America, fourteen sail of the line, would be sufficient to offset any reinforcement the French might have made. Indeed, the instructions given to de Grasse before he left Europe confirm that this was also the size of force the French government had in mind. Rodney was confident that the two British squadrons would unite off the Chesapeake before the French arrived and that this would give the British command of the seas in the area.

The sloop *Swallow* (14) under Captain Wells[14] had been sent ahead to bring Graves information on the course of Hood's squadron. This specified that Hood would first call at the Capes of the Chesapeake and, if he did not find the French or Graves's squadron there, would proceed to the Delaware and finally to New York if the other rendezvous had failed.

The *Swallow* arrived in New York on 27 July only to find Graves absent. The senior officer at the port, Edmund Affleck,[15] made a copy of the letter but did not trouble to inform Wells of the contents of the dispatches and sent the *Swallow* back to sea in pursuit of Graves, who was then cruising off Boston harbor.

The reason why Graves was not in position to meet Hood at the mouth of the Chesapeake was that he was out with his squadron looking for some important French vessels that were supposedly coming from Europe. On 19 July a dispatch from the Admiralty dated 22 May had informed him that American colonel John Laurens was returning from France with a convoy carrying military supplies and money escorted by one ship of the line and two frigates.[16] John Laurens was the son of Henry Laurens, an influential politician from Charleston who had been captured by the British at sea and was being held in the Tower of London. Henry was eventually exchanged for Cornwallis and joined the American negotiating team for the Paris peace conference. John Laurens had been captured at Charleston and held by the British until exchanged, and was now apparently coming home with the French convoy. The Admiralty told Graves that the capture of this convoy would be a serious blow to the Americans.

Graves accordingly took his squadron to sea at once. No blame could attach to Graves, as he would have accepted the priority that the Admiralty placed on intercepting this convoy. To be sure, he might have sent his frigates and 50-gun ships to look for the convoy while keeping his line ships concentrated at New York. However, he was not aware yet of the true situation of Cornwallis at Yorktown, and in any case he was expecting to be joined by a squadron from the West Indies and reasoned that should the French arrive first, they would be closely followed by the British squadron. Had he been ready to sail immediately on Hood's arrival, the British squadron might have got to the mouth of the Chesapeake three days earlier.

He did station frigates along the coast off the Delaware and the Chesapeake to watch for the arrival of either squadron. Having got his forces ready, Graves sailed on 21 July with six sail of the line, later joined by the *Adamant* (50) and the *Royal Oak* (74), which he felt a sufficient force to match the squadron of de Barras, should he meet him, or the convoy escort.

While looking for Graves, on 26 August the *Swallow* attacked and took an American privateer but was then herself attacked by three more privateers. Captain Wells was forced to run the ship ashore on Long Island. Wells and his crew hastily abandoned the *Swallow*, with Wells dropping the packet of dispatches overboard. The *Swallow* was later burnt by the American privateersmen. The upshot was that Graves never did receive the original of Rodney's instructions and received a copy only on 18 August when he returned to New York from his cruise. This was the first of two communications mischances that befell the British preparations for the coming campaign.

The state of Graves's ships—some needing dockyard work, one with holes below the waterline—meant that until urgent repairs were completed, he did not have his full force available for action.[17]

At the time he wrote to Graves, Rodney had been unsure of the departure of de Grasse and of the strength of the force he was to take with him, so he referred only to "a part of" the French fleet "reported to be destined for North America." Thus Graves did not know for certain either the strength of the French coming north or their destination should they come. Both he and Sir Henry Clinton were inclined to believe that the French would concentrate their efforts on New York, the main British base in North America and, it was believed quite correctly, the preferred target of Washington. To preempt the Franco-American move, Clinton and Graves also discussed an attack on Newport, where the squadron of de Barras was based. The French position on Rhode Island was of great strategic value to the Allies. In a realignment of their position in North America, the British had given up Rhode Island—a decision that Rodney called the most "fatal measure" the British could have taken.

As soon as Graves returned from his abortive cruise to intercept the convoy, the project of attacking Rhode Island was once again raised with Clinton. Both commanders felt that British possession of Rhode Island would be a great advantage and would make the position of the French squadron that much more difficult. They agreed that as soon as the *Robust* and the *Prudent* had been repaired, such an expedition would be mounted. Before these plans could come to fruition, the situation was changed by the arrival of Hood's squadron off New York on 28 August.

Rodney had finally left St. Eustatius in the *Gibraltar* on 1 August with the homeward-bound trade. He steered a slightly more northerly course than was usual, hoping that the cooler climate might improve his health enough for him to go to America and take command of the fleet there. By 13 August the convoy and escort were off Bermuda and Rodney made the final decision to return to England. As arranged, he sent the frigate *Pegasus* to New York to inform Graves.

The use of the *Gibraltar* for Rodney to go home was not in fact a loss to the strength of Hood's squadron. The *Gibraltar* was known to be of too deep a draft to cross over the bar and enter New York harbor, though in fact in these urgent circumstances Hood did not try to enter New York but waited for Graves to come out. It was also said that the *Gibraltar* was too much in need of a refit to be of further service. Rodney's former flagship *Sandwich*, also classified as too worn for immediate service, had been detailed to escort the Jamaica trade and then undergo essential repairs in a Jamaica dockyard, so she too was not to join Hood in North America. While the use of the *Gibraltar* for his return home was therefore not a selfish act by Rodney, it did allow him to return in a manner befitting a flag officer. It might be concluded that he chose this to bolster his prestige as he became increasingly aware of the reception awaiting him over the seizures at St. Eustatius. Remembering Rodney's state of health, however, and the arduous service on which he had been engaged for the last eighteen months it is hard to grudge him the extra comfort the *Gibraltar* provided.

On 2 August Hood sailed from St. Eustatius, having sent orders to St. Lucia for Drake to meet him at Antigua. He had also just received the news that a French frigate had arrived at Cap François with some thirty American pilots for the Chesapeake and Delaware coasts. This news, combined with the arrival of a convoy of sixty American merchant vessels, indicated that the French definitely intended to go north and that the destination was not New York. The possibility of decisive events taking place that autumn on the coast of America was in the forefront of Hood's mind. He wrote to Alexander on the day he left St. Eustatius:

Much may depend upon my getting to the coast of America before the enemy, which I shall labour to do.

The Business of America seems at the present moment to be critical. I shall therefore take with me every ship I can, and propose fourteen of the line. I have already despatched a frigate to say I am coming, that I shall first look into the Chesapeake, afterwards proceed to the Capes of Delaware from thence to New York.[18]

Before sailing he promoted his cousin Alexander Hood to be captain of the *Barfleur* in the place of Captain John Inglefield, whom he appointed to the *Centaur* "as I thought 'I' a better Captain for a 74 than 'A.'"[19]

On 3 August the brig *Active* brought Hood dispatches from General Clinton that had been meant for Rodney. Dated 28 June, they gave extracts from intercepted American mail confirming that de Grasse was coming north and conveyed the opinion of Clinton that he would go first to Rhode Island to join de Barras, the French naval commander in the area, and then in conjunction with the land forces of Washington and Rochambeau would mount an attack on New York. As regards the situation of Cornwallis, Clinton wrote that since

> his Lordship's operations in Chesapeake must now cease from the inclemency of the season, I have ... recommended it to him to occupy defensive stations in the York and James Rivers until the season for operations in that climate shall return.[20]

At the time of Clinton's writing, Washington *had* been in favor of an attack on New York. But the arguments put forward by Rochambeau and de Grasse then persuaded him that a concentration at the Chesapeake was the best option open to the Allies. Meanwhile, Clinton had refused Cornwallis's request to take his force back to Charleston to see out the winter.

In accordance with his instructions from Clinton, Cornwallis had taken up a defensive position at Yorktown on 1 August. He would be safe in that position as long as the Royal Navy held command of the sea, which would enable him to be either supplied or lifted off and transported to New York or Charleston. The retention of Yorktown would also give the British an anchorage in southern waters to use when the northern ports were frozen. All would depend on the numerical reckoning of Rodney and de Grasse. While the British commander was making himself secure in his position, it is useful to look at the sequence of events that had brought him to Virginia in the first place.

Cornwallis had served in the war since the beginning, participating in various actions under Howe in the northern colonies. He had been twenty-five years in the army by the time he came to Yorktown and had been aide-de-camp to the Marquess of Granby in the Seven Years' War, taking part in the battle of Minden in 1759.

Like many others, Cornwallis had opposed the rule of Lord Bute, a favorite of George III, and was of a general "Whiggish" disposition which included opposition to the government measures that had led to the break with the colonies. Despite these sentiments, however, he had shown no reluctance to serve in that war and had arrived in North America in 1776 ready to serve under Sir William Howe.

His service in North America was cut short by the illness and death of his wife, and he returned home in 1778. During his time under Howe he had been the victor at Brandywine and occupied Philadelphia. While in England he formed a close association with Lord George Germain and returned to North America with an idea, based on a comment of Germain, that he would soon assume the chief command, as Sir Henry Clinton wished to resign and had suggested Cornwallis as his successor.

By the time of his return to America, the French were in the war openly and a new strategic situation had to be faced. Germain had identified, correctly, the importance of Virginia and the Carolinas to the rebel cause. It was also widely believed in the British government and high command that there was a considerable Loyalist element to be exploited in these areas.

The latter view turned out to be unfounded. The British had never been able to establish the sound base for their operations for which they had hoped. The war had proved costly to both sides, with atrocities being committed, which had never been a prominent feature of the war in the north. The British were solidly ensconced at Charleston, from which the Americans did not have the strength to drive them, and which they were to hold to the end of 1782, when it was given up as part of the Shelburne government's policy of relinquishing all hold on the former colonies.

Cornwallis had won a close-fought engagement at Guilford Courthouse with Nathanael Greene on 15 March 1781. Although he was successful in the action, Cornwallis recognized that the war in the Carolinas was not going to produce the decisive breakthrough that he had looked for. He had two avenues open to him: return to Charleston or go north to Virginia. Above all he wanted to prove to Sir Henry Clinton, of whom he was both deeply suspicious and jealous, that he could bring the present stalemate to an end and achieve decisive results. He wrote to Clinton from North Carolina on 10 April, 1781 that the Chesapeake was a better place from which to conduct operations and that the British should concentrate there rather than New

York.[21] He told Clinton that until Virginia was subdued "our hold on the Carolinas must be difficult if not precarious."

In going north to Virginia, Cornwallis went first to Wilmington, where he rested and reequipped. The British forces he left behind were not sufficient to carry out any offensive action that might have led to the pacification of the area. A much larger force had already proved inadequate for that purpose. Colonel Nisbet Balfour was given the command in South Carolina, a post he held for the rest of the war. The British gave up operations in the interior and concentrated their strength at Charleston.

The British move north to Virginia opened a further field for conflict. The British had two advantages in the present struggle. First, they held a general naval superiority along the whole North American coast which the French had not been able to break. The application of blockade to bring economic pressure to bear on the rebel colonies was telling and bound to become more burdensome as time went on. Washington recognized that "a decisive naval force" was necessary to support the Franco-American operations. So far the French intervention had not achieved this. The second advantage the British held was the general lack of warm feelings and mutual cooperation between the French and the Americans. With a few exceptions, such as Lafayette and Rochambeau, the French military professionals distrusted both the Americans' military reliability and their loyalty as allies, suspecting that they might settle for a separate peace and leave the French to continue the war alone. From what they had seen of the American forces, most French officers had a low opinion of their capacity and refused to commit large French forces to Allied operations such as American proposals to attack the British base at New York or to invade Canada. The French interest in America remained peripheral; what they desired from the war was a successful invasion of Britain, after which they could dictate terms. Despite their overwhelming numbers in the Channel, they had been unable to achieve this and therefore fell back on a colonial war, de Grasse in the West Indies and Suffren in the East Indies. The war in America was a natural adjunct to the naval struggle in the West Indies.

In the situation that now arose with Cornwallis's invasion of Virginia, the British lost their two advantages. Firstly, the French and Americans found a spirit of cooperation and unity of aim which was fostered by the strategic vision of de Grasse, Rochambeau, and Washington (plus the generosity of the Spaniards in supplying the finances to keep the French forces in the field). The rapport and cooperation between Rochambeau and Washington was remarkable. One of his officers said in later years that Rochambeau seemed "to have been purposely created to understand Washington and to be understood by him."[22]

Finally, when it mattered most, the British lost, for the decisive period, the naval superiority they had previously maintained along the North American coast. The strategic ideas of Cornwallis of winning the war in Virginia had placed his army in a situation where he was totally reliant on these two British advantages. When he lost them, the British were not strong enough militarily to both hold New York, which Clinton wished to do, and contend with the opposing forces in Virginia, which was Cornwallis's strategy. And when the navy was not able to drive off the French fleet and establish a link with the British forces, the situation for Cornwallis would become desperate.

The state of Virginia was not a stranger to warlike operations. In 1775 the British governor, the Earl of Dunmore, had issued a proclamation promising freedom to all slaves who joined the British (Loyalist) forces. The question of slavery was a weak point for the rebellious colonists, for they were so dependent on maintaining the attachment of the southern plantation owners that any thought of promising slaves their freedom either during or after the struggle was out of the question. George Washington, who was a slave owner, recognized the danger of a general offer of freedom for slaves and urgently pressed for the expulsion of Dunmore from Virginia as soon as possible. This the rebels accomplished by the end of 1775.

The promise of freedom for slaves if they joined the British cause was an easy card for the British to play, particularly in the southern states, and they played it with some success. At the end of the war in the final negotiations with the Americans they were unable or, more likely, did not care enough to obtain any concessions on this point. In fact Dunmore himself sold a black regiment back into slavery in the West Indies. The question of slavery was to assume greater importance as the century drew to a close with the campaigning of William Wilberforce, but in 1783 there was no public pressure on the Shelburne government to fight for the rights of slaves. The promises the British made to their Indian allies were also not kept in the general scramble of the government to withdraw from America.

The British government had always felt that a base in the Chesapeake area would be advantageous. A British presence there would have the effect of cutting communications between the northern and southern colonies, and a British squadron based on the Chesapeake would be in a position to prevent a junction between a French force coming from the West Indies and the American squadron at Rhode Island. There were, however, not enough troops to spare to secure a base, especially a naval base.

To identify a suitable site for a naval base was one of the tasks given to Cornwallis by Clinton and Arbuthnot. Clinton told Cornwallis that a base for line-of-battle ships in the Chesapeake was of such importance that he was to acquire one "even if it should occupy all the forces at present in Virginia." Any British military presence on the coastal areas of America would be viable only if naval supremacy was kept in British hands. The Spanish campaign along the Florida coast that eliminated the British positions by combined naval and military operations showed how vulnerable British forces were where naval power could not support them.

With the departure of Dunmore from the scene, there was relative quiet until Commodore George Collier[23] with a small squadron raided along the coast and destroyed a large number of privateers and merchant ships and burned a new-building frigate. After that there was a further period of quiet until Benedict Arnold arrived with a force of 1,600 Loyalists, who seized Hampton, Portsmouth, and Norfolk. Arnold then transferred his men up-river by boat and took Richmond. There were no regular troops available to oppose the march of Arnold, only militia, and Washington, on hearing of the incursion in his home state of Virginia, sent 1,200 regulars under Lafayette to strengthen the forces there. Washington realized the importance of the navy to operations in Virginia and, in a move that would mirror the situation six months later, asked the French North American Squadron under des Touches to sail south and try to cut off Arnold from help from the sea.

The British squadron under Arbuthnot, hearing of the French departure, also hurried and met des Touches at sea off Cape Henry. They fought an indecisive engagement in which the French had the better of it but did not press their advantage and retreated, leaving the field to Arbuthnot. This spoiled French intentions and frustrated Washington, though not a ship was lost on either side. Washington was well aware of the necessity of naval superiority for operations along the American coastline, but again it was the British who held it.

When Cornwallis had suggested that Virginia was preferable for the main scene of future operations, he was not entirely whistling in the wind. He had a close relationship with Lord George Germain, who was of the same opinion. Sir Henry Clinton had long resisted shifting the weight of the British effort to the south and had done his best to restrict the number of men available to Cornwallis, preferring to remain strong around New York.

Of the force available to Cornwallis, a good part had been wasted in the Carolinas, which not only had seen significant battle casualties and losses from guerrilla warfare but was a deeply unhealthy station. The southern-most states from the Carolinas to Florida were not a rewarding area for British military effort. The hoped-for Loyalist rising had not come about, and without significantly more troops no success could be expected. Lacking substantial local support, the British forces occupied only the ground they stood on. They remained capable of operations, but their numbers were diminishing with every battle or skirmish, and the victories they did win, such as Guilford Courthouse, did not seriously alter the situation.

What the British government wanted—for Germain had persuaded his cabinet colleagues and the king of the advantages of operations in Virginia—was a significant transfer of troops to the southern theatre. In strictly military terms there was less to be gained by campaigning in the Carolinas than by striking at Virginia, Maryland, and Delaware. All three of these states were important to the structure of the thirteen rebellious colonies and all were "slave states" which offered the British a chance to exploit the natural wish of the slaves to win their freedom. Given the necessity of keeping the richer slave-owning colonies in the alliance against the British, it was not practicable for the Declaration of Independence to be declared applicable to *all* men as "created equal." This would be total anathema to the plantation owners, who could be kept on board only by there being no overt declaration against slavery.

With Cornwallis now operating in Virginia, the first piece of the jigsaw was in place. If he was reinforced sufficiently by Clinton and could rely on support from the sea, he would be in a strong position to strike a damaging blow against the Americans. Without these factors he would be in a very difficult position should the French and Americans combine against him.

On receiving direct orders from the king and government to transfer efforts to Virginia, Clinton had sent 2,000 troops south under Major General William Phillips to meet Benedict Arnold in April 1781. This force defeated the opposing Virginia militia, as we have seen, but after a further advance towards Richmond, Phillips died of typhoid and Arnold was left in command. The appearance of Lafayette in the area caused Arnold to retire to Petersburg following an orgy of looting and destruction. Arnold was subsequently recalled to New York and Cornwallis was left in charge of the united force, which with further reinforcements sent by Clinton now totaled 7,500 men. A good number of slaves fled their plantations to join the British forces, a pointer to what might have happened if the British had operated in strength in the area and won the confidence of the slaves.

For a while Cornwallis endeavored, unsuccessfully, to trap Lafayette's force. The main British force remained generally in the area around Richmond, though independent columns were sent out by Cornwallis to raid across rebel areas in Virginia. One column of 250 men under Banastre Tarleton[24] tried to capture Thomas Jefferson and the Virginia Legislative Council at Charlottesville but missed them by minutes. The British failed, however, to achieve a significant victory in the field, largely because there was not a significant enough number of American troops in the area to make it possible for them to engage with a chance of success. Cornwallis was left with only the loot and plunder that his men had collected and a series of occupied towns, not the decisive battle victory he wanted.

When Clinton ordered him to send troops back to New York to meet what Clinton and the new naval commander, Thomas Graves, believed to be the likely move of the Franco-American forces, an attack on New York, Cornwallis marched to Williamsburg, shadowed by Lafayette with a rather mixed force of militia and a few regulars. From Williamsburg Cornwallis headed for Portsmouth to embark his force. On 8 July he received further orders to establish his force in a position on the James Peninsula at Yorktown. The troops were embarked at Portsmouth and made the short voyage to Yorktown where Cornwallis set up his base. Tarleton was ordered to establish a strong point on the opposite side of the river at Gloucester Point. Lafayette maintained a watching position at Williamsburg, undisturbed by the numerically superior British forces. The decision to station the British army at Yorktown seems to have been a compromise on Clinton's part in the belief that it would be a good base for further operations in Virginia. Cornwallis did not agree with his superior's plan and made a pretty lackluster show of putting the camp into any sort of fortified state, claiming he lacked entrenching tools. It was of course axiomatic that basing the British army on a peninsula as at Yorktown meant that it was wholly dependent on the navy to support it or to rescue it if the situation became unsustainable.

The movements of the French and Americans at this time were orchestrated by de Grasse and Rochambeau. The former, having been persuaded by Rochambeau that he should bring his force to the Chesapeake, was already proceeding north with the promised troops, artillery, and money. Rochambeau was with Washington in the area of New York. Washington, like the British government, was looking for a theatre in which to strike a decisive blow and had long wished to conduct operations against the British stronghold of New York. This was certainly the operation that Clinton expected when the French fleet arrived on the coast from the West Indies.

As commander of the French land forces, Rochambeau had total control over their movements and could have taken them alone to the Chesapeake, leaving the Americans to their fixation with New York. But with persuasive reasoning Rochambeau was able to convince Washington, as he had convinced de Grasse, that the junction of the French fleet and the Franco-American armies at the Chesapeake would produce the decisive result he sought.

With the decision taken to go south, a means had to be found to pin Clinton's force in the north. If Washington and Rochambeau could foster, or more strictly reinforce, the impression of a Franco-American concentration against New York, British forces would not pursue the force going south by either land or sea. In a deception move anticipating World War II's Operation Fortitude, the bluff prior to Overlord to convince the Germans that the invasion was coming in the Calais area, Washington made a feint attack on Staten Island, enough to convince Clinton that the danger to New York was still there, and then on 19 August he and Rochambeau marched south with 6,000 men. Until the latter half of August, then, the British, whatever intelligence they received, could not have known where the expected blow was to fall, as the Allies themselves had not agreed on a strategy for their future operations.

Lafayette was, of course, the first of the Allied commanders to arrive at the Yorktown area, having followed Cornwallis at a discreet distance. Hood was the first British naval commander to arrive there but, not finding the French fleet, he had proceeded to New York. He had overtaken de Grasse en route from the Caribbean, a fact put down by some authorities to the copper bottoms of the British ships but mainly due to his having taken a more direct route north. Shortly after the departure of Hood, on 30 August, de Grasse arrived and began to disembark his troops, being relieved to find that the British fleet was not in possession of the anchorage or in the area.

It might well have been, had the misadventure of the sloop *Swallow* not been compounded by the loss of a second dispatch vessel. This episode began in the Leeward Islands back in the first days of August.

While Hood was proceeding to Antigua he had fallen in with a British frigate that had been on watch off Fort Royal. The captain reported seeing four large ships in Fort Royal Bay, but could not describe them more exactly as visibility was bad at the time. Hood had to reckon on them being ships of the line, which might be destined for a late expedition to St. Lucia. If this forecast was correct, the departure of Drake from St. Lucia to join Hood would leave that island open to attack. Hood decided to send the frigate back with orders for Drake to remain at St. Lucia until the situation was cleared up one way or the other. In the event that the report should be a false alarm, Hood gave St. John's Road in Antigua as the next rendezvous.

The brig *Active*, which had brought Clinton's dispatches from North America, was sent back on 6 August carrying word of Hood's intention to come north. He was unable to give any exact account of de Grasse, as the ultimate intentions of the French commander were still uncertain. If the dispatches carried by the *Active* had reached Graves, they might possibly have alerted him to the sense of urgency that Hood now felt about the situation.

Hood may not have known the ultimate destination or the exact number of the French ships going with de Grasse, or even for sure whether de Grasse himself was going north, but he was sure that a detachment would go and that it was essential for the British cause that the French not achieve superiority in American waters. It was also essential that the British arrive on the coast before de Grasse and that the forces of Graves and Hood be united before the French arrived.

Thus it was a second stroke of bad luck for the British when the *Active* failed to reach Graves. The vessel was captured by the Americans and brought into Philadelphia. By the loss of both the *Swallow* and the *Active*, Graves was deprived of early intelligence of the moves of the French and, more important, of his own side. The commander of the *Active* was held as a prisoner of war but apparently still managed to smuggle out the news he was carrying. Graves received it on 28 August, but it is uncertain whether what he received was the news smuggled out from the American prison or copies of the dispatches the Hood had sent ahead as he neared New York. Whichever it was, the news preceded Hood's arrival by only a few hours.

The dispatches received in early August from Graves and Clinton had given Hood an additional incentive to start for North America as soon as possible, if necessary without waiting for Drake to join him. The ships were all provisioned by 10 August, and Hood gave the order to weigh. As the British were working out of the harbor, strange sails were sighted. On coming closer they were recognized, by an exchange of signals, as the squadron of Rear Admiral Drake. The ships sighted in Fort Royal had proved not to be line-of-battle ships and Drake had therefore followed his original instructions to join Hood, the junction being made just outside Antigua. The force now comprised fourteen sail of the line, steering to the north and to the decisive battle of the American theatre.

Meanwhile de Grasse had left Cap François on 5 August with a force numbering twenty-eight of the line. With the intricacies of the navigation, he was a fortnight threading his way through the Old Bahama Channel and out into the open sea. The French were carrying 3,300 troops to assist in land operations. Hood was carrying the 40th Regiment, which had been embarked on the initiative of Brigadier Christie,[25] the successor to General Vaughan who had gone home with Rodney. It has been said that "the pattern of the British movement was not unlike the French; it was the proportion and the timing which were different."[26] The British had made good time in getting their forces away, but they had not yet realized the scale of the French movements, and it was this difference that was to be crucial to the final result of the campaign.

Hood made good time in his passage north as well, and he sighted the Capes of the Chesapeake on 25 August. Seeing the French had not arrived, and no sign of Graves, he continued to New York. His progress far exceeded the daily rate of the French, who went north by the old Bahama Channel. Here we have the first consequence of the loss of the *Swallow*. If Graves had received the order from Rodney to meet Hood off the Chesapeake, the British could have foiled the intentions of the French and the whole situation would have changed. If de Grasse had found a British fleet waiting for him, either at sea or moored in a defensive position in the Chesapeake, the British would have held the initiative and de Grasse would have had difficult choices to make. If he had taken the option of attacking the British fleet moored in a defensive line in the Chesapeake, it is unlikely that he would have been successful. More likely he would have declined to take the risk. This would have given the British a strategic victory and the opportunity to either embark Cornwallis's troops or to reinforce his operations.

Graves did have cruisers out looking for Hood, but they missed each other and the first warning he had of the approach of Hood's squadron was the arrival of the frigate *Nymphe* on 28 August with the dispatches that Hood had written while off the Chesapeake. Graves quickly replied, telling Hood what he knew, though this included nothing definite about the presence, destination, or numbers of the French fleet, information of vital interest to the British:

We have as yet no certain intelligence of de Grasse; the accounts say that he has gone to the Havana to join the Spaniards, & expected together upon this coast, a little time will show us. I have sent up for pilots to bring your squadron over the bar, which should be buoyed to render it safe. To anchor without would neither be safe at this season of the year, nor prudent, on account of its being exposed to an enemy as well as to the violence of the sea.

My Squadron is slender and not yet ready to move, or I should not hesitate upon your coming over the bar, as we are circumstanced it is a clear point. I meet the general today at Denis's, Long Island, upon a consultation. The *Princessa* I understand draws twenty six feet water, it is too much to come over the bar, therefore I have sent up two transports to come down for her guns. Perhaps to put them in the frigate may save time.[27]

Hood, with his increasing sense of urgency, had no intention of entering New York harbor. Graves's letter did not reflect the same urgency that Hood felt. As we have seen, Graves had just returned from an unsuccessful cruise in search of a French force that intelligence had warned was due from Europe, and his ships were not in a state to get to sea immediately—another consequence of the lost dispatches. If Graves had received either of the missing letters, he would have curtailed his operation off Boston and returned to New York to meet Hood. On return from his abortive cruise Graves reported the state of his squadron as one sail of the line refitting at Halifax and three at New York in need of dockyard attention. The necessary stores for the squadron to put to sea again were also low and would have to be replenished.

The letter from Graves was delivered to Hood as he anchored outside New York. Hood could see that the commanders in New York were no better informed of the movements of the French than those in the West Indies had been. No news had been received or sight seen of the French during the voyage north, though Hood was certain that they would be on the coast of North America soon. Speed was of the essence, and he declined Graves's offer of pilots to see his fleet over the bar into the harbor. Instead he took his boat and went to seek out Graves and Clinton on Long Island. He found them discussing a proposed attack on Rhode Island, where the French North American Squadron under de Barras[28] was based, though information received said that de Barras had sailed on 25 August with his whole force. This attack had been in the minds of both men for some time, and reinforcements that Clinton had received had given the idea fresh impetus. The possession of Rhode Island would be of great advantage to the British. Hood was ready to fall in with such a project, which on its own merits had much to recommend it.

It was obviously necessary to prevent a junction of the forces of de Barras and de Grasse. With time pressing, Hood insisted that Graves should move his ships out of New York to join his squadron as soon as possible. The British would then have their maximum force concentrated and could sail for Rhode Island or the Chesapeake as events might require. Graves was in agreement and promised that he would order his ships to come out of harbor as quickly as they could manage. Even as Graves was struggling to get his ships ready for sea, he received news from Clinton that de Barras had put to sea with eight of the line and a convoy of storeships and transports.[29] It was now clear that the French would not be cooperating in an attack on New York with the American forces.

Hood reported this meeting and its decisions to the Admiralty a couple of days later. He was waiting for the ships in New York, held up by adverse winds, to come out and join him. On that very day, as Hood fretted off New York, de Grasse reached the mouth of the Chesapeake. With the arrival of the French, the strategic situation changed. Cornwallis was now dependent for his survival on the navy establishing command of the sea in the Chesapeake area. The time lost by Graves through the abortive cruise and the failure of the dispatches from the West Indies to reach him had produced the worst possible scenario for the British.

It was not until 31 August that the New York ships were ready and able to make their way out to join Hood. Even at this stage nobody in the British fleet, from admirals down, knew for certain what force the French had sent to North America or where it had gone. The whereabouts of de Barras were also unknown, though he was believed to have sailed south to unite with de Grasse. Graves had hopes that he might meet with the smaller Squadron at sea and destroy it before the two French commanders joined forces.

Some in the force were still hopeful that all would be well. On 2 August, Hood's secretary Joseph Hunt had written to Sir Charles Middleton a letter full of false hopes:

> ... our previous arrival on the coast will operate greatly in our favour, as it will not only effectually enable the Commander-in-Chief to counteract the motions of the enemy, but will also allow of their adopting such measures as will be most efficacious towards preventing a junc-

tion of their squadrons, which cannot fail to lessen the French interest in the Colonies, and will in its consequences, prove a decisive blow to the American cause, which from all accounts, is in a tottering state and verging towards its decline.[30]

Hunt went on in the same tone that he did not believe that the French would be able to send north more than twelve sail of the line after the detachments they would have to make to safeguard the trade. He did not realize that de Grasse had put commercial considerations in second place and suspended the trade to Europe. De Grasse had risen to the challenge of conflicting requirements for limited resources and made the decision that was to change the course of the war.

Up to 30 August the British had no confirmation that the French had arrived off the American coast. On that day Graves received a report from the *Richmond* that the Delaware was clear of the French. The ships in New York had been delayed in from coming out because the wind was not favorable for their passage over the bar. When the wind changed, the fresh ships—*London* (98, flag), *Royal Oak* (74), *Bedford* (74), *America* (74), and *Europe* (64)—were joined to Hood's squadron. As senior officer Graves now commanded nineteen sail of the line, but some of the West India ships were in poor condition from having been long at sea and some were suffering from the degenerative effect that particularly afflicted the early coppered ships.

No orders had been sent by de Grasse for de Barras to join him. De Grasse could not in fact *order* de Barras to do anything, as de Barras was senior to him, so only suggestions could be made. In a generous gesture, realizing that the critical situation needed unified command and that the majority of the French fleet was from de Grasse's contingent, de Barras waived his right to command and signified his willingness to serve under de Grasse. It had been left entirely to his own decision what use to make of his squadron—whether to go south and join the operations on the Chesapeake or to operate in the local area and constitute a diversion. De Barras had been thinking of an attack on Newfoundland, which would keep the British fleet to the south of him, while going to the Chesapeake might very well put the British between himself and his base. He had discussions with Washington and Rochambeau, who strongly pressed him to join de Grasse. De Barras accepted the arguments and promised to bring troops and artillery, though as he pointed out in his letter to Rochambeau, the junction had dangers for his force of which de Grasse was fully aware:

... and he knows better than anyone what forces he can bring to the coast, and what forces Rodney can take there. However, as the opinion of yourself and Washington is opposed to mine, I have decided to go to Chesapeake with my fleet, and bring your artillery and some transports. I must repeat, however, that this is dangerous, and I presume that de Grasse understands its disadvantages, as he has given me freedom not to join him at Chesapeake if I do not think it fit to do so. Graves' fleet, whatever it may be, will certainly not stop me. But according to what Washington says, Digby may reinforce him, and general rumour says that Rodney may appear at any time. It is not 1,000 to 1 against my meeting with one or the other of these squadrons; on the contrary it is to be expected that the enemy, when they know I am at sea, will attempt to intercept my squadron and convoy. However, I will not hesitate to comply with the request of Washington and yourself."[31]

This letter shows the French were already aware that Digby was on his way to North America but not that Rodney had returned to England. De Barras had eight sail of the line under his command and, though he was not worried about meeting Graves's known force of five sail of the line, he had no desire to meet the combined British forces that might soon be operating on the coast. If de Barras was defeated by these, the French would lose the extra troops and the artillery he was bringing.

De Grasse had arrived off the Chesapeake on 30 August, a day before Graves and Hood sailed from New York. The French admiral, bound by his promise to be back in the West Indies by November, was all for immediate action against the British position with the forces now at the disposal of St. Simon and Lafayette. Lafayette argued that they should await the arrival of Washington and Rochambeau, who were known to be on their way. This approach met with the approval of General Duportail, the emissary of Rochambeau and Washington. De Grasse was convinced by the arguments of the military officers and by information contained in dispatches from Rochambeau and Washington. The troops he had brought from the West Indies were landed on 2 September at Jamestown. He wrote to Washington telling him of his arrival and saying he had the York and James Rivers blockaded and was ready to engage any force that might be sent to the relief of Cornwallis.

The reinforcement by de Grasse brought the total Franco-American force to 8,000—and Washington, who was marching south with 2,000 American troops and 4,000 French, comprising almost the entire Franco-American army in North America, had yet to arrive. Cornwallis, with only 6,000 men, was now far outnumbered on land, and his communications with the sea were cut off. His options for offensive action were gone, and he began to fortify his position to defend himself from assault by the Franco-American forces encamped outside. At the moment they did not have enough guns to mount a regular siege (more were coming south with de Barras from Rhode Island) but they were present in sufficient numbers not to be driven off by any sortie Cornwallis might make. With the French fleet now in command of the sea, he had to rely on the Royal Navy to wrest that command back and establish contact with Yorktown so he could evacuate if he wished to.

Graves left New York on 1 September. The British, it has been pointed out,[32] operated under an unwelcome but unavoidable burden: a quarter of the fleet had never worked with the remainder and there was no time for the two parts to get to know each other. Graves had been in command of the North American station for less than two months. He knew that Digby was coming to assume the command and that his position was only temporary. It may be for this reason that he made no great changes to the Signals and Instructions in Addition left by his predecessor, Arbuthnot. He issued these instructions to his own ships when he took over the command, and it may be assumed that copies were hastily written for issue to Hood's squadron when they joined forces along, with a proposed order of battle. The ships that comprised the West Indies Squadron were used to the standard Admiralty Instructions and the Additional Instructions issued by Rodney, which would have been different in some respects from those now issued to them by Graves. Many of the orders would have been the same, but the signal flags to convey them would have been different. The only chance for the two parts of the fleet to get used to each other, and for Hood and his captains to get used to the new instructions, would be on the voyage down from New York. It was, as a recent historian has said, a situation made for misunderstandings.[33]

The situation, as it appeared to Graves, was uncertain. He did not know whether de Grasse had arrived at the Chesapeake or what numbers he had with him. Nor did he know the whereabouts of de Barras or his destination, though the Chesapeake was the most likely. Finally, neither he nor General Clinton knew the destination of General Washington's army. Both feared that the American leader might still make an attack on New York.

Graves did realize that a defeat of the French naval forces or at least a part of them was essential to the British position. It was also essential that the army with Cornwallis be supported rather than left to its fate. If the army could be taken off, it could be used again in either New York or Charleston for the following year's operations. To be sure, Graves could reasonably expect that Cornwallis would do something to help himself rather than wait to be encircled. Consequently the urgency of the need for action was not entirely clear to him.

In New York an officer of the Royal Welch Fusiliers named Frederick Mackenzie was keeping a diary of the events of the time. It is a good record of the thoughts of a young army officer and his contemporaries on these events, and is a great help in the detail it throws open to inspection. On 2 September, the day after Graves and Hood had sailed from New York, he put into his diary the whole situation in a nutshell:

> The French Fleet may be daily expected on the Coast, and there now seems to be no doubt but the Enemy intend turning their utmost force against Lord Cornwallis's Army. If the French come with a Superior fleet, that Army must be left to their own exertions, for there will hardly be a possibility of relieving them, unless by our gaining a victory at Sea.[34]

Two days later, while the British fleet was pressing south under full sail, more information came to the ears of Mackenzie and he duly entered it in his Diary:

> 'Tis said the French fleet in the Chesapeak amounts to 17 sail of the line; as the British fleet is so much superior, and our Admirals are men of tried Courage and acknowledged abilities, there is every reason to expect a most Glorious Victory at last over the French fleet. It is not very probable that M. de Barras has yet joined de Grasse, who not knowing of the arrival of Sir Samuel Hood, will be rather surprized at the sight of so powerful a fleet. The defeat of this fleet will in all probability decide the fate of America.[35]

On 5 September, the very day of the engagement off the Chesapeake, Mackenzie was writing:

> If Admiral Graves is fortunate enough to reach the Chesapeak before M. de Barras, . . . he may be able to destroy the fleet of the Enemy within the Capes, or intercept that from Rhode Island in their attempt

to form a junction. If the wind proves favorable the Admiral will no doubt endeavor to burn the fleet of M. de Grasse. He has a fire ship with him.[36]

One matter of concern to Graves was the condition of some of the West Indies ships. These ships had been the longest from home and had suffered not only long-term wear and tear but structural damage incurred in action with the French—all of which meant that they constituted a weaker unit than was desirable in a line of battle. This irked Graves, for Hood had assured him that the ships of the West Indies Squadron were fit for sea for a month. A foul ship with a leaking hull could slow down the entire fleet and perhaps cause an opportunity to be lost in a situation where speed and handling qualities were at a premium.

Meanwhile de Grasse, on arrival at the Chesapeake, moored his fleet in Lynnhaven Roads near Cape Henry on the south side of the river, with the Middle Ground to the north. He did not, however, anchor his ships in any sort of defensive formation, which would have been a natural precaution if he were aware of a strong hostile fleet in the area, but instead moored in three irregular lines, a totally useless formation for defense should an enemy appear and attack him at anchor. He would be able to get under way, but not easily and not in any regular line, and his fleet would be open to attack as it emerged still unformed into the open sea. Though he detailed two frigates to give him warning of the approach of an enemy fleet, he did not give these frigates orders to cruise in the area to the north from which the British might come, but requested that they stay within direct signaling distance.

The Franco-American operations on land were going very well, and the French were blockading the mouths of the York and James Rivers with three ships of the line and two 50-gun ships detached from the main body of the fleet. The troops under Washington were expected at any time, and until then the forces available were enough to keep watch on Cornwallis. The arrival of Washington could only increase the numerical superiority of the Franco-American army and face Cornwallis with eventual defeat. Before Washington arrived was the time for Cornwallis to attack one or other of the forces facing him.

Out at sea, the frigates *Solebay* and *Richmond* scouting ahead of the British fleet were recalled to within hail of the *London*, where Graves told them to look into the mouth of the Chesapeake to see if any French ships were anchored there.

Captain Charles Saxton of the *Invincible* records that morning as "Fresh Breezes and Clear Weather."[37] The *Solebay* signaled at 6 a.m. that she could see land and later, as she stood into the Chesapeake Bay, that she could see a fleet moored in the river. Charles Everitt, captain of the *Solebay*, was familiar with the area and knew that the local people burned live pine trees to make tar, so he went to the maintop to see for himself that the masts sighted were not in fact bare tree trunks. His personal observation soon satisfied him that they were masts and that they were flying the white Bourbon flag.[38] Initial sightings from the *Royal Oak* counted eighteen or nineteen sail of the line in the southwest.

The French frigates were still cruising off the mouth of the Chesapeake in sight of de Grasse and watching for ships coming from the north. Whether the British frigates or the French in fact spotted their opponents first is not certain. The signal to Graves said that French ships were anchored to the southwest, in the Chesapeake River. It was the fifth of September and the time was 9:30 in the morning.

THE CHESAPEAKE

THE BATTLE JOINED

When the British fleet was first seen approaching, the patrolling French frigates were not immediately certain of their identity. The wind was blowing from the north-northeast and de Grasse was signaled that ships were coming from the north. De Grasse, imminently expecting the squadron of de Barras to join him, thought the ships now sighted were likely those of his compatriot.

Indeed, both Graves and de Grasse were expecting to see de Barras, and both commanders assumed that the ships they sighted were in fact the French North American Squadron. Enlightenment came only when the numbers of the opposing squadrons were signaled. At this time the advantage lay with Graves, who was under sail while de Grasse was still at anchor. Further, Graves knew that any other fleet he sighted would be hostile, while de Grasse could not be sure that it was not de Barras approaching until he received confirmation of the numbers.

As the British commander thought about the situation that now presented itself, it is perhaps time to consider some of the men who commanded the ships and divisions that comprised the British fleet.

All three British flag officers came from the West of England, an area that had supplied many of the most accomplished officers to the navy from the time of Elizabeth I. Samuel Hood, whose career we have followed to this point, had been born in Somerset to a family that originated in Dorset. Thomas Graves was born in Thanckes in Cornwall, the westernmost of the British counties, on 23 October 1725. He came from a naval family and was the second son of Rear Admiral Thomas Graves[1] and a cousin of Samuel Graves,[2] who had commanded on the North American station in the early stages of the war before being superseded by Lord Howe. He was a few months younger than Hood but had far more experience of fleet actions than his subordinate. His professional prospects may have been enhanced by the fact that his wife was related to Lady North, the wife of the prime minister.[3]

Thomas Graves had entered the service very young and by 1741 was serving in the West Indies at the siege of Cartagena under Edward Vernon. In 1743 he was a lieutenant in the *Romney*, the same ship in which Hood started his career, though Hood had left the ship two months before Graves was appointed. In the *Romney* he was present at the ill-fated action off Toulon in 1744 that led to the dispute between two commanders, Lestock and Mathews, and the court-martial and dismissal from the service of the latter. As a lieutenant in the *Monmouth* he took part in the first and second battles of Finisterre in 1747. His service was then interrupted by a period of peace, but in 1754 he was appointed master and commander of a sloop, reaching this level two months before Samuel Hood. Just before the outbreak of the Seven Years' War, in 1755, he became a post captain in the frigate *Sheerness* (20). Graves achieved this promotion a year before Hood and, with promotion coming by seniority, he thereafter held a permanent lead over Samuel Hood.

His career might have finished dishonorably during his command of the *Sheerness*. While in the Channel he sighted a French ship that was identified as a line-of-battle ship. He did not feel, with such a presumed disparity of force, that he could fight the Frenchman, and he therefore declined the engagement and continued on his mission. The Frenchman, who on seeing the strength of the *Sheerness* had brought to to await attack, then also continued on his journey. News of this incident reached the Admiralty, and Graves was brought to a court-martial "for not engaging a ship of assumed equal force." The Admiralty held that the ship was a returning French East Indiaman and that Graves should have taken his ship down to identify his opponent before deciding to decline action. This court-martial took place in 1757 at the same time as that of Admiral Byng. Byng was found guilty under Article 12 of the Articles of War and was, under the regulations in force since the Toulon court-martial, sentenced to death. Graves was found guilty under Article 36 of an error of judgment and was subjected only to reprimand.

The paths of Graves and Hood crossed again when both served under Rodney at the bombardment of Havre. Some sources have him in command of the *Duke* (90) as part of Hawke's squadron at Quiberon Bay, but this was his older cousin Samuel. He became governor of Newfoundland in 1761, a sign that his career had not been adversely affected by the court-martial, and was instrumental in defeating a French attack on the colony in 1762.

With the entry of France into the American War he was part of the squadron under Admiral Byron sent to North America in 1778. On the way the squadron was battered by a fierce gale (as seemed to happen to Byron frequently, hence his nickname Foul Weather Jack) and Graves in the *Conqueror* was driven back to Plymouth. He achieved flag rank in 1779, eighteen months before Hood, and served briefly with Sir Charles Hardy in the Channel. While serving under Hardy he collaborated with Richard Kempenfeldt in experiments to devise a more flexible manner of signaling. He was then ordered to join the reinforcement to North America in 1780 under Vice Admiral Arbuthnot and fought in the action against des Touches off the Chesapeake on 16 March 1781. That action, though indecisive, was enough for the British to keep control of the seas off the Virginia Capes. Now Graves was back in the same area again with another action to fight. He was only in temporary command of the station pending the arrival of Admiral Digby from England, and was slated to go on to Jamaica as second in command to Sir Peter Parker. While serving at Jamaica he was sent home by Rodney in charge of the prizes from the battle of the Saintes, but the squadron was overwhelmed by a hurricane and Graves was fortunate to escape from the catastrophe.

After the American War he was employed in various posts, but on the outbreak of war with France in 1793 he was made second in command to Lord Howe in the Channel Fleet. This was a sure sign that the Admiralty had full confidence in him and that his career had not suffered because of the propaganda put out by Hood and his supporters. He fought in the action of the Glorious First of June and was wounded in the arm. After the action he was created an Irish peer but, because of his wound and his age, he never served actively again before his death in 1802. If he had not been wounded, it is possible that he and not Alexander Hood would have become the commander of the Channel Fleet during the increasing periods when Howe was too ill and, later, retired.

The commander of the rear division at the Chesapeake was Francis Samuel Drake, who came from the village of Buckland Monachorum in Devon and who was believed to be was a collateral descendent of the famous Elizabethan sailor. He was four years younger than Graves and therefore the youngest of the three rear admirals. His early career is obscure, but he was in command of the frigate *Falkland* (50) at the action in Quiberon Bay in 1759. His service in the Seven Years' War ended in the West Indies, where he was present at the capture of Dominica in 1761 and of Martinique in 1762. Like Graves he was part of the squadron under Byron that was sent to North America in 1778, and like Graves he was forced back to England by the storm. He was then sent to join Rodney's fleet sailing for the relief of Gibraltar and took part in the two actions fought in that operation before returning to the Channel.

When he and Samuel Hood (to whom he was four months junior as a post captain) were raised to flag rank in September 1780, they both went out as reinforcement to Rodney in the West Indies. In fact, Drake was offered the post of second to Rodney before Hood, but turned it down. After taking his full share in the disappointing 1781 campaign in the area, Drake now commanded the rear division of the British fleet, though circumstances would conspire to give him the position of honor in the van when Graves reversed the order of sailing during his maneuvers before the battle. Later he was with Hood at St. Kitts and with Rodney at the Saintes, where again the order of the fleet was reversed and his division led the fleet into action. In the general distribution of awards after the battle he was given a baronetcy for his efforts. His flagship, the *Princessa* (70), had been a prize taken by Rodney in his action off Cape St. Vincent in January 1780. In August 1789 Drake was appointed a commissioner at the Admiralty, but he died three months later.

Both Samuel Hood and Thomas Graves had family members serving with them in their flagships, and Graves had his cousin, another Thomas Graves, in command of the *Bedford*. This second Thomas Graves was also to achieve a measure of professional distinction. Born in 1747, he had entered the navy during the Seven Years' War. He had been in the expedition to the Arctic in 1773, serving in the *Racehorse* under Captain Constantine Phipps[4] looking for the Northwest Passage. The other ship in the expedition, the converted bomb vessel *Carcass*, had Horatio Nelson on board.

In the present war he had served on the North American coast and had been made a post captain in 1779. Influence had achieved for him the command of the *Bedford*, which he retained through the three fleet actions of Chesapeake (where his brother David was flag captain on the *London*), St. Kitts, and the Saintes. He was then appointed to the frigate *Magicienne*, in which he fought a desperate action with the French frigate *Sybille*. The two frigates were of equal force and battered each other into virtual wrecks. Graves was able to get his ship back to Jamaica, but the *Sybille* was later captured by a British battleship.

The younger Thomas Graves had no immediate employment in the French Revolutionary War but was finally awarded his flag in 1801. He served briefly in the Channel under St. Vincent in the blockade of Brest before being detached to go with Hyde Parker to the Baltic. He was second in command to Nelson at Copenhagen, then served again in the Channel under Cornwallis on the resumption of the war in 1803, but in January 1805 a French squadron under Missiessy escaped from Brest and Graves seems to have been held responsible. The French had judged their escape for the moment that they could see Graves's squadron at anchor in Quiberon Bay taking on water. Whether for this reason or for ill health—blockading was extremely wearing on reserves of physical and nervous energy, and Graves was once described as "thin as a shotten herring"—for the rest of the war he had no further active service. He died in 1814. Samuel Hood had two cousins serving on the *Barfleur*. There had been three, who were brothers, but Arthur had drowned in the West Indies in 1777. The elder surviving cousin, Alexander, was serving as flag captain, and young Samuel was a lieutenant in the same ship. Both brothers had been brought on in the service by their older namesakes. Influence had secured for Alexander a place on James Cook's second voyage round the world in 1772. He remained flag captain during the following three engagements before being appointed to the frigate *Champion*.

Captain Alexander Hood was killed in April 1798 in a single-ship engagement between the *Mars* (74) and the French ship *Hercule* (74). In that contest the state of the wind precluded any maneuvering, and the outcome was decided by the superior British gunnery, inflicting casualties of more than 300 on the *Hercule* while the *Mars* lost fewer than 90. Alexander Hood was injured early in the action but lived long enough to receive the French captain's sword in surrender. The *Hercule*, coincidentally, was one of the ships serving at the Chesapeake under de Grasse.

Samuel Hood must be considered, after his older namesake, the most talented of the Hood family. He was a well-educated man who spoke several languages, and a good seaman and fighting captain who commanded the *Zealous* at the battle of the Nile. He lost his arm in an action in the Channel in 1806 but continued to be employed, most notably in the Baltic. The Admiralty regarded him as one of their most able and reliable officers, and together with Pellew and Saumarez he made up a triumvirate of first-class commanders who rendered great service in the post-Trafalgar period. He died as commander in chief in the East Indies in 1814 of a fever.

Another protégé of Hood in the fleet was John Inglefield, in command of the *Centaur* (74), a former French ship which had been a prize of Boscawen after the action off Lagos Bay in 1759. Inglefield had been in the retinue of Hood since his time as commissioner at Halifax. He had accompanied Hood back to Britain in 1770 and been with him in the various appointments he filled in the guard ships. At the outbreak of the war with the French he had been appointed a lieutenant on the *Robust* with Alexander Hood and was present at Keppel's engagement off Ushant. He had been made post captain in October 1780 and served as Hood's flag captain in the *Barfleur*. However, on Alexander Hood's being made post, Inglefield was appointed to a vacancy in the *Centaur* while Alexander became flag captain. Inglefield went on to command the *Centaur* in the actions of 1782 and then accompanied Graves to England with the prizes from the Saintes. When the fleet was struck by a severe hurricane, the *Centaur* was one of the ships that were overwhelmed and sunk. Although Inglefield got away from the ship and was eventually rescued, the experience seemed to mark him for the rest of his career. He did serve with Hood in the Mediterranean in 1793–94 but came home in 1795 and later declined promotion to flag rank. He accepted a post as dockyard commissioner and served in this position until 1811. He died in 1828.

Leading the British fleet into action was the *Alfred* (74), a relatively new ship commanded by William Bayne, a fifty-one-year-old Yorkshireman. Bayne was by now a senior post captain with a seniority date of 1760 and had seen service in the Leeward Islands in the previous war. He had come out with Hood's reinforcement in 1780. After the Chesapeake he commanded the *Alfred* at St. Kitts, where his ship was involved in an unfortunate collision that foiled Hood's plan of attack. Despite this collision Hood praised the quick and professional way in which Bayne got his ship repaired and ready for action again. In the engagement with de Grasse on 9 April 1782, which preceded the battle of the Saintes, Bayne received wounds from which he bled to death.

Another captain with the hand of fate on him was Lord Robert Manners of the *Resolution*. Unlike Bayne, he had risen rapidly through family influence. He was the son of the Duke of Rutland and had been the subject of a pleading letter from Lord Sandwich to Rodney in 1780 to "do something for him" to relieve the pressure the Admiralty was under. Something was done for him: he was made a post captain that year. Rodney took Manners and the *Resolution* back with him to the West Indies after his visit to the North American station in 1780. Lord Robert told his brother that he longed to be away from the North American station and had no doubt that he would be going to the West Indies with Rodney.[5] However, it was not a case of unwarranted advancement, for he proved himself a good officer and was spoken of as one of the forthcoming "stars" of the navy. He was about the same age as Nelson but did not live long enough to invite comparisons with his contemporary, for he was injured in the battle of the Saintes and died on his way back to England.

The list of officers commanding the French ships indicates the grip that the aristocracy had on the quarterdeck in the French service. The French navy had never been better prepared or equipped than in the present war, but it still suffered from two flaws in its manning system. The route to command in the service was not open to all men of talent regardless of rank, and the ability of the government to find seamen to man the ships declined as the war progressed. The pool of seamen open to the Royal Navy was larger than that available to the French navy, and despite the iniquities of the press system it did, with other methods, continue to provide men for the manning of the rapidly expanding fleet.

The French admirals opposing Graves were an unusual trio in that de Grasse and Vaudreuil were what might be called "bred to the sea," but Bougainville had started as a diplomat, then joined the army before finally settling on a career as a sailor when he made his voyage round the world in 1766–69. A transfer from the army to the navy was not unknown, for one of his contemporaries, the comte d'Estaing, had made the same journey.[6]

De Grasse had been chosen for his command in preference to the more experienced and senior de Barras, who was already serving in North America. So far the French Admiralty had no reason to think they had made a bad choice. De Grasse had been born in 1723 and entered the navy in 1738. He was present in Galissonière's fleet at the capture of Minorca in 1756 and later in that war served under d'Aché in the East Indies and fought in the actions against the British squadron of Sir George Pocock. In the present war he had command of the rear division of de Guichen's fleet in the action with Rodney in April 1780. Now he commanded that fleet and faced a critical situation.

Through his present handling of the fleet and marshalling of resources he had achieved a preponderance of force at the vital spot. He was to emerge from the campaign as the final arbiter of the fate of British North America, but from this peak the fates turned against him. Although he carried out one further successful campaign in the West Indies, he was unable to crush Hood's squadron either at St. Kitts or in the preliminary skirmishing to the battle of the Saintes. If on either of those occasions he had inflicted a destructive defeat on the British, it is unlikely that they could have carried the war on beyond 1782. As he proved in all his engagements, he lacked the killer instinct to seek a decisive action with a view to achieving naval superiority with all that that entailed.

After his defeat at the Saintes, de Grasse lost his reputation in the French service, but at least the Americans continued to esteem him and his part in their successful struggle for independence. When, after a period as a prisoner on parole in England, he carried Lord Shelburne's peace proposals back to France, his career was effectively ended.

Louis-Antoine de Bougainville, born in 1729, was a noted mathematician, with published works on the subject to his credit. He was so highly thought of in this field that he had been a member of the British Royal Society since 1756. He had also been a representative at the French embassy in London, which had made him a familiar figure in London society. In the Seven Years' War he served as aide-de-camp to the marquis de Montcalm in the Quebec Campaign of 1758–59. Following the loss of Canada he was with the French army on the Rhine until the end of the war.

In 1764 Bougainville took to the sea and established the French colony in the Falkland Islands before undertaking his voyage round the world in 1766–69, in the course of which he came close to sighting the coast of Australia. During this voyage he achieved a form of immortality by having a new (to Europeans) species of plant named after him, bougainvillea. In 1772 he was made secretary to the king, Louis XV, but with the outbreak of hostilities against Britain in 1778 he volunteered to serve in North America. In the investigation held in France to enquire into the defeat at the Saintes, Bougainville was largely blamed by de Grasse for not supporting him properly. With the end of the war he returned to France, but he seems to have taken no active part in either opposing or supporting the Revolution and apparently lived quietly on his estates in Normandy concentrating on his scientific research. He was made a count and a member of the Légion d'Honneur by Napoleon and died in 1811.

Louis-Philippe de Rigaud, comte de Vaudreuil, was born in 1723, the eldest son of the last governor-general of French Canada. He entered the French navy in 1740 and achieved the rank of post captain by 1754. The similarity to Hood in age and naval service will be noted, except that Vaudreuil achieved post rank earlier. He served with the fleet under d'Orvilliers in the Channel in 1778. Now he was second in command to de Grasse and like him was to find his career terminated by the defeat by Rodney at the Saintes. Although he was not forced to surrender his ship, he was court-martialled for his actions, but he was acquitted. He had no further active service. In

1789 he was a Member of the Estates General when that body assembled. However, as the Revolution got more extreme, he fled to London in 1791 and remained until 1800. Feeling the situation with Napoleon in control was more stable and acceptable, he returned to France, where he died in 1802.

On the quarterdeck of the *Ville de Paris* along with de Grasse was Pierre-René-Marie, comte de Vaugiraud de Rosnay, serving in the capacity of what in the Royal Navy would be called Captain of the Fleet. He was just under forty years old and had entered the navy in 1755. He had an eventful career in the Seven Years' War, serving on the *Eveillé* (64) off Santo Domingo when a French squadron captured the *Greenwich* (50) on 16 March 1757 and on the *Orient* (80) at Quiberon Bay on 20 November 1759 when Hawke destroyed the fleet of Conflans and therewith the French invasion hopes.

In the present war he had taken part in the battle of Ushant in the *Couronne* (80), and in the campaign of 1779 he was promoted to serve in the *Bretagne* (110), the flagship of d'Orvilliers. In 1781 he sailed to the West Indies with the fleet under de Grasse and was on the *Ville de Paris* at the engagement with Hood off Martinique. After the Chesapeake he served at St. Kitts and the Saintes, becoming a prisoner of war upon the surrender of the French flagship.

In the years before the Revolution he held various posts, but with the advent of the Revolutionary government he fled to Britain and took part in various ineffective attempts to assist the Breton royalists in their revolt against the Revolutionary forces. He remained in Britain even after the Peace of Amiens and the adoption of the imperial title by Napoleon. It was not until 1814 that he finally returned to France, where he died in March 1819. It is interesting to speculate that, with such a prolonged period of residence in Britain, he may very well have become acquainted with Hood and discussed past campaigns together.

Of the other commanders of the French ships, François-Hector, comte d'Albert de Rions, of the *Pluton* was one of the most distinguished. He was a friend of Suffren, who described him as "brave . . . full of zeal and ardour and a good seaman." Now fifty-three years old, born at Avignon, he had entered the Gardes-Marin in December 1743 and seen service in both the Austrian and Seven Years' Wars. He had commanded the *Sage* in the French expedition under Dubois de La Motte to relieve Louisbourg in 1755, but in the engagement with the British squadron under Boscawen he was forced to surrender and became a prisoner of war. On being exchanged he served in the Mediterranean but was again made prisoner in 1758. He was appointed to the command of the 50-gun ship *Sagittaire* in d'Estaing's squadron in 1778 and took part in the operations against Lord Howe on the coast of North America. While serving in the *Sagittaire* he captured the British 50-gun ship *Experiment* commanded by Sir James Wallace, which was taken into the French squadron. When d'Estaing took his fleet to the West Indies, d'Albert de Rions went with it and was present at the actions with Barrington and Byron. He was appointed to the *Pluton* (74) in 1781 and commanded the ship at the Chesapeake, St. Kitts, and the Saintes.

D'Albert de Rions was made commissioner at Toulon in July 1784 and appointed a commodore to command a squadron in August of that year. He was given command of the fleet at Toulon in January 1788 but he was arrested by revolutionary dockworkers in December 1789. Eventually released by order of the National Assembly, he was given the command at Brest in an attempt to restore discipline and order at that port. In 1792 he fled the country to join the forces opposed to the Revolution. He did not return to France until 1801 and died in October of the following year.

In command of the *Languedoc* was François-Aymar, baron de Monteil. He was fifty-six and had entered the navy in 1741, seeing active service in both the Austrian and Seven Years' Wars. In the latter war he had served under the comte d'Aché in the East Indies in the battles against Sir George Pocock. Returning to Europe, he was sent with Ternay on the raiding expedition against Newfoundland in 1762.

He had a varied career between the wars, including being made inspector of forests in 1769. In 1774 he was sent to the Eastern Mediterranean in a bid to increase French influence in that area. When war with Britain resumed in 1778, he was present at the battle of Ushant in the *Conquérant* and remained with the French Channel Squadron in 1779. In 1780 he went to the West Indies with de Guichen in the *Palmier* and fought in the battles against Rodney in April and May 1780. At the request of the Spanish he led a French squadron in a successful attack on the British base at Pensacola, Florida. From the *Palmier* he was transferred to the *Languedoc*, in which he fought at the Chesapeake. He survived the war, though ill health forced his return home from the West Indies. He died in France in 1787.

In command of the *César* was another officer from the French aristocracy, Jean-Louis-Charles-Régis de Coriolis, marquis d'Espinouse, usually abbreviated to Coriolis d'Espinouse. He had entered the navy in 1741 and commanded the *Fantasque* (64) in the action between de la Clue and Boscawen at Lagos Bay in 1759, where he was fortunate enough to bring his ship safely out of the battle.

Between the wars he was employed on various occasions in the Mediterranean, but on the outbreak of war in 1778 he was appointed to the *Caton*, followed by the César, his command at the Chesapeake and then at St. Kitts. Promoted to the equivalent of rear admiral in January 1782, he flew his flag in the *Duc de Bourgogne* at the battle of the Saintes. In the aftermath of this action, a 1784 enquiry into the reasons for defeat held him responsible for not doing everything he could to support de Grasse. He then left the navy. His date of death is uncertain.

*   *   *

The situation of the French fleet was serious. De Grasse, through the faulty disposition of his frigates, had been caught unawares by the arrival of the British. He had nearly sixteen hundred officers and men ashore engaged in various tasks. The recall signals that he hoisted were largely ineffective, as they were too distant to be read by the men on shore. He was unable to muster his full strength, with three ships of the line detached to assist the army by blockading the York and James Rivers. The situation was urgent, and he could not wait for the return of the missing men or ships.

He could not wait, but he could not move, either. The tide was still flowing strongly in. If the British arrived early enough to take advantage of this flood tide, the French fleet would be exposed to attack while it was still anchored in Lynnhaven Bay. In addition, though the British *might* not attack de Grasse in his present position, they were between him and de Barras, which placed the latter in the position of having to either withdraw his squadron or be overwhelmed by the superior numbers of the British.

A British blockade of the mouth of the river would have permanently kept the two elements of the French fleet separated. As the French fleet was not moored in a position to repel any attack made on it, de Grasse had no option but to get to sea as soon as possible with whatever force was available to him. The manning situation in one ship, the *Citoyen* (74), was said to be so critical—five officers and two hundred seamen short—that there were not enough crew left to man the ship efficiently in action, and in fact the upper-deck guns could not be fought.

It is hard to understand why de Grasse was so unprepared for the appearance of a British fleet on the coast. It was known that the British had come north and that, with unencumbered passage, they would probably have arrived earlier than his own fleet. Given the fifty-fifty chance that the next fleet he saw would be hostile, a prudent commander would have moored in a more defensible manner and had his frigates more widely spread to give adequate warning.

The presence of the French fleet inside the Capes was reported to Graves by a signal from the *Solebay*. Graves described it later as "a number of great ships." The British fleet was then still some fifteen leagues from Cape Henry. Hoping it was the squadron of de Barras, Graves pushed on with a favorable wind and with the tide, making into the bay. At 10:30 a.m. he flew the signal to prepare for battle, eager to attack what he thought was a detachment of the French fleet. It was at 11 a.m. that the number of ships in the Chesapeake convinced him that he was approaching the French main fleet and not just de Barras' squadron. His frigates confirmed that he faced a French fleet of twenty-four sail of the line. He could not yet tell if de Barras had joined de Grasse, as neither he nor Hood knew exactly how many ships the French had brought north.

The discrepancy between the fleets did not rest entirely on numbers. The French line-of-battle ship carried a heavier weight of firepower than its British equivalent. The French also had four ships of 80 guns, which were reckoned to be the equivalent of a British 98-gun ship. Included in the British fleet was a solitary fireship, the *Salamander*, commanded by Edward Bowater. Such ships were a hangover from the Dutch Wars of the previous century and had little place in the type of naval engagement that was about to take place, but nevertheless Graves ordered Bowater to "prime" his vessel. Bowater was to have a long career in the service, achieving the rank of Admiral of the White before his death in 1829 at the age of seventy-seven, but that career seems not to have been distinguished, and the fact that he was still master and commander at thirty-one would suggest neither influential patrons nor the talent to rise without one.

As the British steered southward with a moderate breeze, at 10:40 Graves signaled for line ahead at two cables. Given the time factor, the British probably had no chance of engaging the French at anchor but, despite the odds against them, they had every chance of engaging and defeating the van of the French fleet as it emerged from the bay before the ships of the center and rear divisions could come to its aid. By noon the ships of the British van under Hood were estimated to be ten miles from Cape Henry.

The French were unable to move until the coming of the ebb tide at about noon. At 11:30 a.m. de Grasse made the signal for his fleet to unmoor and proceed to sea. The only way out of the bay was through the narrow channel between Cape Henry and the Middle Ground. Situated as they were, moored in no particular order, the ships did not have the time or space to assume the designated order of battle. In these circumstances de Grasse ordered that they form a line of battle in the order in which they emerged from the bay and proceed line-ahead on the port tack. The rearmost ships were well into the bay and would have to tack several times to get clear.

The whole process made for extreme confusion in the French fleet. The leading ships emerged from the bay in an irregular line with large gaps between the various groups. If the British had been nearer and able to take advantage of this confusion, the French force could have been defeated in detail before it could properly unite. By contrast, one French observer noted the British "were in the best possible order" while bearing down on them.

The difficulties of getting to sea were appreciated by no one more than Bougainville, the second in command. His flagship, the *Auguste*, was moored to windward of almost all the rest of the fleet and was blocked in by a shoal. Foreseeing a need to get to sea quickly from such a position, Bougainville had rigged a stern cable that could be used to swing the head of the ship around to miss the shoal. When the signal came to make sail, the *Auguste* was one of the first ships to get under way, and Bougainville claims that the *Auguste* became in fact the leading ship of the French line. Appendix 2 gives the generally accepted order of battle for the French when the engagement commenced.

Many ships had difficulties in avoiding the shoals and getting to sea. At one time the *Souverain* was in only four fathoms of water, while the *Citoyen* was warned by the frigate *Aigrette* that unless she tacked immediately she would be aground on a sandbank. There was a certain amount of competition among the French captains to lead the line against the British, and some jostling occurred before an irregular line formed. Monteil in the *Languedoc* found himself ahead of the *Ville de Paris*. The *Languedoc* had originally been one of the ships designated to lead the van of the fleet into action, but in the order that now prevailed she was to the rear. De Grasse appreciated that Monteil was entitled to the honor of leading the fleet, but he also knew that the rear was without an officer of flag rank, and he hailed Monteil and asked him to take charge of the rear division. This change was effected just before the two fleets engaged at 3:30 p.m. The French formed on a line bearing northeast-to-southwest as they were able to get clear of Cape Henry.

The log of the *London* records the French starting to get under way at 12:30 p.m., and at 12:45 Graves signaled for the distance between his ships to be reduced to one cable. The French remarked upon the compactness of the British line as they bore down. At about 1 p.m. the signal was made for the British fleet to form an east-west line of bearing. This put them on a course roughly parallel to the French but closing slightly and still heading into the mouth of the bay.

A French account later published in Jamaica says that while the French were recalling their men and getting ready to sail, the British were "forcing sail" and forming line of battle "ahead on the starboard tack" with the heaviest ships—presumably referring to the *Barfleur*—in the van. (The order of battle for the British fleet is shown in appendix 1.) Aboard the *Ville de Paris*, it was thought that the confident approach indicated that the British did not know the strength of the fleet which they were attacking.

Graves needed to take advantage of the situation while it was still favorable to him. The French would be some time in getting out of the bay, and until they could form a regular line of battle, they would be open to defeat in detail. They were vulnerable, and an attack on the van as it emerged into the open sea looked the best course. Hood was certainly of the opinion that there was enough time for the British to attack and crush the French van before the center and rear could assist. In this case speed of action would not have been foolishly precipitate, as in Byron's action off Grenada. Speed and the rashness of his attack against a superior fleet had been the ruin of Byron, but speed could have been the saving of Graves. It would have meant an attack with his line unformed, on the basis of a "general chase," as had occurred at such notable actions as Quiberon Bay and Rodney's Moonlight Battle off Gibraltar. Instead Graves noted that the French center and rear were far astern of their van, which theoretically gave them an opportunity of "doubling" the British rear—that is, attacking on both sides. He therefore delayed his attack to let the French ships come more abreast of him. He may also have seen in Byron's actions a warning about a precipitate attack on a superior fleet. Further, Graves had reason to feel unsure of the quality and reliability of his captains, for most were strangers to him.

As Graves later told Sandwich, "My aim was to get close, to form parallel, extend with them, and attack all together." His intention was not to attack ship for ship all along the French line but to bring a compact formed line onto the van of the French before they could be assisted by the center and rear. The opinion of Hood, and others, was that the attack should have been made direct on the French van as it emerged from Lynnhaven Bay. "Had such an attack been made, several of the enemy's ships must have been inevitably demolished in half an hour's action, and there was a full hour and half to have engaged it before any of the rear could have come up."[7]

The weather by this time was described as squally by the master's log of the *London*, and Graves ordered a reef to be taken in on the topsails. The

British line was now not so well formed as before, and the rear division had to be signaled to make more sail to maintain station. The French noted several signals flying from various ships of the British line as the two fleets approached each other, indicative of the efforts Graves was making to control his fleet and keep his line well formed.

On their east-west course the British ships were still heading into the bay, led by the *Alfred* of Hood's division. By 2:00 p.m. the British were nearing the shoal of the Middle Ground, which represented a significant navigational obstacle. The French were some three miles distant to the south, as the log of the *London* recorded, "standing to ye eastward with their Larboard tacks on board in a line ahead."

With the approach of the Middle Ground, the signal was made at 14;09 for the fleet to wear together, which brought the British onto the same tack as the French. Graves had signaled this alteration because he thought the van was too near to the Middle Ground, but the log of the *Barfleur* records the distance to Cape Henry as six miles, and this shoal was about three miles from the Cape—still plenty of distance, at a speed of only four or five knots, to have closed with the French and fought the action in the regular order. Whether the result would have been different if Hood had been leading the fleet is impossible to say. The maneuver chosen, bringing the fleet onto the same tack as the French, reversed the order so that Drake's division was in the leading position and Hood's in the rear. Drake's was the weakest part of the British fleet, yet when the action came it would be exposed to the brunt of the French fire.

As they came onto the new course the British were in some disarray, and Graves brought to to allow his ships to form their line better and to allow the French to draw further ahead. This placed the center of the French fleet, now coming clear of the bay, approximately level with the British center, the two fleets on roughly parallel courses but about four or five miles apart. The intention of Graves was to follow the ideas of Howe and concentrate his force on a straggling French line, but being careful not to allow the more numerous French fleet to overlap his own.[8]

With both fleets now proceeding on parallel courses, Graves made the signal for the leading ship, the *Shrewsbury*, to lead more to starboard—that is, to close the French line. Just before four o'clock the signal was made to form line at a distance of one cable's length.

If the signal had been understood and the ships had all turned *together*, the result of the day might have been different. The signal made was one from the instructions that Graves had issued to the West Indies ships. What happened was that the ships turned towards the French in succession as each reached the point where the leading ship, the *Shrewsbury*, had turned. Graves had used Signal 10 of Arbuthnot's Additional Instructions, which he adopted when he took over the command and which he had issued to all the captains. This signal read: "If at any time I would have the leading ship in the line alter course to starboard, I will hoist a flag half red, half white at the main topmast head."[9]

It is plain that there was a danger of the various captains interpreting the signal as they did. This situation would have been avoided if the British commanders had discussed together the signaling system to be used and the general tactical principals to be followed. There had been no time for this at New York, and the chance doesn't seem to have arisen during the voyage down together. With the signal misunderstood by the leading ships, Graves's plan had gone immediately awry. All the leading ships were from the West Indies Squadron and made the same mistaken interpretation of the signal. Many signals were made—to the *Royal Oak* to keep her station in the line; to the *Princessa*, the *Alcide*, and the *Terrible* to lead more towards the enemy—as Graves wrestled with the situation, still trying to get the individual approach to the French that he desired.

The *Terrible* was by far the worst-conditioned ship in the fleet and was to suffer severely because she now occupied a leading position in the action. The poor condition of the ship was probably due to the coppering. It had been found in earlier coppered ships that there was an adverse effect, electrolysis, on the iron fittings, particularly the bolts that held the structure together. The condition was so serious that coppering was later suspended until a remedy could be found. But for the duration of the war Middleton, the comptroller of the navy, pushed forward an increased coppering program, relying on a compound mistakenly believed to be a suitable agent for protecting the iron fixtures from the effect of the copper.[10] A satisfactory solution was found only when the iron fastenings were replaced with copper, but this was a massive undertaking and could not be done in time of war when ships were wanted urgently.[11]

Those ships that had been coppered under the earlier program, like the *Terrible*, could only wait until they got back to a home dockyard for expensive remedial work or gradually deteriorate until they were longer seaworthy. Lord Robert Manners later remarked on the poor condition of the *Invincible*, which he described as almost as bad as the *Terrible*.[12] The *Terrible* was letting in so much water that the pumps had to be kept going just about permanently to keep her afloat. It was reported by the French that during the British approach to action the *Terrible* was in fact fired on by Drake to get her to go back to her place in the line, but there is no confirmation of this from the British side.

It is recorded in the log of the *Barfleur* that, at 3:09 p.m., "the Admiral made the *Princessa*'s, *Alcide*'s and *Intrepid*'s signal to alter their course." These ships were in the van division and were among the leading ships in the line. The signal to steer to starboard was repeated at 3:17 p.m.

The van of the fleet, having made two changes of course to starboard and following the misinterpretation of the signal to bear down on the French, was now closing the van of the French line, with the center in fairly close support. But it had become plain that a fault was developing in the British plan.

The British battle line was now a "dogleg," with the Van angled towards the French, the center not yet turned, and the seven ships of the rear division increasingly lagging the rest of the fleet. According to Captain Saxton of the *Invincible*, the *London* flew a "Chequered Blue and Yellow Flag at the Foretop Great Mast Head and a White Pennant Open" recorded as "each ship to steer for and engage his opponent in the enemy line." This was followed by the signal to prepare for battle.[13]

The time was now about 3:45. The log of the *London* states that this signal was made purely to the van, yet the signal, which was one of those introduced by Arbuthnot, was for the *fleet* in line of battle to alter course to starboard. This is certainly more likely to have been the intention, as Graves must have seen the gap developing between the rear ships and the rest of the fleet. There followed a signal for the fleet to form line of battle at one cable's length from each other.

It was clearly Graves's intention that all ships in the line should alter course towards the French at the same time. The signal was meant to produce a "lasking" movement in which the ships approached the enemy in line abreast sailing at a slight angle. This was the tactic employed by John Byng at Minorca and attempted by Rodney in his engagements the previous year and by Nelson at Trafalgar. It had the effect of bringing all the ships down together but not leaving them as exposed as in a direct head-on approach. If this signal was made and the interpretation was available to the van ships, why did they not use the approach ordered by Graves?

The French too were having their troubles. Between a fickle wind and the action of the current and the difficulties of getting out of the bay, the leading ships wound up too far to windward for de Grasse to form a good line. He had to signal these ships to bear up two points so that they could all engage together.

Action was now imminent as the respective vans were very close. Graves hoisted his colors in the *London*, and the rest of the British ships followed suit. Just before 4 p.m. Graves signaled for the fleet to close up the line to half a cable's length.

Judging the moment right to engage, Graves hauled down the signal for altering course to starboard and replaced it with one for close action, each ship to steer for and engage her opposite number in the line. The moment Graves had been waiting for had arrived. The *London*, which Graves had brought to during the process of marshalling his fleet into a good line, now filled her sails and went down on the French line towards the *Ville de Paris*. By the log of the *London* the time was 4:03 p.m.

Up to now the *London* had been flying the signal for the fleet to maintain the line of battle—and, according to Hood and the rear division, this still continued flying when the signal was hoisted for all ships to engage the enemy. The log of the *London* records the signal for the line as being hauled down at 4:11 p.m. "that it might not interfere with ye signal to engage." According to Hood and the ships of the rear division, it was not hauled down until more than an hour later—Hood gives the time as 5:25—and consequently he could not go down to engage the enemy without, he claimed, disobeying the signal to maintain the line.

This situation has been put down to Hood's time spent under the strict regime of discipline in fleet training with Rodney. There is enough evidence given by other witnesses to support the contention that the signal was hauled down sometime after 5 p.m. but before 5:30, despite the statement in the log of the *London* giving an earlier time.

There was, however, no doubt of the intention of Graves to bring his whole fleet into action. Drake in the van division recognized this and acted accordingly. Yet he brought his ships into action in a sloping line, not adopting the lasking approach but following the lead ship, turning in succession at the same point as the *Shrewsbury* as they steered to close the enemy. Hood, with the ships of the rear division, did not engage at all. He certainly did not follow Nelson's belief that to place your ship alongside the enemy cannot be wrong!

There seems to be general agreement that the two sides opened fire about 4:10 p.m., commencing with the leading ships in the van and going back along the line as the engagement became more general. While the van was engaged at what was described as "musquet shot," Hood considered that the *London* and the ships of the center were engaged at a "most improper distance." The rear division was out of range entirely and did not fire a shot. The problem with the center was that the *Montagu* had luffed up and opened fire at too long a range, which meant that the ships astern of her, including the *London*, had to do likewise or they would have crossed the fire zone of the *Montagu* and come between her and the French line. In bringing his division into action, Graves was not helped by the fact that the French line was in a similar shape to his own, with the van closer to the British than the center, and the rear even further out, like Hood's division.

The leading ship of the British line, the *Shrewsbury*, began a close engagement with the *Pluton*. In the early exchange of fire the commander of the *Shrewsbury*, Mark Robinson, lost his left leg, while his first lieutenant was killed. The British were under the handicap of firing from their lee ports, as they were coming from the windward gauge. This meant that the ships heeled slightly towards the water, interfering with the rate and accuracy of the shooting except at the very closest range. The French, on the other hand, were firing from their windward ports, so their ships heeled away from the British line and kept their ports clear of the water. This did, however, give the British gunners the opportunity to score hits between wind and water as the French heeled over in the breeze.

It is generally stated that, both in the American War and in the subsequent Revolutionary and Napoleonic Wars, the French liked to direct their gunfire high so that the spars and rigging of their opponents were damaged, immobilizing them for a period. It is true that this practice was generally followed, but not always, and certainly not to the exclusion of firing at the hulls of British ships. The damage inflicted by the French on Hood's squadron off Martinique earlier in the year and that inflicted on this occasion show that the French gunners were decidedly capable of causing casualties in the crew and serious structural harm. Firing at the rigging did succeed for the French on many occasions, and it has been said that the French tactics were sounder, as a British ship immobilized could then be battered into submission from angles to which she could not reply.[14] However, this contention does not bear close examination. At no stage in the American War did the French capture a British line-of-battle ship, except for the *Ardent*, which had accidentally sailed into the middle of the Franco-Spanish armada in the Channel in 1779 when the *Ardent*'s captain mistook the enemy fleet for his own. This fact alone must suggest that the French tactic of firing high was wrong, for it was not producing the most desirable result, the destruction and capture of British ships. The French made no attempt to "take, burn, or destroy" as was the policy of the British navy. They were content to play for a stalemate, which in the conditions of the American War was as good as a victory for them. The British policy of shattering the hull and killing the crew proved decisive in the long run and led to the British victories in the following war.

At the Chesapeake the French secured the land victory at Yorktown by their success at sea. They inflicted a tactical defeat on the Royal Navy, which led to the fall of the government of Lord North and ultimately the independence of the United States. The capture or destruction of any ships of the British fleet would have been a bonus, but incidental to the ends for which the French had come to North America—a serious, and possibly fatal, blow to British power on the Continent. This they achieved. It was a great achievement for an afternoon's fighting.

The *Shrewsbury* was disabled in the exchange of fire with the leading French ships, having her fore and main topsail yards shot down and her mizzenmast damaged in two places. In addition, hull damage that caused her to take in water was making it difficult for her to keep her place in the line, and she gradually dropped away, leaving the ship next astern, the 64-gun *Intrepid*, exposed to the fire of two French ships, her existing opponent the *Marseillais* and the *Pluton*, which had been engaging the *Shrewsbury*.

The commander of the *Intrepid* was Anthony James Molloy, who in this engagement achieved a reputation in the service for his "spirited behaviour" in the defense of his ship against these two opponents. He had also commanded the *Trident* in Rodney's action against de Guichen on 17 April 1780 and had likewise been commended for his conduct on that occasion. Thirteen years later after the Glorious First of June, where he commanded the *Caesar* (80), Molloy was court-martialled for failing to do his utmost to engage the enemy when leading the British line. He and his ship were subjected to very hard handling in the battle off the Chesapeake, and the mental effect may very well still have been with him when he came to take part in the action under Howe. Courage in action can be likened to a reservoir, which can be drawn upon until eventually it is empty and the combatant, no longer able to face life-threatening situations, places self-preservation first. Possibly Molloy at the First of June found his reservoir empty and could no longer steel himself for close action again. The situation is very similar to that which faced Sir Thomas Picton prior to the battle of Waterloo. When Wellington asked him to join the army mustering in the Netherlands for the campaign against Napoleon, Picton told Wellington he was certain the campaign would be fatal for him, though he had served in the Peninsular War with conspicuous bravery and without serious injury. He did overcome his fears and join the army, only to be wounded at Quatre Bras and killed at Waterloo.

The *Intrepid* was only a 64-gun ship, but for some time she kept up a good defensive fire against the two French 74-gun ships she opposed. Hood claimed in a letter to Lord Sandwich that Molloy in fact made the two French ships "turn their sterns to him." This was true, for both the French ships had suffered in their engagement with the two leading British ships, and de Grasse ordered them to bear away to leeward, which action exposed them momentarily to British raking fire.

The fourth ship in the French line, the *Réfléchi*, was also badly hit and had her captain killed, and others of the leading French ships were hard pressed. In his despatch to the Admiralty, Graves did Molloy full justice, saying that he had behaved with the "utmost gallantry" in trying to cover the disabled *Shrewsbury*. The *Intrepid* received sixty-five shot holes in the starboard side, many lying between wind and water. Her masts and yards were also badly damaged and in danger of falling. With such damage the *Intrepid* was temporarily out of the fight.

With the vans of the two fleets engaged at close quarters and the center divisions cannonading each other from long range, Hood thought that Graves should have signaled for the center to advance and go to the support of the van. He said as much in a letter to Lord Sandwich a day after the action:

> . . . the signal was not thrown out for the van ships to make more sail, to have enabled the centre division to push on, instead of engaging at such an improper distance (the *London* having her main topsail to the mast the whole time she was firing, with the signal for close action and the signal for the line ahead at half a cable flying, though the French ships pressed on) that the second ship astern of the *London* received very little damage, and the third ship from the *London* received no damage at all, which most clearly proves how much too great the distance was the centre division engaged.

Now, had the centre of the British line gone on to the support of the van, and the signal for the line been hauled down, or had Rear-Admiral Graves set the example of close action even with the signal for the line out, the van ships of the enemy must have been cut up; and the rear division of the British fleet would have been opposed to those ships the centre fired at, and at the most *proper* distance for engaging, or the Rear Admiral commanding it would have had a great deal to answer for. Instead of that, our centre division did the enemy very little damage; and our rear ships being barely within random shot, only fired a few guns.[15]

The rest of the ships of the British van did not suffer to the same extent as the *Intrepid* and the *Shrewsbury*. The *Alcide* had her masts and rigging damaged and some shot below the waterline. The *Ajax* had her mizzen topmast shot through, her mainmast damaged, and the rigging cut. Neither of these ships, however, had any trouble in keeping her place in the line.

Rear Admiral Drake in the *Princessa* was opposed to the *Réfléchi* and seems to have maintained a superior rate of fire. The French ship, as we have seen, was roughly handled and her commander killed. The fire of the *Princessa*, severe enough to drive her opponent out of the line, was then turned on the *Caton* (64), which too was driven from the line. The outstanding performance of the *Princessa* and her crew was not ended: after the *Caton* she came to such close action with the *Diadème* that the wads from the British guns kept setting fire to the French ship. Drake seemed to have the measure of this opponent also.

The commander of the *Saint Esprit*, de Chabert, apparently saw the danger to the *Diadème* and came to her assistance, steering across the stern of the *Princessa* and firing into the British ship a raking broadside "that the gentlemen of Albion could not stand, and had to haul their wind." The *Princessa* shook herself free only to find another French ship approaching, the *Auguste*, flying the flag of Bougainville. It is reported that Bougainville tried to board the British ship but was foiled at the last moment, whereupon he left the *Princessa* and turned his attention to the *Terrible*.

The performance of the *Princessa* was indicative of what a well-trained and disciplined guns crew could achieve. Had the British concentrated on the French van as Hood wanted (and Graves strove to do), they would have been in a strong position despite the damage received by the *Intrepid* and the *Shrewsbury*.

The *Terrible*, however, was in a bad situation. Leaky and shaken before the battle, she was feeling the effects of her own broadsides as well as the return fire from the French. The *Auguste* was an 80-gun ship with the broadside power of a British 98. The effect on the *Terrible* was shattering, and it was plain that she was overmatched. The return fire of the British was not, however, totally ineffective and some damage was done to the *Auguste* in both rigging and crew.

The ships of the center division were still engaged with their opposite numbers in the French line, but not at close range. The *London*, though frustrated by the position of the *Montagu* in closing the French center, was some way nearer to the French line than other ships ahead of her in her division. It was the backing of the *London*'s main topsail to avoid interfering with the fire of the *Montagu* that had caused the ships behind her to do like-wise and led to the bunching that masked the fire of certain ships. At 4:22 p.m. Graves had made the signal for the ships to form line ahead to clear this bunching and enable the ships to obtain a clear field of fire. According to log of the *London*, the signal was hauled down at 4:27 and replaced by that for close action again.

De Grasse had the worry of a British concentration on his van, for part of his center and the whole of his rear division were still not in the open sea and able to support the van ships while they were heavily engaged in this opening phase of the battle. The unengaged French ships were carrying all the sail they could, but the wind remained fickle. Their slowness in coming to the support of the van lends more support to the contention of Hood and others that the van should have been subjected to an immediate and heavy attack without forming a regular line of battle. It is quite plain from the maneuvers carried out that Graves intended a measured approach that would bring a well-formed line onto the French van, but was foiled by the misunderstanding of his signals.

A change of wind to the east-northeast about 5 p.m. took away from the British some of the advantage they had enjoyed in the windward position. The wind shift, however, was not enough to help de Grasse; in fact it placed his van further to windward of the center, leaving it unsupported. De Grasse signaled for the van to steer further off the wind, enabling his line to be bet-ter formed. According to French accounts, this move was intended to allow the British to close so that the engagement could be made "general," which it was said de Grasse ardently desired. The leading French ships therefore bore away, firing their broadsides as they went, while the crippled ships of the British van were unable to follow. Or, as a French account put it,

> with much eagerness he [de Grasse] desired a general engagement, he signalled to the Van to go more freely in order to invite Admiral Graves to follow, but as the English fleet was already severely pun-ished, the latter determined to keep the advantage of the wind and

fight at a greater distance in order to avoid the fire of the last French ships which were approaching.[16]

The British, understandably, took the retreat of the French van ships from close action to mean that they had driven them off, whereas the French took the reluctance or inability of the British to follow and close again as proof that the French had inflicted a defeat on the British van.

The captain of the *Citoyen* formed this impression of the action so far, particularly the conduct of the British van ships:

> the vans were fighting at very close range . . . but the enemy, instead of fully engaging themselves, hauled their wind at the moment that they fired their broadsides. Their admiral himself, for fear of approaching too close, laid everything against his mast at 4:30 p.m. The action commenced at the center of the fleet from the van and to the rear of Admiral de Grasse. The enemy, although master of the wind, only engaged from far off and simply in order to be able to say that they had fought. In that part of the line it was not at all the way it was in the van of the two fleets, where one could see only fire and smoke billowing on both sides.[17]

The ships in the rear of the fleet still had to fire a shot. According to an officer on the *Invincible*, George Grey,[18] Hood tried a broadside from the *Barfleur* at about 5:20 p.m., "at which time we were exceedingly close on the *Barfleur*'s lee quarter and could easily observe the shot fall considerably short, therefore we persisted in not firing a single gun."[19]

Hood and the ships of the rear division were still sailing in strict line of battle. Hood would not leave the line to close with the French because it would have meant disobeying the signal that he claimed was flying from the *London* and breaking the line of battle. An example that should have come to his mind was Lord Hawke, then just a captain, at the battle of Toulon in 1744. The flag for the line was kept flying by Admiral Mathews as well as a later one to engage the enemy. Hawke, as captain of the *Berwick*, decided that it was the intention of the admiral to engage the French and chose to disobey the signal for the line and to obey only that for engaging the enemy. This is what Drake had done with his squadron.

The failure to break their own line and close with the enemy shows a distressing lack of initiative on the part of Hood and his captains. It must be counted the blackest moment of his career. He had come to North American waters to counter the French concentration and to meet and defeat that concentration. He was part of an inferior fleet that needed all its strength to defeat its opponent, and his division was not taking any part in the action. Whatever he may have thought of the missed opportunities of the morning, his own feelings must have told him that his place was alongside the enemy. The appearance of the fresh ships of Hood's division on the scene of the action might have been enough to crush the van and to seriously maul the ships of the French center that had managed to get close to the action. At 4:22 p.m. the rear division was still three-quarters of a mile from the French line and at two cable lengths' distance from each other. By the time the line had been adjusted and the approach made, it would have been nearly five o'clock before Hood could have engaged, and at this stage it was too late to overwhelm the French van and center.[20]

In the postmortem that followed the action, Hood always attacked Graves on the grounds that contradictory flags were flying from the *London*. There is too much evidence from the ships of the rear division not to believe that they were sincere in their statement that the flag for the line was still flying, unless one accepts the unlikely idea that there was a wholesale conspiracy by Hood and his captains to protect their own position by falsely declaring the signal to be still flying. Such a conspiracy would have had to include all other officers, as witness the remarks of Thomas White,[21] who was serving as a midshipman in one of the rear ships, upon the statement that the signal for the line had been hauled down:

> I shall be induced to fancy that what I that day saw and heard was a mere chimera of the brain, and that what I believed to be the signal for the line was not a union jack, but an ignis fautus conjured up to mock me.[22]

Hood's own journal records that the signal for the line was hauled down in the *London* at 5:25 p.m. and the one for close action was left flying. With this Hood took his division down to the action. Lieutenant Grey in the *Invincible* records:

> Admiral Hood, the *MONARCH* and ourselves very close together, bore down a little and then Brought too again together.[23]

The act of bringing to after the initial movement indicates that Hood wished to come down in a concerted body. An officer on the *Barfleur*, Lieutenant Shivers,[24] records that the ship hauled its wind and tacked "to regain our station."[25] At this stage ranging shots were tried from the ship, probably the broadside mentioned earlier by Lieutenant Grey as occurring at 5:20 p.m. The shots were seen to fall short of the French line, whereupon Hood ceased firing and closed a little further before trying again. From this volley the shots just about reached the French line. The French seem to have had the range rather better, probably because they were firing on the upward roll. The log of the *Barfleur* notes that French shots passed over the ship at 5:45 p.m. The time of the *Barfleur* first opening fire is variously recorded as being between 5:50 and 6:15.

The ships of the rear division never got to close action, for soon after six o'clock Graves signaled for the fleet to maintain the line ahead, parallel with the French. The decisive moment for intervention had probably passed in any case. Hood could see from the damaged state of the van ships that they were unlikely to take any further part in the action that day. The advantage the British had enjoyed had vanished and now lay with the French. The ships of the French rear division were beginning to clear the bay and would soon be able to join the action.

As seen from the French fleet, the refusal of the British ships to accept a close action with the French rear could have only one interpretation. The Swedish volunteer Tornquist thought that the "English rear had no desire to keep within our range."[26] The comte d'Ethy, commanding the *Citoyen*, noted the approach of the *Barfleur*:

At 5:45 p.m. the three-decked ship commanding the enemy rear came up, as well as the two ships ahead of her, opposite the *Palmier* and *Solitaire*. Some moments after their arrival, they hove to and experimented to see whether their cannonballs would reach our ships. The enemy admiral began by firing several shots and the other ships, which had also hauled their wind, followed suit. The ships of the enemy rearguard always held the windward position; their fire became general up as far as my ship, but it did not last long, the enemy remaining hove-to. . . . I had much the better of the exchange with the three-decker, for it appeared to me that nearly all her cannonballs fell into the sea before they reached us, while the few that we fired were not wasted, or if so, it was because they overshot the enemy.[27]

A French account of the action says that de Grasse was pleased to see Hood and the rear division coming down into the action. To counter this movement he planned to tack his fleet together and bring it onto a northwest course "which would inevitably have thrown the English fleet into confusion." This intention on the part of de Grasse seems to have been foiled by Graves's decision to signal for line ahead at half a cable's length, replacing the signal for close action. This kept the British fleet in the windward position and caused the action in the van to gradually cease by about 6:30 p.m. The signal for engaging the enemy had been hauled down on the *London*, and the battle of the Chesapeake was over.

THE WORLD TURNED UPSIDE DOWN

The prospects for the British fleet were not entirely black. It is certain that Graves had it in mind to engage the French the following day despite the odds against him, as his disposition of the fleet attests. Captain Everitt of the *Solebay* had hailed Saxton as Everitt passed heading towards the van of the fleet and said he was to tell the Drake that Graves intended to renew the engagement in the morning and that the line of battle should be kept.

In order to maintain his position relative to the French fleet during the night, Graves sent the frigate *Solebay* to carry the night orders to the ships in the rear and the *Fortunée* to the ships in the van. The disposition Graves chose was for the fleet to cruise at a separation of two cables (though some witnesses say that the fleet was at one cable's length) and to keep abreast of the French. Some of the signals made at this time could not be discerned by the ships of the rear in the increasing darkness. The French fleet was seen by the British, presumably because the French were showing lights, with the van bearing south-southeast and the rear southwest-by-south. The signal for battle was hauled down in the *London* at 6:30 p.m., and a few minutes later all firing between the two fleets had stopped. Some twelve hours had passed since the two sides first sighted each other, some two hundred people on each side had lost their lives, and the war had changed course forever, though neither side yet realized it.

During the night, however, reports began to come in to Graves on the state of the ships of the van division. The leading ship, the *Shrewsbury*, which had suffered 14 dead and 52 wounded, was forced during the night to make the signal of distress. The *Intrepid* had also taken serious damage. Both ships had shot holes along the waterline, which necessitated continuous pumping until the holes could be stopped. Worst of all was the condition of the *Terrible*, which was making two feet of water every fifteen minutes. There was nothing to do but destroy her, as she was in no state to fight another action or to go back to New York. It was just a matter of time before she sank of her own accord, and the decision was later taken to strip her of all items of use and then to burn her. All these ships were of Drake's division, but even the *Montagu* from the center division, the very ship that had prevented the *London* from going down to engage the *Ville de Paris*, signaled that she was having difficulty keeping in line. With all these reports as evidence of the reduced fighting power of the van ships, Graves had no option but to spend the rest of the night and the following day in repairing damage.

A list of the casualties and damages suffered by each ship of the fleet shows:

Shrewsbury - 14 killed, 52 wounded.
　　Masts, yards, and sails shattered.
　　Ship leaking on the larboard tack.
Intrepid - 21 killed, 35 wounded.
　　Masts and yards damaged. Sails and rigging much cut.
　　Nineteen holes below the waterline.
Alcide - 2 killed, 18 wounded.
　　Masts, yards, sails, and rigging damaged.
　　"Many" hits below the waterline.
Princessa - 6 killed, 18 wounded.
　　Masts, yards, sails, and rigging damaged.
　　Holed under the waterline.
Ajax - 7 killed, 16 wounded.
　　Masts, yards, sails, and rigging damaged.
Terrible - 4 killed, 21 wounded.
　　Masts, yards, sails, and rigging damaged.
　　Holed below the waterline. Pumps blown. Made 2 feet of water in
　　　　25 minutes.
Europe - 9 killed, 18 wounded.
　　Masts, yards, sails, and rigging damaged.
　　"Ship strains and makes water."
Montagu - 8 killed, 22 wounded.
　　Masts, yards, sails, and rigging damaged.
　　"Hull much shattered."
Royal Oak - 4 killed, 5 wounded.
　　Some mast damage.
London - 4 killed, 18 wounded.
　　Masts, yards, sails, and rigging damaged.
Bedford - 8 killed, 14 wounded.
　　Some mast damage.
　　Some hull damage.

Resolution - 3 killed, 16 wounded.
   Negligible damage.
Centaur - no killed or wounded.
   Negligible damage.
Monarch - no killed or wounded.
   Negligible damage.
Barfleur, America, Invincible, Belliqueux, and *Alfred* -
   No casualties or damage.

During the hours of darkness Graves must have had many things on his mind. The fair prospect that had presented itself in the morning was gone, along with the advantage of surprise that he had held. His plan of attack had not been understood, and his ships had failed to get into action as he intended. Facing a superior fleet now fully at sea and formed in line of battle, even if he was able to force another action, it was possible that the French would survive his attack in better condition than his own fleet. If de Grasse was determined enough, he could inflict a clear defeat on the British and throw the whole British strategy for the war into ruins.

Graves had sought to engage a superior enemy fleet and had maneuvered to bring about a concentration of force on a part of the French line in accordance with the tactical ideas of Lord Howe. It was not the full-scale head-on attack that Hood would have made, but it was tactically sound and should have been successful. The plan failed because of misunderstandings by his subordinates. Only about eleven of the French ships had been engaged, including those that came up late. These had been engaged by ten British ships, and both sides had suffered damage and casualties accordingly. How much more could have been achieved if the British had had their missing nine ships in action!

The British must also have felt the lack of the ships left in New York in the dockyard or in the West Indies for convoy duty to Jamaica. If Graves had had twenty-three ships instead of nineteen to give more equality on the day of action, it might have made the result more favorable—*if* all of them could have been brought into the action. By sending only fourteen ships under Hood as a reinforcement, the two British commanders showed that they were unaware of the concentration being planned by their opponents. They did not realize the importance that Rochambeau and Washington attached to achieving a decisive land victory in North America and the necessity of achieving naval superiority off the Chesapeake to do this.

The French were sighted at daylight the next morning, three or four miles to the southward. Saxton remarked on them as "in no exact order" and with no appearance of having sustained much damage. On this day, 6 September, Graves issued a memorandum to all flag officers and captains. It was an attempt to clarify his position and contained the mildest of rebukes to Hood for his failure to act as Graves intended. The relevant part was quite straightforward, and it was plain to all that criticism of the rear division commander was implied:

> When the signal for the line of battle ahead is out at the same time with the signal for battle it is not to be understood that the latter signal shall be rendered ineffectual by the strict adherence to the former
>
> . . .

The next part of the memorandum covered the confusion that occurred in the center division in which ships got in each other's way and blocked the field of fire:

> Admirals and captains of the fleet are desired to be attentive not to advance or fall back, so as to intercept the fire of their seconds ahead and astern, but to keep as near the enemy as possible, whilst the signal for close action continues out.[1]

Hood did not formally react to this document, but when Graves had issued it for a second and third time he appended the endorsement "It is the first time I ever heard it suggested that too strict an adherence could be paid to the line of battle. . . . According to Mr. Graves's Memo, any captain may break the line with impunity when he pleases."

The Graves interpretation of the line of battle would have been fully understood and endorsed by Nelson (as witness his action at Cape St. Vincent) in the succeeding wars and had been accepted by Edward Hawke in the action off Toulon nearly forty years before. The interpretation by Hood was not one that would win battles or inspire others. It has been observed that if the remarks issued by Graves had been written by Nelson, they would have been acclaimed as an indicator of the offensive spirit on which Nelson relied so much.[2] Issued by Graves, they do not have the same resonance, because his contemporaries and later historians have condemned him for his "failure" at the Chesapeake. If Hood had acted with the same spirit as Nelson at St. Vincent, the final result might have been different.

There is therefore the question of why Hood acted as he did. Even if it is accepted that the signal for the line was still flying from the *London*, as Hood said it was, until almost 5:30 p.m., why did he fail to realize the necessity of the rear ships getting into close action with the enemy? Was he influenced by the Rodney regime of strict obedience to the signals of the admiral? Did Hood and the other captains really think that in keeping the line of battle sacrosanct they were behaving according to Graves's wishes, let alone the interests of the British position in America?

The Additional Instructions that Graves had taken over from his predecessor Arbuthnot were not models of clarity. The British might, with advantage, have adopted the West Indies signals, with which the majority of the ships were familiar. It would have been even better if the two parts of the fleet had had time to drill together and if all the commanders had decided on what was to be done in the various circumstances in which the French might be met. This could have happened if the two fleets had met off the Chesapeake on 25 August, which would have given them nearly a week to settle in together and agree on their tactics for engaging de Grasse. Here can be seen the fatal ramifications of the false intelligence the government sent to Graves, which caused him to undertake a fruitless cruise looking for the ships said to be coming from Europe. Still, the French were at an obvious disadvantage when they were taken by surprise, and it did not require signals to point out that the obvious course was to attack those ships of the French fleet that had got out of the bay before those in the rear could come to their aid.

Could Hood's failure to come into action with his division have been occasioned by a fit of pique? Did he feel that, as Graves had rejected immediate assault for the line of battle's more formal concentration of force, he would merely obey the orders from the *London* but do nothing more? Could he have been just an angry man with an axe to grind?

Or was there no reason for his action other than what he stated? He was obeying the signal for the line that he claims was flying from the *London*. He could see that the situation required his action, but he was unwilling to break the line and go to the assistance of the hard-pressed van ships. The reason *may* have been the "schooling" that he and his captains had received from Rodney. This schooling, however, did not affect the actions of Drake, who, even though misinterpreting the approach line that Graves intended, did take his division into action.

Whatever may be the truth, Hood's action, or lack of action, was to have fatal consequences for the war in North America. Efforts by Hood—and he made plenty in his letters home—to explain away his actions by sticking to the sanctity of the line of battle and denigrating the performance and capability of Graves are hollow. He must have been fully aware, if not at the time then certainly later, that he had substantially contributed to the poor result of the day's action.

Of the three rear admirals present on that day, Drake had done the best. He had taken his division into action and fought his own flagship magnificently, causing serious damage to the French van ships. Graves had done his best, with a less than perfect signal book and handicapped by his unfamiliarity with most of the captains who comprised his fleet. The *London* had never engaged in really close action, for which he must accept some share of blame, but his intentions were good. In Hood, however, there had been a total failure of initiative. By his inaction he had worsened the numerical inferiority that Graves already faced. He was correct in his desire to attack the French as soon as possible, but he made no effort, as Graves's plan matured, to understand the intention of his commander and bring his division into action in support of the others.

After the battle, and for the next few days, Hood wrote accounts of the engagement to friends in England. It was the start of his campaign to vindicate himself and to attack the conduct of Graves. On 13 September he wrote to George Jackson:

> we plainly discovered 24 sail of French ships of the line and 2 frigates at anchor about Cape Henry, preparing to gett under sail; at noon they began to come out in a line of Battle ahead, but by no means regular and connected which afforded the British fleet a most glorious opening for making a close attack to manifest advantage, but it was not embraced and as the French ships came out close upon a wind, and the English line steered large, the action commenced towards the Van, that part of the enemy's fleet being to windward of their Centre, and the Centre to windward of their Rear. Our Centre then upon a wind began to engage at the same time, but at a most improper distance (though *London* had the signal for close action and the signal for the line ahead at half a cable flying, was under Topsails, with the main topsail to the mast, notwithstanding the French ships were pressing on) and our rear being barely within random shot, did not fire while the signal for the line was out.[3]

To Sandwich he wrote on 6 September:

> Yesterday the British fleet had a rich and most delightful harvest of glory presented to it, but omitted to gather it in more instances than one.

First, that the enemy's van was not closely attacked as it came out of Lynnhaven Bay.

Secondly, when the enemy's van was greatly extended beyond the centre and rear, that it was not attacked by the whole force of the British line. Had such an attack been made, several of the Enemy's ships must have been inevitably demolished in half an hour's action, and there was a full hour and a half to have done it in before any of the rear could have come up.[4]

This is the crux of the whole matter! If "the whole force of the British line" had attacked the French, victory would have been theirs! If Hood was able to recognize this fact a day later in writing an exculpatory letter to Lord Sandwich, why did he not recognize and act on it the previous day? There is no answer to this question, as we cannot read the mind of Samuel Hood. His defense was the signal for the line that Graves still kept flying from the *London*. His instinct and his professional training told him that the correct course was to bring his division into action. His later remark to Graves that "the signal for the line was enough for me" does no credit to his intelligence or his professionalism as a naval officer. His behavior is inexplicable for one of his talents.

The controversy over the battle was to reverberate through the years and the discussion still continues today. More than twenty years after the battle, Captain Thomas Graves, the cousin of Admiral Graves who commanded the *Bedford* in the action and who later served as a flag officer under Nelson at Copenhagen, gave his thoughts on the action. They were not supportive of Hood's case:

It would have ended gloriously and fortunately for Great Britain, notwithstanding the decided superiority of the enemy, had the zealous endeavours and example of Admiral Graves been imitated; and had the judicious signals made on that day by him, been obeyed as they ought, and instantly executed. That they were made in the most favourable and critical moment, and must have overthrown the enemy, who were only saved by the rear division of our fleet not bearing down and engaging agreeable to the signals so aptly made.[5]

Even twenty years later, then, there was ill feeling remaining about the action, or inaction, of the rear division. It came from a member of the Graves family who must have been irritated by the general impression, given by

Hood's supporters, that the lack of success was due to the failings of Graves. The attitude of the Admiralty to Graves does not seem to have been affected by the denigration of Graves's leadership. Sandwich defended him against an attack by Germain and the suggestion that he should be recalled to face a court-martial. He was not recalled, and his transfer to Jamaica went ahead even though Graves complained of his being sent to a station where he would be second in command or even third, while Hood and Digby were commanders on their particular stations. The Admiralty assured him that no reflection on his conduct on 5 September was intended.

The verdict of history has largely gone with the Hood version, perhaps lent more credence by his later actions in the American War. The influence of Hood, which was considerable, was able to persuade more people, especially among his contemporaries, that the day had been lost because of the tactical ineptitude of Thomas Graves. The justification of Hood came down to the fact that Thomas Graves was not considered equal to the command of a British fleet.

If it is accepted that the signal for the line of battle to be maintained was flown in the *London* all the time Hood said it was, then the course of the battle was altered by the mistake of a signal lieutenant and by the action of Hood himself, who could not see where the proper place for his division was, despite the example of the van division.

When news of the engagement reached Britain, one of those who read the official dispatch was Rodney, who was convalescing at Bath. The letter he wrote to George Jackson shows that Rodney too must have felt that he had his own position to defend,

for tis impossible for me not to feel most sensibly any news which appears to me of the most fatal consequences to my Country, and more especially where the Navy has been concerned. In vain may plans be concerted to defeat the designs of the Public Enemy, if inferior officers will take upon them to act in direct opposition to the Orders and Letters of their Superiors, and lay idle in port when their duty ought to have obliged them to have been at sea to watch the motions of the Publick Enemy and prevent the junction of their squadrons. Had Mr. Graves attended to the intelligence I sent him six weeks before I left the West Indies as likewise two other expresses I sent him. Pressing his junction with his whole squadron with Sir Samuel Hood off the Cape of Virginia, he had been on that station long before de Grasse, and of course prevented the latter landing his troops in Virginia. The Commanding Officer, likewise at Jamaica had no right to detain the *Torbay* and *Prince William*, whose Captains had my positive orders, not to lose a moments time (after seeing the Jamaica Convoy safe at that Island) in joyning Sir Samuel at or off the Chesapeake. I likewise pressed Sir Peter Parker to send some more ships with them, as I was assured the French Fleet were intended for that coast, and that in all probabality the fate of the War depended upon His Majesty's Fleet being in full force, and that the Blow on which depended the Sovereignty of the Ocean, must be struck off the coast of Virginia. I advised Sir S. Hood by all means to guard the mouth of the Chesapeake, to anchor in Hampton Road if occasion, to keep his frigates cruising off the coast to the southward, that he might have timely notice of the enemy's approach, and to despatch one of his frigates to Mr Graves acquainting him with his arrival and pressing a speedy junction, no one thing of which has been regarded. . . .

His [Graves's] letter I cannot understand and his terms, particularly his Cut Up, a term neither Military or Seaman like, it must have been a Mistake in printing, he meant Cut off the Van from the Centre. The other parts of the letter contradicts itself, and his mode of fighting I will never follow. He tells you that his Line did not extend so far as the Enemy's Rear. I should have been sorry if it had, and a general Battle ensued, it would have given the advantage they could have wished, and brought their whole twenty four ships of the line against the English nineteen, whereas by watching his opportunity, if the Enemy had extended their line to any considerable distance, by contracting his own he might have brought his nineteen against the enemy's fourteen or fifteen, and by a Close Action totally disabled them before they could have received succour from the remainder, and in all probability have gained thereby a compleat Victory. Such would have been the battle of the 17th April [of 1780 against de Guichen] had I been obey'd, such would have been the battle off the Capes, and more especially if all the line of battle ships had (as they ought) been joyned, our numbers then had been twenty-five, viz four of Admiral Graves and my two from Jamaica. In my poor opinion the French have gained the most important Victory and nothing can save America, but the instant return of the Fleet from New York with 5,000 troops, and Digby's Squadron, but even then the French will have done their business and gone, if not, block them up to eternity; suffer none to escape from the Chesapeake, they will soon be tired of their station and wish they had never taken the part of America.[6]

There is much in this letter that bends the truth to fit his case. We have seen, although Rodney might not have been aware of the facts when he wrote his letter, the series of accidents that prevented Graves from bringing his squadron to meet Hood off the Chesapeake. This failure to bring about an early concentration off the Capes was certainly a significant factor in the outcome of the campaign. It is true that the ships on Jamaica convoy duty had not been sent on by Parker as promptly as they might have been. We know also that when the intelligence first arrived Graves was absent from New York, cruising to look for a French force that the Admiralty had told him to expect from Europe. This intelligence proved false, so the unfortunate absence from New York served no useful purpose. With regard to whether Hood should have stayed in the area of the Chesapeake once he had arrived rather than go on to New York, it is true that some advantages would have accrued from staying. However, Hood arrived before the French and saw no sign of either Graves, whom he expected, or the French. Given those circumstances, he was right to go to New York, as that was known to be an alternative destination for the Franco-American forces and he might expect to meet Graves there or possibly coming south from New York in response to the dispatch from Rodney. It could have been disastrous if Hood had waited at the Capes while Washington and Rochambeau with the Franco-American land forces besieged New York with de Grasse blockading by sea.

Of all the possible alternative hands that could be dealt, those the British were dealt were the worst. The two best-case situations for the British would have been for Hood to have met de Grasse on the way north while he was still encumbered with his convoy or to have formed a junction with Graves's squadron off the Chesapeake before de Grasse arrived. In either of these situations the result would likely have been vastly more favorable to the British than the engagement of the fifth of September.

For the rest of the night the two fleets sailed in the presence of each other. In accordance with usual practice, Graves rejected a night action. Apart from the need to repair some ships of his fleet, he would have considered the chances of a successful action slight, and he therefore resolved to renew the action in the morning.

The sixth of September dawned with only a light wind, which continued until about 4 p.m. No move was made by either side to renew the engagement, while both took the necessary steps to repair damage. From the British viewpoint the French seemed to have suffered hardly at all, but the Swedish observer with the French fleet noted with satisfaction "by the sailing of the English fleet that they had suffered greatly."

Graves kept the line of battle at half a cable, but reports reaching the *London* showed that the damage suffered by the fleet the previous day put an immediate renewal of the fighting out of the question. In the van, Rear Admiral Drake was forced to shift his flag from the *Princessa*, which had been severely damaged in the action, to the *Alcide*.

That evening Graves signaled for Hood and Drake to come to the *London*. At the meeting the atmosphere must have been rather more than difficult. An account published later said that Graves asked Hood why he did not bear down to engage. Hood replied that the *London* had been flying the signal for the line. Graves then turned to Drake and asked how he had come to bear down, and Drake said that he had come down in accordance with the signal for action flying from the *London*. Graves then turned to Hood again, and one suspects that there must have been a hint of triumph in his voice. "What say you to this, Admiral Hood?" Hood seems to have been unperturbed. "The signal for the line was enough for me."

Hood wrote to George Jackson with an account of the meeting of 6 September but seems to have confused it with at least two subsequent meetings with Graves, for he refers to intelligence received by Graves from the *Medea* and the *Iris*, which had been sent to look into the Chesapeake. In fact Graves had ordered the *Medea* to carry out that mission only on the sixth, and it was not until the following day that the two frigates actually entered the bay. They could not possibly have returned to Graves with any intelligence until late on the seventh or even the eighth. Hood also mentions the detachment of the *Richmond* and the *Iris* to carry a letter from Clinton to Cornwallis, but these two frigates were not to leave the fleet until 8 September.

Either at this meeting or some later one Hood put forward a plan of startling boldness. He must have had it in mind ever since he saw the result of the fighting on the fifth and the stalemate that existed. His suggestion was that the British fleet should make for the Chesapeake and anchor there before the French could return. It was a bold move, but it was the only way that he could see of retrieving the situation and bringing aid to Cornwallis and his army. Instead of fencing with de Grasse at sea and trying to hold the windward gauge, the British should stake everything on the scheme to seize the anchorage and force the French to fight for it.

It is a matter of history that Hood succeeded in carrying out a similar maneuver at St. Kitts. The suggestion therefore cannot be rejected out of hand. What discussions took place, if any, between Hood and Graves and Drake on this matter is not known, but in the end Graves decided not to accept the advice, and no move was made to seize the anchorage. Graves may have been thinking of the misunderstanding of signals shown on the fifth and of the vital part that communications would play in such a maneuver as Hood proposed.

Any fleet anchored inside Lynnhaven Bay on a line from just inside Cape Henry to the shoals of the Middle Ground would be in a strong position. To attack a fleet so anchored, the attacker would have to round Cape Henry, exposed to the fire of the anchored fleet, and then pass along the line to the selected anchorage position. Once anchored and engaged, there would be no opportunity for the attacking fleet to withdraw. It would have to be a fight to the finish, with the advantage to the anchored fleet and not the attacker. The situation could be reversed. What if the French had chosen to adopt such a formation, especially if they had done so on their first arrival in the area? In the present circumstances, if de Grasse had returned to the anchorage and assumed a defensive position, it would have been a problem for Graves when he returned from New York, in the event that Cornwallis was still holding out.

The result of such a scheme, if it had been carried out by the British, is debatable. It assumes in the first place that the British ships could outsail the French fleet, if it came to a race for the anchorage. This Hood did manage to do at St. Kitts, but it was a close-run thing and it was accomplished by a fleet that had not been damaged in a previous action, which was not the case at the Chesapeake. The British fleet was not entirely composed of coppered ships, and even some of those that had copper had been long at sea and were slow and leaky. The fact is that the British commander did not have a fleet with a significant advantage in speed and maneuvering ability over his French opponent. It is more likely that the British could have succeeded if they adopted the same tactic as de Grasse and steered for the anchorage at night when their movements would have been to a large extent hidden from the French.

Mahan considers that if the British fleet had seized the anchorage in the Chesapeake, de Grasse would have withdrawn from the area after his junction with de Barras, and the British could have evacuated Cornwallis in safety.[7] However, the fleet could not have escaped if de Grasse had decided to blockade the entrance to the river. The situation would have been exactly the reverse of that postulated by Rodney with the British blockading the French in the river. The British fleet would have been heavily outnumbered, supplies could run short if the blockade was prolonged, and a Franco-American army on shore could begin to erect batteries to shell the British out of their position.

The loss of Cornwallis's army at Yorktown by surrender of the garrison would be a serious blow to the British ability to continue the war in America, but, as later events demonstrated, the British were still able to continue fighting elsewhere. The loss of the fleet would have meant the irredeemable loss of the war. To end hostilities on satisfactory terms, it was essential for the British to restore a position of equilibrium where the French and American successes in America were offset by a British naval superiority that would deny the French and Spanish the other advantages they sought from the war.

The total success Hood wanted could only be achieved if de Grasse sooner or later acceded to the British seizing his anchorage. The British had to hold on long enough for de Grasse to reach the deadline for his promised return to the West Indies. French relations with the Americans would be seriously damaged if he left the coast without achieving the ends they hoped for, but if he failed to meet his promises to the Spaniards, this too would have consequences for Allied relations.

The character of de Grasse should be considered in this equation. Would he, as Mahan suggests, have simply quitted the scene if the British had seized his anchorage, or would he have been willing to delay his return to the West Indies in order to blockade the British fleet in the Chesapeake? In his whole period of command since arriving in the West Indies, even while he had numerical superiority, he had never shown the slightest desire to fight a decisive action at close range and finish the war at a stroke. One solid indicator of the likely behavior of de Grasse is that after the action of 5 September, when he eventually returned to his anchorage, he was very disturbed to find that ships were occupying it, and he immediately cleared for action. Fortunately for the French, the "intruders" turned out to be not the fleet of Graves but of de Barras, who had lately arrived at the Chesapeake. If de Barras had been a couple of days later, he might have found de Grasse at anchor and Graves in the area with his superior fleet.

Given that de Grasse did not immediately give up the attempt on St. Kitts in January 1782 when Hood carried out such a maneuver as he suggested now, there is some reason to believe that he would not soon have given up in a similar situation off the Chesapeake. At St. Kitts, time was not a factor for the French, though reports reaching the British indicated that de Grasse, after failing to dislodge the British by direct action, was somewhat impatience with how long the capture of Brimstone Hill was taking. At the Chesapeake, time parameters did operate and it would have been difficult for de Grasse to either go or stay. Whether the British could have held their position until the French had to depart, which could have meant at least another month, is a moot point. The British would not have been able to take on fresh supplies in their position, so they would have had to rely on whatever they had. The blockading French might very well have been able to make supply arrangements with the Americans. Viewed as a practical alternative, the suggestion by Hood does involve more risk than Graves might have felt justified in running with the care of the only fleet the British had to maintain their position in both North America and the West Indies.

The partial success by Hood at St. Kitts was achieved under different circumstances from those that Graves would have faced at the Chesapeake. The seizure of the anchorage at Basseterre Road, St. Kitts, was a brilliant tactical stroke. It has to be remembered that Basseterre Road was a much easier anchorage to leave than the Chesapeake, as de Grasse had already demonstrated. Hood carried out the St. Kitts operation with a fleet that was not hampered by battle damage and with ships that had had time to become used to operating together, and the movement followed a period of consultation between Hood and his subordinates at all levels.

De Grasse had achieved strategic successes with the actions off Martinique and the Chesapeake, but he had not sought to destroy the British fleet so that they could never again be a threat. He had shown a superior strategic vision by taking his whole force to North America. He had, however, been surprised at anchor, which was a temporary tactical defeat. Though he recovered from this through the mistakes made by his opponents and managed to fight a partial action that served his purpose and put the British at a disadvantage, he made no move to seek action again the following day while the British were hampered by damage already incurred. He was again to show this reluctance to finish off an opponent when he neglected the opportunity of overwhelming Hood's squadron in the engagement prior to the battle of the Saintes. That was his last chance before fate ended his career in defeat. If he had sought an action with Graves on either 8 or 9 September, it is likely that with his preponderance of numbers he would have defeated Graves. Such a defeat not only would have removed any possibility of Britain retaining a naval capability on the North American coast but would have crippled the British government strategy for the following year of building up the strength of the fleet in West Indian waters. If Graves had been decisively beaten, there could have been no battle of the Saintes to restore the British position in 1782.

Would de Grasse have recognized the chance being presented to him and seize it? He had promised to return to the West Indies by November, which would seem to be ample time for starving the British fleet into trying to break through his blockade and offering him the chance, perhaps with his fleet enlarged by the ships of de Barras, to fight a close action with Graves and destroy British power at sea. The chances are that he would not have stayed to carry out this strategy, but it will always be a matter for conjecture when considering the risks inherent in seizing the anchorage as Hood suggested.

The two fleets remained in sight of each other during the sixth of September. Bougainville, for one, thought it unlikely that the British would fight again on that day, in which assumption he was proved right. With the wind still favoring the British, the frigates *Medea* and *Iris* were sent into the Chesapeake. There they managed to cut away many of the buoys that the French had attached to their anchors when they cut their cables to get to sea. They counted three large ships still at anchor in the bay. These they reported to Graves to be a ship of the line, a 40-gun ship, and a frigate.

On the seventh the wind shifted to favor the French, but de Grasse did not try to close with the British, and the latter were too damaged aloft to regain the windward position. De Grasse had the greater reason for optimism, for he knew that de Barras would arrive soon and increase his numerical superiority. He could also see that the British ships were not yet fully recovered from the action of the fifth and represented no immediate danger. He wrote a cheerful letter to Bougainville saying that if the British did not escape during the night he would close with them the next day, which he hoped would be "a happier one." He considered that the junction with de Barras would be a "body blow" to the British, and a decisive one at that. The condition of the British fleet made him cheerful too:

I have great hopes based upon the damages to the enemy which I can see. I judge by them that they are not as well-outfitted as we are, and by the slowness of their movements that they are not as ready for battle. If we can have a sample we shall become better informed about this.[8]

What did de Grasse means by "a sample"? Did he mean that he wished to try to take one of the injured British ships? If so, this would have brought on the action he professed to be seeking.

On the eighth the wind still favored the French, but they made no effort to come down and fight. The wind was getting fresher by this time, and there was some thunder and lightning.

Hood was called aboard the *London* for another conference. The meeting was held at 7 a.m. and continued for approximately half an hour. Again the question of what to do with the fleet was raised, but no definite plan of action was decided, and Hood returned to the *Barfleur* more agitated than when he left.

Graves had more than the French to concern him. He had to consider what to do with the *Terrible*. The ship had been in poor condition before the action, but now the effects of firing her own broadsides and the damage from the French guns had made her condition critical. At 11 a.m. the *Terrible* made a signal of distress and Graves sent the *Fortunée* and *Orpheus* to her assistance. The water continued to gain, and on the tenth the decision was made to destroy her after the boats of the fleet had removed her crew and all the stores that might be of use.

On the ninth the wind still favored the French, and for that day the two fleets continued in sight of each other. Tornquist says that the wind changed during the day to favor Graves again, but statements of Hood and other eyewitnesses say the French had a favorable wind that took them in the direction of the Chesapeake. Hood wrote to Jackson on 13 September:

> On the 9th the French fleet carried a press of sail which proved to me beyond doubt, that de Grasse had other views than fighting and I was distressed to see Mr. Graves did not carry all the sail he could also, and gett off the Chesapeake before him as it appeared to me to be a measure of the utmost importance to keep the French out, and if they did get in, they should first beat us. Instead of that Mr. G put His Majesty's Fleet on a contrary course just at dark, and at 8 o'clock made the signal to lay to.[9]

That Hood was still hoping his idea of seizing the anchorage might be acted upon implies that Graves had not rejected it outright, but the question became academic after the British lay to for the night. In not following up the action of 5 September, both Graves and de Grasse were lacking the killer instinct. There seems to be no doubt that Graves did wish to attack again on 6 September, but as the deficiencies in his fleet became clear, he rightly decided that no such move was possible. Hood did have this instinct, but he did not have the direction of affairs and had blotted his copybook by not engaging on the fifth.

With a fleet that by all accounts had not suffered to the same extent, de Grasse had the leeward position to account for his inaction, but when he did have the windward gauge he still failed to attack. De Grasse did not feel that he had anything to gain by renewing the action. He was expecting reinforcement by de Barras, which would further strengthen his position. Until then he had achieved enough. He, and his American allies, held all the aces.

The impression of events on the ninth given by Tornquist is that Graves and de Grasse fenced for the windward gauge, and that at one time the British bore down towards the French line with the intention of renewing the action. It is possible that Tornquist might be referring to the previous day, for he also remarks that "the following day towards evening Count de Grasse once more won the luff back again, because he had a smaller number of damaged ships." If the remarks of Tornquist are taken to apply to the eighth and ninth they are quite logical, but if taken to apply to the ninth and tenth they are impossible, for all British reports agree that the French fleet was out of sight from the British fleet on the tenth.

On the evening of the ninth de Grasse made sail for the Chesapeake. It was a logical move if he did not intend to renew the action and was worried that the British might seize the anchorage before he could get back. He would also be able to pick up the men who had been left behind in the hurried sailing on the fifth, and he would be in the best position for a junction with the squadron of de Barras. Finally, he would still be between Cornwallis at Yorktown and any relieving British fleet. Graves, unaware of the French move, made no attempt to follow and remained hove to all night. The following morning there was no sign of the French. Hood gave vent to his feelings to Jackson:

nothing was seen of the Enemy's fleet from the *Barfleur* which alarmed me exceedingly, and I debated with myself some little time whether I should venture to write Mr.G a few lines or not, as it is rather awkward and unpleasant to send advice to a senior officer. [10]

Hood did send a note to Graves to ask news of the French:

I flatter myself you will forgive the liberty I take in asking whether you have any knowledge where the French fleet is, as we can see nothing of it from the *Barfleur*.

By the press of sail de Grasse carried yesterday (and he must even have done the same the preceding night, by being where [he] was at daylight), I am inclined to think his aim is the Chesapeake, in order to be strengthened by the ships there, either by adding them to his present force, or by exchanging his disabled ship for them. . . .

I trust you will pardon the offer of my humble sentiments, as they are occasioned by what passed between us when I had the honour of attending your summons on board the *London*, on the 8th, in the evening.[11]

In consequence of this letter, another summons was sent for Hood to go on board the *London*, where he and Graves and Drake discussed the next moves. Hood continued to press his opinion that the fleet should make for the Chesapeake. He was astonished, he said to Jackson, "that Mr. G was as ignorant as myself, where the French fleet was." He complained that Graves had been deficient in not keeping a proper watch with his frigates. He did admit to Graves, however, that if they went back to the Chesapeake they would already find de Grasse in occupation and the entrance barred against them.

The French had come within sight of the Chesapeake on the morning of 10 September. There was a moment of concern in the fleet when mast tops were sighted over the land as they approached, and de Grasse was afraid that Graves had seized the anchorage from him. He gave the order to clear for action, but as the fleet advanced, it was found that the ships in the anchorage were those of de Barras. The latter had avoided the British by taking a wide sweep out to sea before setting course for the Chesapeake. This junction of de Barras with de Grasse, further reinforcing the numerical superiority of the French, put the final seal on British hopes of relieving Cornwallis. The shocked reaction of de Grasse at the possibility that the anchorage had been seized does lend credibility to Hood's suggestion that this was the best option for the British.

When de Barras arrived, he had found the British frigates *Richmond* and *Iris* engaged in cutting away more of the French anchor buoys. Confronted with overwhelming force, they had to surrender.

It was on the evening of 11 September that the fleet headed for the Chesapeake with the *Medea* scouting ahead. On the morning of the thirteenth the *Medea* signaled that the French were anchored in the bay. The *Medea* did not, however, signal the number of French ships present, so the Graves remained in ignorance of the arrival of de Barras until the numbers could be counted by direct observation from the *London*. De Grasse now had thirty-six ships of the line—double the force available to Graves. It was obvious that nothing could be done in the face of such odds. Graves wrote to Hood informing him of the information relayed by the *Medea*:

> Admiral Graves presents his compliments to Sir Samuel Hood, and begs leave to acquaint that the *Medea* has just made the signal to inform him that the French fleet are at an anchor above the Horse Shoe in the Chesapeake, and desires his opinion what to do with the fleet. . . .[12]

This letter displays a certain lack of self-confidence in Graves. It is hard to imagine either Rodney or Hood asking the opinion of other flag officers on the handling of the fleet!

The sighting of the French in the Chesapeake was not a surprise to Hood, for he had predicted that action at the meeting with Graves. He composed the following well-known formal letter, the final sentence of which might very well serve as an epitaph for the whole campaign:

> Rear Admiral Sir Samuel Hood presents his compliments to Rear-Admiral Graves. Is extremely concerned to find by his note just received that the French fleet is at anchor in the Chesapeake above the Horse Shoe, though it is no more than what he expected, as the press of sail the fleet carried on the 9th and in the night of the 8th made it very clear to him what de Grasse's intentions were. Sir Samuel would be very glad to send an opinion, but he really knows not what to say in the truly lamentable state we have brought ourselves.[13]

A further council was summoned, which decided that in view of the condition of the fleet and the superiority of the French, no other course was available but to return to New York. The French saw the British approaching from the north and feared that an attack was intended. De Grasse gave the signal to prepare to weigh, but as the British ships turned away northward the signal was rescinded.

The following day Graves sent his account of the action to Sandwich. Considering the events of the battle, it was remarkably moderate in tone, for it allotted no blame: "The signal was not understood. I do not mean to blame anyone, my Lord. I hope we all did our best." This was a generous gesture by Graves and a sentiment that is unlikely to have ever appeared in a dispatch by Rodney! Graves would have been less than human if he had not felt deeply let down by Samuel Hood and the ships of the rear division.

Graves never commanded in a fleet action again and will never find a place among the great fleet commanders. His best, indeed his only, chance of fighting a successful action had been a failure. It had been brought to that state by others. His initial approach to the engagement forsook the tactic of immediate attack, which would have involved considerable risk, and opted to fight the action by bringing down a superior force onto a part of the French line.

As has been mentioned, recent historical opinion has pointed out that the tactic of attacking the French van as it emerged from the bay did involve a certain amount of risk and it assumed that the ships of the French van would wait to be assailed. It is more than possible that de Grasse would have directed them to bear away with the wind to draw the British down after them, which might have given him the chance to gain the weather gauge with his center and rear divisions. Graves did not lay blame where he might have fairly done, on the shoulders of Hood. Hood was to have another chance to make a name for himself, but no such opportunity was given to Graves. Middleton told Hood, who was certainly apprehensive that some criticism would be leveled in his direction, that the official account had "very little implication of censure" and the "not doing more" was due to the numerical inferiority of the British squadron.[14]

The situation on land was also developing, with the French and Americans hurrying their forces to the scene. By the eighth of September Washington was at Baltimore, and on the ninth he went home to Mount Vernon in Virginia, where Rochambeau joined him the next day. The Allied armies were assembling at Williamsburg and by 26 September had 15,000 men concentrated there. Two days later the formal siege opened. Cornwallis was soon forced to abandon the outworks of his position and withdraw his force into the main defended area. The decreasing number of men under his command did not allow him to man the extended lines properly. Indeed, he soon reduced his numbers further by expelling from the camp the runaway slaves who had joined the British while they had been campaigning in the countryside earlier in the summer. Now they were just extra mouths to feed, and Cornwallis made the logical if inhumane decision to expel all those who could not be considered on the fighting strength of his force.

The siege guns that had arrived with the ships of de Barras were unloaded and brought into position before the British works. The siege at

Yorktown was conducted according to the formal rules that had existed for many years in Europe, though here the Franco-American commanders were not facing the same problems.

With the construction of parallels, the French sappers were gradually working their way nearer to the British fortifications. Against a traditional fortress, such as had existed at Louisbourg in the two previous wars, these activities were the necessary preliminary to any assault. At Yorktown, where the besiegers were faced not by masonry and long-established earthworks but by hastily thrown up trenches and outworks, they were something of an overinsurance on the part of the French engineers.

In addition to his troubles with the besiegers outside his camp, Cornwallis had to contend with disease. All the usual illnesses that afflicted any army of the time, including smallpox, affected his force, and the number of men fit for duty decreased daily. By the time of the final capitulation, only about half of Cornwallis's force remained available to fight.

The besiegers enjoyed a far better situation than the besieged as regards health and provisions. With the whole country to draw upon, the French army and fleet could expect to be well fed while they did their duty to their allies. In the hands of Rochambeau the siege remained an Allied operation, and the Americans were encouraged to play a significant role, though present in far fewer numbers than the French. The situation was similar to the European command of General Eisenhower after D-day, where the overall preponderance of force would ultimately rest with the United States but the British and Canadians played their part as significant if minority contributors to the Allied effort. Rochambeau needed all the diplomatic qualities of Eisenhower to keep the alliance with the Americans strong and effective, particularly in a situation where the two sides did not have much of a sense of comradeship—where, in fact, in some cases there was outright distrust! In George Washington the French commander found a leader with whom he could work and who had all the qualities necessary to unite his rather disparate forces and to work with his French allies. The distrust was not difficult to understand, for only twenty years earlier the French had been the enemy and the British the allies. It is certain that the principles the Americans claimed to be fighting for would have had little appeal to the officer class of the French army.

A recent history of the American Revolution has pointed out the mix of nationalities involved in this dramatic scenario. While there was no doubt on which side the British and French regulars fought, the same could not be said of other elements, as a quarter of the Continentals were African Americans. . . . the all black 1st Rhode Island Regiment [were] "the most neatly dressed, best under arms, and the most precise in its manoeuvres" (according to a German observer). . . . There is food for thought here—Germans fighting for both the French and the British, Irishmen serving in all three armies, almost as many white Americans in the British as there were in a Continental Army in which, of three divisional commanders, one was a French nobleman and another a Prussian mercenary, and which was becoming increasingly dependent on slaves volunteered by their owners to take their place, or by African American paid substitutes.[15]

After the departure of the British fleet, Cornwallis still had nearly a month to watch the forces gathering around him before the first shots of the opening bombardment were fired into the British position on 9 October. If all had gone to plan in New York, this might have been just about the date that Graves arrived back for the new rescue attempt. But, as will be seen, in New York all was not going well for the British cause.

As the British sailed north after the failed attempt to establish contact with Cornwallis, it was the start of another far longer campaign. Over the succeeding years the two admirals Graves and Hood fought a campaign in the press to put a favorable light on their own behavior and blacken the other. Hood was the more successful, for his version held the more prominent position in the public mind and he was more influential in high places. The *Political Magazine* for January 1782 said in a pro-Hood article that Graves "had not the abilities for his station" and that Sir Samuel was "a most excellent and experienced officer" and "deserves to command an English fleet." When he returned home with the laurels of Frigate Bay and the Saintes, he stood in a much more exalted position than Graves, and historians since have tended to look at the situation through the criticisms of Hood and to stigmatize Graves as hidebound and conventional. In recent years, however, the pendulum has swung the other way and Graves has received more favorable treatment from historians.[16]

For more than a week New York had been without news of the action fought on 5 September. On the very day that the fate of the American War was being decided, as we have seen, Frederick Mackenzie was writing in his diary:

If Admiral Graves is fortunate enough to reach the Chesapeak before M. de Barras, . . . he may be able to destroy the fleet of the Enemy within the Capes."[17]

THE WORLD TURNED UPSIDE DOWN 173

The twelfth was a day of hopeful rumors:

> There was a report current in the town last night that Admiral
> Graves had destroyed Six French ships of the line in the Chesapeak. It
> is certain that some persons who went from hence yesterday in a flag
> of truce to Elisabeth-town, were suddenly ordered off without being
> permitted to speak to their friends; which seems to imply that the
> Rebels had received some unfavorable news.[18]

On the thirteenth came the first definite news with the arrival of the frigate
Pegasus from the fleet with Captain Stanhope:

> Tho' Captain Stanhope would not give us any information respect-
> ing the fleets, it was soon afterwards learnt from persons who had
> been on board the *Pegasus* that she came from Admiral Graves's fleet,
> that as soon as our fleet appeared off Chesapeak, M. de Grasse, who
> had been joined by M. de Barras, weighed anchor, and came out with
> 24 sail of the line, leaving a 64 and 3 frigates to continue the blockade
> of York River. That the two fleets having got near each other a partial
> action ensued, particularly between the *Shrewsbury* & *Intrepid*, and
> two French ships, that nothing decisive had happened, but that as
> the fleets continued in sight of each other, a general action was ex-
> pected.[19]

It will be noted from this last extract that Mackenzie was relaying the
belief in New York that de Barras and de Grasse had joined before the action of the fifth. The *Fortunée* arrived with more news on the night of the
seventeenth, and by the eighteenth Mackenzie was able to give a fairly accurate summary of the action and subsequent events and to record that the
British fleet was returning to New York to refit and await reinforcements.
On the nineteenth he wrote:

> All the Shipwrights and Carpenters belonging to the Dock yard, are
> now very busy in making yards and top Masts for the fleet. . . .
> I fear the fate of the Army in Virginia will be determined before our
> fleet can get out of this harbour again.[20]

Graves arrived back at New York on 20 September. All possible speed
was necessary in refitting, but New York was not well supplied with naval
stores for such a number of ships. Among the senior officers in New York
there was a divergence of opinion as to how the situation should be tackled.

Hood was all for getting back to the Chesapeake immediately, considering time to be the most precious element and not to be wasted.

On the day of his arrival, Graves received a letter from Clinton asking for a meeting to work out a strategy for the rescue of Cornwallis. Clinton wanted to await the arrival of the new naval commander, Rear Admiral Digby, to make up some of the numerical deficiency from which the British had suffered on 5 September. The admiral replied the next day that his squadron was badly damaged and he intended to come into port to effect the necessary repairs. After this he would be willing to cooperate in any action the army proposed. The belief in New York was that Cornwallis would be able to hold out until the end of the month. The scale of the French and American forces gathering against him was not yet realized. This slightly optimistic picture was dispelled on 23 September when Clinton received two notes from Cornwallis dated a week previously. Cornwallis said that he had six weeks' supplies left but that his defenses would not be able to resist a determined assault and that if he could not be relieved soon "you must be prepared to hear the Worst."[21] These two notes were discussed by Clinton with his senior officers, and it was agreed that an attempt should be made to rescue Cornwallis by landing a force near Yorktown and marching to his relief. This must be done quickly or Cornwallis would be forced to surrender, which would have "fatal consequences," so the attempt should be made whatever the risk.

On 24 September at a further meeting that included the naval commanders, it was proposed that the fleet take with them three or four fireships which, if the French should be found still at anchor, could be launched at them in an attempt to cause damage and confusion. The proposal was agreed by the others present, and it was further decided that 5,000 troops should be taken on board as a relief force. A letter to this effect was sent to Cornwallis, expressing the hope that the relief expedition would start from New York on 5 October.

This plan represented the last hope the British had of carrying out a rescue of the besieged forces in Yorktown. However, it was a venture with a high degree of inherent risk. There could be no delay in the timing of the expedition: speed was essential. The buildup of the Franco-American forces meant that at any time the British defenses could be stormed and the defenders overpowered by weight of numbers. The British would be operating in the face of a superior army and navy, and although over a long period the British had acquired expertise in carrying out amphibious expeditions, this operation was going to require more than its share of good luck—something with which the British actions so far in this campaign had not been blessed. The success of the operation was extremely doubtful, and it could well end in complete disaster, with not only Cornwallis's army trapped but Clinton's forces and Graves's fleet. This outcome would mean the end of everything, not just British control of America but even the continuation of the war.

In the middle of these deliberations came the welcome news that Digby had arrived off the bar with the long-awaited reinforcement of three ships of the line, the *Prince George* (90), the *Lion* (64), and the *Canada* (74). Among the crew of the *Prince George* was Prince William, whom Hood had last seen at Portsmouth when he was assisting the king to get his son fitted out for the navy. The captain of the *Canada* was the Hon. William Cornwallis,[22] brother of the general and one of the most accomplished and popular officers in the navy. Cornwallis was a man in whom Hood was to place a good deal of trust and friendship in the future, which was fully reciprocated, and the pair remained firm friends until Hood's death in 1816.

Lord Robert Manners told his brother that the arrival of Digby "has given great hopes" to many people, especially among the army officers. He went on to say that he saw no reason for this hope, as de Grasse and de Barras combined would still have such a superiority that it would be impossible to force de Grasse's position so long as he remained where he was and was not forced out by bad weather or lack of provisions.[23]

The arrival of Digby would mean the imminent departure of Graves for Jamaica. The thought of leaving a station in which he was de facto commander for one where he would be second or even third in command grated on Graves's professional self-esteem. He felt so strongly on the matter that he wrote to the secretary of the Admiralty, Philip Stephens, on 26 September:

> I beg leave to state to their Lordships on my own behalf, that being superceded by a junior officer, and sent to another station where I can only be second and possibly third in command, after having been nearly four years upon severe and critical services, imply much disapprobation of my conduct as will certainly discredit me in the opinion of mankind who are generally inclined to construe mens real sentiments from their actions. I dare hope their Lordships will not suffer me to remain long in so painful a situation.[24]

Stephens was able to reassure Graves that the Admiralty did not hold any such opinion on his conduct and that he was not under censure in any way. However, when the next flag officer promotions came round in which

Graves could have expected his promotion to vice admiral, the list stopped just short of him. He did not achieve this step until 24 September 1787, though it is impossible now to say whether this was an act of censure or not. He did find employment as second in command to Howe in 1793–94, and but for his serious wound received at the First of June he might have succeeded Howe when the latter retired.

Hood was for a speedy return but was not very sanguine about what could be accomplished in view of the massive superiority the French enjoyed. Graves had returned with eighteen of the line, which, with the three ships from Digby plus the two ships from Jamaica that Rodney had asked Sir Peter Parker to send on and would arrive soon, meant he could muster twenty-three of the line, still well short of the French squadron. Clinton, aware from his contact with Cornwallis of the French superiority, claimed that the admirals had assured him that the French fleet of thirty-six sail of the line could not, from the position in which it had last been seen between the Middle Ground and Horseshoe Shoal, prevent the passage of a British fleet into the York or James River.

Digby immediately joined the deliberations of the senior British officers. At a meeting with Clinton that was also attended by Hood, Digby pressed for another council of war to examine every aspect of the operation. Clinton stated that it was required for the navy to land the relief force in the Chesapeake Bay in order to attempt a junction with Cornwallis. He further told Digby that the navy's role would not be restricted to putting the army ashore but would entail supporting the troops and supplying them or the operation would fail. Digby next asked the most important question of all: What was to be done if the operation succeeded and Cornwallis was rescued? Were the troops to stay in Virginia or be withdrawn? The question needed to be asked, for the reembarkation of the troops would be a difficult operation with the strong French and American forces in the area. Even if they had been defeated after the initial landings of the British, they would not be likely to depart, given their strength and the importance of the objective. And in addition to supporting the army, the navy would have to face a superior French fleet, which would make the embarkation and transporting of the troops a daunting operation.

While these discussions were going on, Lord Robert Manners wrote his brother a long letter that covered the events of 5 September and the subsequent return to New York. It is worth quoting at length as the considered opinion of one of the most capable captains in the fleet:

As soon as we arrived off Sandy Hook from the West Indies, we were ordered to sea without crossing the bar, to look for the Viscomte de Barras with the Rhode Island Squadron, consisting of seven sail of the line, and after being out a few days to the southward, on the 5th saw Le Comte de Grasse at an anchor in the Chesapeake, where he had arrived two days before us with twenty eight sail of the line from the West Indies, twenty four of which were actually with him. When he perceived us he stood out, forming his line, and an action commenced at four o'clock in the evening which lasted till sunset, when both sides desisted firing. The next day on our side was chiefly spent in repairing our damages. The enemy, partly by carrying more sail and partly from a shift of the wind, gained the winds of us, where they remained three days afterwards, and though they constantly had it in their power to give us battle the whole time—our fleet being to leeward and under very little sail—yet they uniformly declined it. It appeared extraordinary at the time that the enemy, with five sail of the line superior, should avoid an action, but they had a deeper stake; their object was Lord Cornwallis and the Chesapeake, where they had disembarked, as we afterwards found, 3,000 men, and had left four sail of the line, which they soon regained, leaving us indeed the sea, but at the same time a disabled fleet and incapable of acting offensively, therefore we proceeded to New York, where we arrived on the 20th.[25]

Manners mentioned that the *Resolution* was one of the ships more or less seriously damaged in the action on 5 September, but he expressed doubt that the New York yard would have the resources to complete the repairs.

The feelings of Digby and Hood on the matter were probably clear to Clinton. They were very concerned about the prospects of mounting a successful rescue of Cornwallis. The more they discussed the details with Clinton, the less they liked it. Clinton relayed the feelings of Digby and Hood to other senior army officers at a meeting and also told them that the likelihood of meeting the 5 October deadline for departure was considered poor and that if the rescue operation had not started by that date, Cornwallis should be told to act on his own account and carry out any measures he thought could save his army. Graves was then asked when he thought the refitting of the fleet would be completed. He immediately replied that he did not expect to be able to proceed before 8 October.

A few days later yet another meeting, this time attended by both services, agreed that an amphibious operation to rescue Cornwallis was to be the objective of the British at New York "without suffering any circumstances to divert the attention from it." Graves informed the meeting that his revised date for the fleet to sail was now 12 October if the winds were favorable "and no unforeseen accident happens."

There was a general suspicion forming in the mind of Clinton that the relief of Cornwallis might have to be attempted by the army alone without the assistance of the navy. He got the impression from the three admirals he had spoken to that the refitting was likely to take longer than first hoped and that, even if that were not an obstacle, the sailors did not view the operation's success as very likely. He had told Cornwallis that if the amphibious operation was delayed, he would try to create a diversion by mounting an attack through New Jersey towards Philadelphia, which he hoped would draw the Americans away from Yorktown.

Clinton was quite correct about the feelings of Graves on the matter. The admiral had not previously known how critical Cornwallis's situation was, and he now questioned the possibility of relieving him at all. Graves had sown further doubt in Clinton's mind by asking whether, if the expedition was unsuccessful and nothing could be done to assist Cornwallis, Hood's squadron might be ordered to sail direct from the Chesapeake to the West Indies with Clinton's relief force still aboard. Graves later explained that this line of thought was mere speculation, but it could only have been mentioned with the intention of undermining the resolve of Clinton to pursue the operation. Clinton replied that the operation was to be carried out by "our joint exertions" but if the relief failed he hoped that the whole fleet would return to New York. Any other possibility would be disastrous for the British position in America and would lead to the loss of the army in Virginia and the possible loss of New York. The responsibility for these consequences, he implied, would be on the shoulders of Graves. However, if Graves wished to provide transports for the troops being shipped from New York, Clinton would be equally happy with that solution. The idea of transports accompanying the fleet south was not considered feasible because, even if they could be provided, they would unduly slow the fleet. Having failed to get Clinton to reconsider the operation, Graves convened all flag officers and senior captains on 8 October. At this meeting, according to Hood, he proposed to reduce to writing whether the relief of Cornwallis was "practicable." Hood, who was probably the most enthusiastic of the flag officers about the operation, wrote of this meeting and Graves's proposal to his correspondent George Jackson:

This astonished me exceedingly, as it seemed plainly to indicate a design of having difficulties started against attempting what the generals and admirals had *most unanimously* agreed to, and given under their hands on the 24th of last month, and occasioned my replying immediately that it appeared to me a very unnecessary and improper question, as it had been already maturely discussed and determined upon to be attempted with all the expedition possible; that my opinion had been very strong and pointed (which I was ready to give in writing with my name to it), that an attempt under every risk should be made to force a junction with the troops the commander-in-chief embarks in his Majesty's fleet with the army under General Earl Cornwallis at York . . . and the provisions landed, I was also of opinion the first favourable opportunity should be embraced of attacking the French fleet. [26]

In the face of the hostile opposition of Hood, Graves backed down and it was not discussed. However, whatever his reason for raising it at the meeting, the question Graves asked was a critical one and should have been asked by all the senior officers of both services, for the course of action decided upon was one that entailed a high degree of risk. They were aware that they would be seeking to land 5,000 troops in the Yorktown area in the face of a French fleet of thirty-six sail of the line and a combined Franco-American force of almost 20,000 troops and militia. It was not an operation that would stand close scrutiny, and it can only have been agreed upon because it was thought necessary for British prestige to try to effect a rescue whatever the consequences. The French and Americans held all the aces. To effectively negate the desperate moves of the British, they needed to do nothing beyond perhaps forming a defensive line of their ships across the mouth of the Chesapeake. Even if the British were successful in fighting their way in, they would be left several ships seriously damaged and unable to operate efficiently. They would also probably have incurred large losses in the troops that were embarked, and this would further reduce the numbers to face the still superior Franco-American forces.

At this meeting Digby, the senior of the admirals present, waived his right to command and agreed that Graves should lead the fleet in any rescue attempt at the Chesapeake. When these operations were over, Graves would then leave for Jamaica to become second in command to Sir Peter Parker as had always been intended by the Admiralty. Hood did not think much of this arrangement, as he wrote: "It would, in my humble opinion, have been a most fortunate event if Mr. Graves had gone off to Jamaica upon Mr. Digby's arrival." He gave Jackson his opinion of Graves:

> I own to you I think very meanly of the ability of our present com-
> manding officer. I know he is a *cunning* man, he may be a good theo-
> retical man, but he is certainly a bad practical one, and most clearly
> proved himself on the 5th of last month to be unequal to the conduct-
> ing of a great squadron.[27]

Frederick Mackenzie writing in his diary seems to have picked up on the mood of some naval officers:

> It appears very doubtful that the Navy will after all attempt . . . the
> relief of Lord Cornwallis. The general conversation among them from
> the Captains downwards, is, of the great superiority of the French
> fleet, the impossibility of destroying any of them by fireships, or forc-
> ing them in the position they have taken, and the certainty that they
> will come out immediately on the appearance of the British fleet, and
> attack it. They talk very freely of the conduct of the Admiral on the 5th
> of September, and appear more ready to censure the conduct of others
> than to refit their own ships.

MacKenzie added in disgust:

> Several of the Captains spend more of their time on shore than they
> do on board, and appear as unconcerned about the matter as if they
> commanded Guard ships at Portsmouth.[28]

Two exceptions that Mackenzie was able to make to this blanket condem-
nation were Lord Robert Manners of the *Resolution* and Thomas Graves of
the *Bedford*. He does not mention William Cornwallis, who must have been
more than anxious about the fate of the army at the Chesapeake.

Hood, who had got to know and admire Captain Cornwallis, was able
to let him have some news of his brother. A Major Cochrane,[29] a scion of
Lord Dundonald, had got into the besieged British camp to deliver a message from Clinton to Cornwallis. Unfortunately, Cochrane was killed in a
subsequent bombardment of the British camp. Hood wrote:

> Major Cochrane got safe to Lord Cornwallis, and the boat in which
> he went is come back. She left New York the 9th at night. The *Charon*
> is burnt by red hot shot, and the enemy throw shells into Lord Corn-
> wallis's works but cannot move his Lordship, who is in high spirits, he

has plenty of provisions, and the only man he has lost of any consequence is the head commissary. This is all I yet know, which I thought would be some satisfaction to you. I expect to hear more tomorrow from headquarters. The ships are mostly at Staten Island and will be here tomorrow if the wind permits.[30]

The *Charon* (44) had been one of a squadron of ships trapped in the Chesapeake by the French fleet on one side and the Franco-American army on the other. The others were the *Guadeloupe* (28), the *Fowey* (24), and the fireship *Vulcan*. All were destroyed by red hot shot, but the *Bonetta* (14) was captured by the French when Yorktown finally fell.

Despite the feelings of Mackenzie that Manners was one of the more enthusiastic of the captains for the attempt to force the French line and rescue Cornwallis, his real feelings were relayed to his brother in the letter of 27 September:

it is reported that it is determined to make an attempt on their line, and a desperate one it will be if put into execution, and, if not, Lord Cornwallis and his army, I am afraid are in a most perilous situation, from which they cannot be extricated by any other means; in short, it is so melancholy a prospect to look forward on that I wish to drop the subject and wait calmly for the event, which one way or another must soon happen. If we don't succeed in our attempt, and are repulsed, the fate of America is decided and the West Indies will be left an open prey to the French arms; and should we succeed so as to open a passage and throw in succour, I fear it would be only a temporary relief as probably in the course of things such superiority must at last carry the point.

I had as nigh an escape in the last affair as I ever wish to have; the peak of my hat was shot off by a ball; I felt a slight inconvenience from it for a few moments but no injury.[31]

The refitting the fleet proceeded slowly, and the proposed sailing date of 5 October came and went. The shortage of masts and spars was the main cause of the delay. Hood said the repairs went on "unaccountably tedious" and he feared for the safety of Cornwallis. On 13 October the *Torbay* and the *Prince William* finally arrived in New York from Jamaica. The two ships were hailed by Hood as "a noble acquisition that makes my heart bound with joy." The delay by Sir Peter Parker in sending them on as Rodney requested has been much criticized, both at the time and since. The arrival of these ships must have been some relief to Graves, who was aware of the odds he still faced.

Graves told the Admiralty that the want of stores at New York, which also lacked a dockyard, was the reason that the squadron could not yet sail again. He recounted a list of unfortunate incidents and ended on the pessimistic note that he saw "no end to disappointments." The paucity of stores in New York was partly attributable to the visit of Rodney's fleet the previous year, when he had largely stripped the dockyard of such items, for which replacements ordered from Britain had yet to arrive.

Mackenzie entered in his diary on 16 October:

> If the Navy are not a little more active, they will not get a sight of the Capes of Virginia before the end of this Month, and then it will be too late. They do not seem to be hearty in the business, or to think that the saving that Army is an object of such material consequence. One of the Captains has exposed himself so much as to say, that the loss of two line of battle ships in effecting the Relief of that Army, is of much more consequence than the loss of it. Sir Samuel Hood appears to be the only man of that Corps who is urgent about the matter, and sees the necessity of doing something immediately. The others think too much of the superiority of the French fleet, and say ours is by no means equal to the undertaking.[32]

If what Mackenzie writes is a true reflection of the feelings of the captains of the fleet, it shows a very bad spirit abroad. The prospect of facing the superior French fleet seems to have been viewed in a very pessimistic mood. Experience had shown them that an engagement with the French did not bring the decisive victory that the public expected and the navy ardently desired. It produced hard fighting and a stalemate at the end, with serious damage to masts and yards to repair. The feeling seemed to prevail that the French were so superior in numbers that nothing could be done against them and that the rescue of the army was not worth the loss in lives and possibly in ships. This attitude contrasts starkly with that prevailing at the time of the Dunkirk evacuation in 1940 with Admiral Bertram Ramsay and of Admiral Andrew Cunningham in 1941 at Crete, who both took the decision to hazard their ships and suffered serious loss in coming to the aid of the British army. The latest intelligence from Cornwallis conveyed his opinion that only a landing in the York River and a successful naval action could save him. His position was now further endangered by the commencement of formal siege operations with the digging of parallels. Forty cannon and sixteen mortars were firing regularly on his works, which were not constructed to withstand such a bombardment for long.

By 17 October the ships were ready to take the troops on board. General Clinton had allotted 7,149 men for the relief force, and the embarkation was not completed until the following day. Unknown to anyone at the time, the man who embodied the spirit of the navy in the previous war and would serve as the example to the navy in the following wars died at his home in Sunbury on that day. Lord Hawke was the fighting admiral par excellence, and his achievements were contrasted by Horace Walpole with the present reality. Having heard of the action off the Chesapeake and the death of Lord Hawke, Walpole commented:

> The Admirals Graves and Hood have attacked a superior French fleet at the mouth of the Chesapeake, and have not beaten it. . . . Lord Hawke is dead and does not seem to have bequeathed his mantle to anybody.[33]

The fleet now consisted of twenty-five sail of the line, with four rear admirals—Graves, Digby, Hood, and Drake. Graves, who was now familiar with the officers, would command. The fleet sailed on 19 October, carrying the hopes of the British in North America. Clinton considered that if Cornwallis could not be rescued and was forced to surrender, there was no hope of ever forcing America back into the British dominions. As Mackenzie noted, the captains of the British fleet may not have been hopeful of success in the enterprise, but the army officers were determined to do all that was possible to save Cornwallis. The general was a popular man in the army, and it was felt that he could not be left at the Chesapeake to be forced into surrender.

Graves was by now fully aware of the gravity of the situation. He had considered the events of 5 September and issued new signals and instructions that made it plain what his intentions where when they next met the French. It is obvious from the signals that he intended to enter the river and go up to Yorktown, getting above the French fleet. With the serious situation of Cornwallis now known in New York, Graves seems to have been determined to fight an action if necessary to achieve his purpose, and the new signals were designed to make this action more successful than the last.[34]

De Grasse knew that Digby was coming and could be bringing as many as ten sail of the line, which would give the British a much greater numerical strength. Worried lest he once again be caught at anchor, de Grasse told

Washington that he proposed to go to sea, leaving enough ships to blockade the York and James Rivers. The mere suggestion that the French fleet might leave the Chesapeake put the Allied land commanders in a panic, and they appealed to de Grasse to stay in the river. After further consultation with his flag officers, de Grasse agreed.[35]

Graves's new determination might have served the fleet if it had come to an engagement with the French. It was all too late, however, for on the very day on which the fleet left New York and made its way southward again, Cornwallis was forced to surrender.

With an effective force of only 6,000 men, Cornwallis had been obliged to restrict his defensive perimeter, but he remained optimistic, convinced that the position was not hopeless. The Allied forces with nearly 14,000 men enjoyed a massive preponderance not only in men but, more important, in guns, especially the heavy siege pieces that the French had brought with them. Their overwhelming firepower began to destroy the British earthworks and to cause casualties among the men. Cornwallis was not entirely passive and mounted sorties to drive the Allies from their defenses and to spike their guns, but these were only temporary measures. The pressure was soon resumed. As a last resort Cornwallis tried to ship his whole force across the river and get away to the north. Rough weather frustrated this attempt and it had to be abandoned. With the failure of this final chance, which might go down as yet another piece of bad luck that the British suffered during the campaign, the only course left was to surrender. In a letter sent in these last days he told Clinton that his position was so bad that he could not recommend that the fleet and the army run any risk to save him.

However, with the British numbering barely 3,000 fit men and with their defenses in a condition that invited assault, Cornwallis had no alternative but to negotiate a surrender. On 18 October the British laid down their arms to the Franco-American forces.

Graves heard the news from three refugees who had escaped from the Chesapeake in a small boat. He relayed these escapees' stories in a report to the Admiralty on 29 October:

> James Rider a black man, says he left Yorktown on Thursday 18th in a four oared boat in company with a Captain and people belonging to the Sloop *Tarleton* . . .
>
> That they left Yorktown to make their escape as it was said the troops were going to give it up; there had been no firing for a day

and a half before he left it, and it was reported that Lord Cornwallis was making Terms to be sent to England and also respecting private property.

He gives an account of his being taken twice and of his escaping to a Despatch Boat sent from the Fleet the day before yesterday.

James Robinson [a Black] Pilot to the *Charon* Man of War left York-town with Rider because he heard there was a treaty to surrender the place. On Wednesday the firing ceased and a Flag of Truce was sent out, which returned and the firing began again, that it ceased a short time afterwards and he has not heard any since tho' he was near the place for two days.

The soldiers were all standing on their works during the time the Flags were out. That the merchants were getting all their things on shore as the shipping were to be given up to the French.

About eight or nine days ago the enemy made an attack on our left and carried two of our Redoubts and killed most of the people that were in them. . . .

On Wednesday night he said he saw a large bonfire in the enemy's camp. One of the Magazines had blown up.

Robert Mayse left Yorktown with the above. He was told the Army had surrendered Prisoners of War according to the terms granted at Pensacola. That all the people that could were making their escape. He is very positive that they have capitulated and therefore the place was to be given up on Friday at one o'clock; there has been no firing since.[36]

The British ships were seen briefly by the Allies on 29 October but were observed to turn northwards to New York. One account says that Hood and Drake wanted to remain off the mouth of the Chesapeake to blockade the French in the river (the suggestion of Rodney in his letter to Sandwich) but Graves and Digby dissented from this proposition. The suggestion is certainly in the Hood manner and would have seized the initiative, forcing the French to fight if they wished to return to the West Indies. With the fleet crammed with troops, and with winter weather approaching, it is doubtful how long such a blockade could have been enforced. But with de Grasse anxious to get to sea and back to his station, it might very well have been the best card that the British had left to play.

Hood wrote to his friend George Jackson that same day regarding the surrender at Yorktown:

. . . a most heartbreaking business. And the more so to my mind as I shall ever think his Lordship ought to have been succoured or brought off previous to the return of the French Fleet to the Chesapeake and which Mr Graves has in his power to effect at his pleasure after losing the glorious opportunity of defeating its intentions on the 5th of last month.[37]

At New York Hood was anxious to get back to his command with the largest force he could raise. He believed that any ships kept on the North American station would be wasted during the coming months, for he was in no doubt that the French would make their next major move in the West Indies and that the British should concentrate all their forces there to match it. He informed the Admiralty on 3 November that Graves had given him back all the ships he had arrived with and that he would be returning to his station as soon as the task of disembarking the troops had been completed. At the same time he was making every effort to increase the strength of his fleet. He had begun this process while the fleet was still at sea when he wrote to Digby from the *Barfleur* on 31 October:

> With your assistance in aid to the present force under my command, I shall be put in a very respectable state for acting offensively against the enemy, but without it I must be upon the defensive only, and possibly shall not be able to prevent mischief.
>
> I can only, Sir, most humbly suggest and solicit, which is what my duty calls upon me to do in the most pressing manner; and it must rest with you to decide. If I cannot do as I would, I must be content to do as I can—a man can work only with the tools he has. But I cannot refrain repeating that not a moment is to be lost in taking your resolution either way, as I think it necessary I should return to my station at the Leeward Islands so soon as the troops, army provisions, etc. are disembarked, unless you have commands for me to the contrary.[38]

When Hood learned that Graves was going to proceed to his new station at Jamaica in the *Torbay*, one of the ships that Hood had brought with him from the West Indies, he was indignant. He wrote to Graves on 3 November:

> I cannot hear of your intentions of taking the *Torbay* to Jamaica without remonstrating against it, in the strongest manner, as His Majesty's islands committed to my care are surrounded with such appar-

ent danger that I have thought myself obliged to solicit Rear-Admiral Digby to strengthen the squadron under my command.

Under these circumstances it is very much my duty to object in the most pointed terms against parting with a seventy-four gun ship, to attend you to Jamaica, where she cannot be wanted.[39]

Hood won his point, and the *Torbay* stayed under his command. He had more trouble with Digby, who was naturally reluctant to give up most of his force for the West Indies. Digby made Hood the generous offer of four of his ships, which would bring Hood's force to eighteen of the line.

Hood wished there to be secrecy about the force that was going with him to the West Indies, but he heard that some of the captains of the ships allotted to him had been indiscreet in writing to their lodgings in New York and ordering their belongings sent to their ships, as they were bound for the West Indies. Hood unburdened himself to Digby:

This is to me very extraordinary, as it was so easy a matter to have prevented any captain from knowing it [the destination in the West Indies] till his ship was at sea. I am most exceedingly sorry for it, because it is very immaterial whether de Grasse knows of my going with fourteen or eighteen sail, as he will naturally take care in either case to be four or five superior. Now, had he understood that I sailed with only fourteen, and was found with eighteen by the enemy, great and manifest advantage to the King's service might have arisen therefrom, but it is a great satisfaction to my mind that I have been in no way instrumental in letting the *important* secret forth.[40]

Hood sought to reassure Digby that his giving up his ships would not endanger New York and that they could be far more usefully employed in the West Indies. The letter included an offer to share with Digby any prize money that the ships might make on the West Indies station. This was a generous offer, for Hood was by no means a wealthy man, but it proves his zeal for the public service. Hood's letter to Digby was a logical restatement of his views on where the best use could be made of the ships:

I cannot see it of the least consequence to *you* . . . whether you know that the French fleet has left the Chesapeake or not before the fleet of his Majesty separates; as nothing can, in my humble opinion, be apprehended from *it* upon this coast for some months to come, and it appears to me of very little consequence whether De Grasse leaves more or less force in the country, since Sir Henry Clinton without hesitation declares he has no fears for New York.

Where can the advantage be in locking up a considerable part of your squadron in Oyster Bay, in the Sound, which is the only place of safety you have for the ships from the weather? And I very much doubt whether they would be *there* safe from the enemy's fire-vessels. Let the army establish what *posts* they may for their protection, and if your ships must cruize in the winter months, where can they be sent *more* for his Majesty's service or your own advantage than to the *southward?*[41]

Digby informed the Admiralty that he intended to send four or five of his ships with Hood. He would reserve the rest until the movements of de Grasse were known for certain. Digby said that with the reinforcements given him, Hood would be superior in coppered ships, whereas even if Hood had taken all the other ships as well, he would still not be superior to the whole French fleet. Hood had to rest content with what he had got, and he left New York on 11 November.

De Grasse had already sailed on 5 November with a force of thirty-six of the line. He left four of these at Cap François to escort back to France the trade that had been held up pending the operations in North America.

The one British gain of 1781 was St. Eustatius. This gain was lost on 25 November to a surprise French expedition of the marquis de Bouillé. The year therefore ended most favorably for the French. They had inflicted a tactical and strategic defeat on the British and changed the course of the war in America. For this success, de Grasse earned a good share of the credit by concentrating all his forces at the decisive spot. Hood and Rodney, on the other hand, had misread the situation and believed that de Grasse would not make such a move. As a consequence the British found themselves outnumbered when the day of decision came. The failure of both Rodney and Hood to defeat or seriously damage the French fleet in the two chances they had in the year must also be considered a factor. If the French had been beaten decisively in the West Indies, they would never have been strong enough to go to North America.

While Rodney bears the responsibility for underestimating the French response, Hood bears the responsibility for the failure of the action. His refusal to bring the rear division down cost the British dearly. The French achieved their objective of repulsing the British fleet, while the British failed to achieve theirs of defeating the French and relieving Cornwallis. Hood returned to the West Indies still with his professional reputation to make.

The echoes of the Chesapeake and the fall of Yorktown rumbled on in Britain. In the dying months of the North ministry there was a suggestion by Germain to bring Graves home and try him by court-martial for his actions on 5 September. Sandwich, mindful of the split that followed the Keppel and Palliser court-martials, did not agree, arguing that mere want of success did not warrant court-martial proceedings, and the matter was allowed to drop. In the months following Yorktown, not only was the newly captured St. Eustatius lost but also St. Vincent, St. Kitts, and Minorca. Gibraltar remained threatened and was known to be a prime Spanish objective. Jamaica too was known to be one of the objectives for which the Spanish had entered the war. The government thought it a likely target of the French and Spanish forces in the coming campaign of 1782. The loss of Jamaica would dwarf all other losses in the West Indies, and steps were taken to reinforce Rodney at the expense of strength in the Channel. In the East Indies Sir Edward Hughes was contending manfully with the threat of the French fleet under Suffren.

The government had, therefore, to find reinforcements for both the East and the West Indies. Thanks to Sandwich's building program, this could be done. Indeed, it was the revival of British naval power, and the decline of the French, that would enable the war to be ended on satisfactory terms. The Admiralty was determined to have naval superiority in the Leeward Islands. Rather than match French moves as they had been doing, they followed the policy of accumulating a force that would give Rodney numerical and qualitative superiority over de Grasse and remove once and for all the French threat to the British position in the area.

In assessing the Chesapeake campaign, there are several factors to be considered. First of these was pure luck! Under this heading is found an extraordinary run of good fortune that followed the movements of de Grasse.

The British government was well aware of the reinforcements that were preparing at Brest for the West Indies. The time of de Grasse's sailing from Brest was such that the Channel Fleet under Sir George Darby had a good chance of intercepting him. Had Darby, commanding the fleet involved in the second relief of Gibraltar, not been diverted to Cork, his force would have been in a position to meet de Grasse in the mouth of the Channel. Whatever the result of such an engagement, it would certainly have had an effect on the strength and capacity of the force that was bound for the West Indies.

The second element of luck came with the loss of the *Swallow* and the *Active*, the first carrying Rodney's dispatch to Graves and the latter Hood's letter advising Graves of his course and the news of the French. Although the *Swallow* did reach New York, she was sent on by Affleck to look for Graves, and when she was subsequently lost in an action with U.S. privateers, Rodney's dispatch was lost with her. With the *Active* also lost, Graves had no news of Hood's coming to New York until a few hours before his arrival.

The fact that Graves's squadron was not at New York but pursuing a French squadron that the Admiralty, erroneously informed, had told him was crossing the Atlantic to Boston was another piece of good fortune for de Grasse. If the British admiral had been in port when the *Swallow* first arrived on 28 July, he would certainly have been able to sail in time to meet Hood off the Chesapeake with his whole force of six of the line.

There were also elements in which luck played no part. These comprised poor operational decisions by the British commanders. The first was the close blockade by Hood's squadron at Martinique when de Grasse first arrived in April 1781. This was chosen by Rodney so that the convoys sailing from St. Eustatius would not be interfered with by any of the ships present at Fort Royal prior to the arrival of de Grasse. If Hood had been stationed which he wished, he would have been better positioned to engage de Grasse despite the superior numbers of the latter. If the French fleet or the convoy accompanying it could have been successfully attacked, it might very well have altered the whole course of the campaign of 1781 and given the British the initiative. The safe arrival of the French fleet and convoy was a significant strategic and tactical success for de Grasse and consequently a defeat for the British. It has to be admitted that Hood did his best from the position he was placed in, but with his disadvantageous position and numerical inferiority he was never able to seriously threaten de Grasse.

A further chance for a fleet action came at the French capture of Tobago on 5 June. When the British sighted the French, they had the windward gauge and were in a regular well-formed line, while the French were in some confusion. It was 4 p.m., hours before dark, but Rodney refused to attack, fearing that the French would not wait to fight an action but would merely draw the British more to leeward. The opportunity of an action was there but was not seized, and again the French were able to achieve their objective—albeit their secondary objective, St. Lucia having been the first—

without serious loss. The fall of Tobago in itself was not significant, but the British failure once again to press home an attack on the French fleet when they seemed to have an advantage was another lost opportunity.

The final example of bad practice by the British was the failure to station a frigate to keep a close watch on the movements of de Grasse when the campaigning season in the West Indies was over. De Grasse had been seen leaving Fort Royal and, as has been stated, was correctly assumed to be bound for Saint-Domingue. No British frigates seem to have been off Havana, the final stopping point for de Grasse, to count his numbers or note his course when he finally sailed for the Chesapeake on 17 August. The British had already sailed a week before from Antigua, having no further intelligence of the French numbers going north. It was certain that the British, with their coppered ships, would make a faster journey than the French. Could a couple of days have been better spent in seeking more information on the French movements or numbers? Hood still had five days in hand over de Grasse when he arrived in sight of the Capes of the Chesapeake on 25 August despite his somewhat longer voyage.

The most important areas of failure for the British lie in the conduct of the battle itself. There was the difficulty of two squadrons trying to work together without time to get to know each other. There was the fact that the signals Graves proposed to use were unfamiliar to the majority of his fleet. There was the omission to haul down the signal for the line of battle, exacerbating an already critical situation. And there were the failures of Samuel Hood, amply covered in the narrative above. Controversy will continue to rage over the tactics used by Graves. He came from the Channel Fleet and was probably familiar with the thinking of Lord Howe in such a situation. He had chosen, however, not to issue his own signal book when command on the station fell to him, but merely to endorse those of his predecessor. He was only an interim commander and may have felt that he would not be in post long enough to impose a new code of signals. Whether it would have made any difference to the result of the action is difficult to say, but at least the signals and the Standard Fighting Instructions and Additional Fighting Instructions would have been familiar to the members of Hood's squadron, as shown by his own later proposed attack at St. Kitts, which was based on Lord Howe's Instructions.

The two commanders who emerged from the whole affair with their reputations enhanced were de Grasse and Rochambeau. The former had had a successful five months campaigning in the West Indies against Rodney and Hood, with the success at Martinique and the capture of Tobago to his credit, and had generally been able to impose his will on the British. Now he had brought his whole fleet and troop reinforcements to the crucial spot in cooperation with Rochambeau and Washington. It was a decisive act which yielded one of the most successful combined operations in the period of sail.

Rochambeau had been given the difficult task of commanding the French troops in North America. Relations were bound to be strained. The French officers, representatives of the ancien régime, could not be expected to feel any personal sympathy for the ideas and aspirations of the American Revolution except insofar as they would welcome the split from Britain as revenge for the humiliations of the Seven Years' War. On the American side there were likewise many men in the Continental Army who had spent years fighting the French and their Indian allies and to whom they must have seemed a natural enemy. There was certainly a lack of trust on the French side, among both military and naval officers, of the Americans and a suspicion that they might make a separate peace and leave the French to fight on alone. The French had been surprised and shocked by the savagery with which the war was carried on by the Americans and the Loyalists. It was not the sort of warfare they were used to, though perhaps those with campaigning experience in Canada might have found it familiar.

With the exception of men like Lafayette—who, apart from his attachment to the American ideals, also had his own desire to get revenge on the British for the death of his father in the previous war—there can have been very few French officers who heartily endorsed the principles the Americans said they were fighting for. There was no natural meeting point between the officers of the French and American armies. After the surrender at Yorktown, the French officers entertained their defeated opponents to dinner. This hospitality amazed and angered the Americans, who were not schooled in the ideas of chivalry that predominated in European warfare. One French officer, when asked, explained this treatment by saying that the French were aware that the Americans did not like them, and so it should not be surprising if they associated with the British officers, with whom they had much in common. Rochambeau, however, while he could not be said to endorse democratic principles, was a natural conciliator. He made this "unnatural alliance" of the two armies hold together. He treated Washington and other American generals with respect. In the case of the Yorktown operations, he had been able to persuade Washington to give up his ideas of an attack on New York, and once the operations were under way he gave the American army the greater part of the action, even up to insisting that the American army should accept the surrender of Cornwallis. The achievements of Rochambeau throughout the war are significant enough to make him a decisive influence in the successful outcome.

British policy in America had been one of dispersion of their forces, which relied very largely on the Royal Navy keeping command of the sea. This policy had proved dangerous in the Gulf of Florida, as the Spanish had swept up various British settlements where they met no opposition from the British navy. The British had persevered with this policy and had now found its true cost in the surrender of Cornwallis. The military campaign was virtually over on the American mainland, but in the naval campaign there was still a lot to play for, and at last the British had decided to pursue a strategy of concentration and naval superiority by reinforcing the force under Rodney in the West Indies. This was where the next round would be fought.

The Rise and Fall
of an Admiral

When Samuel Hood left New York to return to his station in the Leeward Islands, he again assumed responsibility for the most important area for British trade and wealth. For the eighteenth-century governments of Britain—and France—the wealth generated by the West Indian possessions exceeded all other sources of revenue.

In the North American theatre he left behind, the war was rapidly becoming unwinnable. It had always been balanced on a knife edge, and it had progressively deteriorated after Sir William Howe failed to deliver a death blow to the American cause in August 1776. The decision not to destroy Washington's army in the operations at Long Island and a similar failure in the Pennsylvania Operations in August and September 1777 led inexorably to the surrender at Saratoga, the entry of the French into the war, and the surrender at Yorktown. The British forces could never be numerous enough, no matter how many engagements they won against the Americans, to subdue the country.

Hood returned to a command that had been, and was, under serious threat from the French and Spanish forces, which intended the seizure of all the remaining British possessions, including Jamaica. The loss of colonies on such a scale was seen by the Bourbon powers as a means of inflicting a swift defeat on Britain, an ideal revenge for the humiliations of the previous war. To counter this threat, the British government had decided to reinforce the fleet in the Leeward Islands to the point where it held both numerical and qualitative superiority. Its mission would include intercepting French reinforcements from Europe. Until superiority was attained with the return of Rodney, Hood had to carry on with the numbers he had brought back from America.

The repercussions of the action of 5 September now began to reach him. An account critical of Hood in the *Morning Chronicle*, written by "an officer of the Squadron," had reached his notice. It had been read to a gathering of captains and "heartily laughed at" except, it seems, by the captain of the ship from which the account was said to have emanated, who was furious that such "a farrago of absurdity" could come from his ship. The captain promptly placed a letter in a Barbados newspaper that had reprinted the London article and also sent one to England. All such criticisms were treated by Hood with great disdain, as he showed in a letter to Alexander:

> . . . my conscience is perfect clear and I bid defiance to the utmost malice can do; and though the times are, I confess, full of calamity and danger particularly for Military Men, I have naught to fear. But admitting the partisans of Rear Admiral Graves, could fix delinquency upon me, it must be from the private representations of the Rear Admiral, and which must prove him a delinquent in a very high degree, not only for not making my failure of duty known in his public letter, but for calling on me, three several times after, for my opinion and advice; and more especially when I was so candid to tell him, where I thought he had been mistaken in a conversation we had together the evening after the action. How our friend could take it into his head, that I should apply to go home upon Sir George Rodney's return, astonishes me much, it is a measure I could not have the shadow of pretence for and thought he knew me better.
>
> Being almost the youngest Flag Officer in His Majesty's Navy, how could I imagine a fleet of that vast magnitude, which must be employed in these seas, could be placed under my direction. Be assured I shall descend with as much pleasure to serve as *second*, as by accident I rose, to be *first* in command. I will most cheerfully, and to the utmost of my poor abilities support Sir George, as it is my duty to do, as I also would any other Admiral, to whom Government should think fit, to commit the care and protection of the Islands.[1]

It is probably fair to say that the four months that stretched from his return to Barbados on 5 December to the battle of the Saintes on 12 April 1782 were the high point of his professional career. It was this period that cemented his reputation, both among his contemporaries and with historians, and it was in this period that he was able to demonstrate the talents he possessed—talents that make his actions at the Chesapeake all the more inexplicable. In early 1782 he commanded in one action and took a prominent part in another. In order to fully appreciate the talents of Hood, which he had not shown to advantage in 1781, it is useful to examine these two actions, the action at St. Kitts and the battle of the Saintes (which in fact consisted of two engagements).

The Battle of St. Kitts (Frigate Bay), 24–25 January 1782

Despite the loss of the *Terrible*, Hood could, by drawing ships from North America and counting the two now returned by Parker from Jamaica, muster a force of twenty-two sail of the line.

One of the first pieces of intelligence he received on his return to the West Indies was that a squadron of some ten or twelve of the line was soon to sail from Brest with a force of troops destined for the conquest of the remaining British islands in the West Indies. Hood "would do a great service to the Kingdom" if he could intercept this force, which would add to his popularity, "already on a very respectable footing."[2] The Admiralty information was only partially correct. The force in fact comprised nineteen sail of the line, including a detachment from the Brest Squadron, destined for cooperation with the Spanish at Gibraltar.

British plans were on the same lines as those of the French. Significant reinforcements were to go to the West Indies with Rodney. As the government's major concern was for the security of the West Indies, the squadron there would be reinforced at the expense of the Channel Fleet. Superior numbers, it was hoped, would give the British the edge in the West Indies. This was the last throw of the government of Lord North before the effects of Yorktown undermined its support in the House of Commons.

The year 1781 had ended on a hopeful note for the British when Rear Admiral Kempenfeldt intercepted the French reinforcement of which the Admiralty had warned Hood. Despite being outnumbered, Kempenfeldt was able to attack the convoy and capture fourteen ships because de Guichen had placed his escort to leeward of the convoy. Kempenfeldt sent the *Tisiphone*, under the command of James Saumarez,[3] to the West Indies to warn Hood of the approach of the French force.

Hood felt that after the action Kempenfeldt should have proceeded across the Atlantic and joined him in the West Indies. This would certainly have altered the balance of power in the theatre. However, as James Saumarez arrived in the area only after Hood had taken up his position at St. Kitts, it is doubtful if Kempenfeldt could have arrived any earlier and prevented the captures of St. Vincent and St. Kitts when de Grasse returned. In fact a sizeable French reinforcement never reached the West Indies. A severe gale scattered the force, and only two line-of-battle ships, the *Brave* (74) and the *Triomphante* (84), succeeded in reaching their destination.

Hood's fleet needed extensive repair and refitting, in an area with a shortage of all types of naval spares. Food was another problem. There was a desperate shortage of bread, and the local contractors were not able to supply the amount he wanted, a twenty-day supply. If Hood could not stay at sea for a sufficient period, he would not be able to seek out the French or to cruise off Fort Royal. Lack of provisions would force him to surrender the initiative to de Grasse and merely react. The resources of St. Eustatius were no longer available to the British. The French had taken the opportunity of the British fleet's absence in North America to mount a small expedition of four frigates and three hundred men. A garrison of eight hundred men had been left there but had surrendered without too much resistance. Lord Robert Manners was reluctant to cast any shadow on the ability or integrity of the commanding officer of the garrison but thought that the surrender "was very injurious to his character."[4]

To strengthen his force Hood requisitioned the battleship *St. Albans*, which had arrived as the escort to a convoy from Cork. His force was already reduced from the numbers with which he had left New York. The *Royal Oak* and the *Monarch* had lost touch with the fleet on the way south in a gale. They would rejoin, he trusted, but in the meantime any accession of strength was useful.

The French made the first move of the new campaigning season. Their intended objective was the capture of Barbados. This they hoped to achieve without waiting for reinforcements from Europe. They had 6,000 troops available and a numerically superior fleet. Hood was still at Barbados when he received news of the French leaving Fort Royal and standing to the northward.

Hood put to sea immediately with a force of eighteen sail of the line. The *Monarch* and the *Royal Oak*, which latter had struggled back in a damaged condition, were included in this total. The elements came to the assistance of the British, as the French were reported trying to beat to windward to get to Barbados. Foiled by strong contrary winds, de Grasse gave up the attempt and made for Fort Royal to prepare for another attempt, on an island that would be easier to get to. Two of Hood's frigates cruised off Fort Royal waiting for the French to come out.

The French sailed again on 5 January with the intention of attacking St. Kitts and Nevis. One of the surveillance frigates was dispatched to warn Hood while the other tracked the French fleet. The course steered by the

French told Hood that their ultimate destination was either St. Kitts and Nevis or Antigua. He warned the governors at both place that the French were at sea and said that as soon as he knew their destination he would come to the aid of the island under attack. On 14 January came news that the French were off St. Kitts. Hood immediately sailed from Barbados with twenty sail of the line. He was unsure of the strength of the French but assumed it would be superior to his own force. He had only managed to accumulate a sixteen-day supply of bread for his fleet and intended to call at Antigua for flour. Hood received late reinforcements of the *Russell* on the fifteenth and the *Prudent* on the twenty-first, which raised his total to twenty-two ships of the line, with which he assured Sandwich he would "give battle to the Count De Grasse, be his numbers as they may!"

Hood felt a confidence in his own ability, and he knew from past meetings with de Grasse that the French commander was reluctant to engage in a destructive close action. However, Hood hoped to catch him by surprise at St. Kitts and force him to fight in conditions of Hood's choosing.

Hood learned on 16 January that the French were investing St. Kitts by sea and land and that the British garrison had retired to the fort at Brimstone Hill. The French had twenty-six sail of the line and 6,000 troops aboard, outnumbering any forces Hood could bring. The recovery of the island— for the planters had accepted the French surrender terms—depended on the arrival of the British fleet and sufficient land forces to attack the French forces already landed. There had been much discontent at St. Kitts since Rodney's seizure of St. Eustatius, and the French were welcomed almost as allies! The guns that Rodney had left to strengthen the garrison had not been dragged up to Brimstone Hill and mounted, as the planters had not supplied the labor to do so.

To ensure the success of this operation, Hood would have to defeat the French fleet and thereby isolate their forces ashore. The British troops could then be landed and attack the French force there. To be sure, the British were unable to muster enough troops, even including those already serving in the fleet, together with the marines, to match the French force. They could put ashore only 2,400 men against the reported French total of 6,000. This inferiority reduced the options open to the British commander, for he could not both operate ashore and force the French to stop their seige of Brimstone Hill. In any case, no success ashore could be achieved without a victory over de Grasse to cut off the French troops from their fleet support. It was this operation that Hood planned to carry out.

Hood knew that the French were anchored in Basseterre Roads, but he did not yet know that they were not in a defensive formation. De Grasse may have assumed that his frigates would give him ample warning of the approach of the British. Like his military colleague, he was much superior to the British force that opposed him, twenty-nine ships to Hood's twenty-two. Hood planned to deny de Grasse the opportunity of using his numerical superiority by denying him the opportunity of getting to sea. Hood would attack him at anchor.

His plan was to approach St. Kitts under cover of darkness, following the trade winds in time to reach the French anchorage at dawn. Hood issued instructions to all his flag officers and captains describing his intention of attacking the three rear ships in the French formation, a maneuver based on Article 5 of Lord Howe's Additional Instruction of 1777 for attacking the rear ships in succession. Having carried out this attack, each ship was to stand out to sea and, should the French remain at anchor, repeat the process. This attack on the French rear could not be countered by the French ships further down the line. If the plan had come to full fruition then, Hood would doubtless have extended his attack, like Nelson at the Nile, as the rear ships were successively battered into submission.

Unlike Graves at the Chesapeake, Hood intended to rely on a set of signals and instructions that had been issued to all ships. To further clarify his intentions, Hood consulted his officers, especially Drake and Edmund Affleck, his division commanders. It is quite possible that Hood discussed the tactics to be employed in attacking the French at anchor with both his friend William Cornwallis, who had served with Howe, and Edmund Affleck, who had served with Kempenfeldt. The maneuver he intended to carry out required initiative from each of his captains, something that he and Rodney had not been keen on allowing previously in the fleets under their command.

Hood sailed on 23 January just as it was getting dark. He had fifty miles to cover to the French anchorage and, given favorable winds, he should be there by the opening hours of daylight. The plan went smoothly until about 4 a.m. on the twenty-fourth, when the *Alfred* (74), the leading ship in Hood's line, ran into the frigate *Nymphe* (36). For some reason the officer of the watch on the *Nymphe* had caused her to heave to. The *Alfred* was taken completely by surprise, and a collision was unavoidable. Captain Saxton, who recorded the visibility as foggy and said it was difficult to see any other ships, described the result at 6:30 a.m.: "saw the *Alfred* astern with . . . Foresail up; Top Gallant Masts struck and Topsail down."

The damage to the *Alfred* was considerable, and she fired several guns for assistance. After inspection it was decided that she was unable to continue in her present state. Hood was unwilling to engage with anything less than his full force, and the carpenters of the fleet were summoned to undertake the necessary repairs. The *Nymphe* was so seriously damaged on the starboard side that she had to be patched up and sent back. Hood's decision to wait until the *Alfred* could rejoin his force presents an interesting parallel with Graves's reluctance to attack de Grasse headlong at the Chesapeake.

Another interesting parallel is the reaction of Hood to the failure of his attack plan through the failure of one individual. At the Chesapeake, it was Hood who had wrecked the plans of his superior, and even allowing for the claimed extenuating circumstances, he had been treated with more leniency than he was to show to the lieutenant of the *Nymphe*, who was ordered to face a court-martial.

By daylight, after heroic efforts, the repairs to the *Alfred* had been completed, but the British fleet was not where Hood had intended it should be, and was therefore in danger of discovery by the French. At 8:45 the *Convert* reported to Hood the strength of the French fleet. This Hood reported to the squadron by hoisting "a Red and White Chequered Flag at the Main Topmast Gallant" twenty-eight times.

Two French ships were sighted from the fleet at 11:30 that morning, and Hood's own frigates reported a French force now counted as twenty-six sail of the line and four frigates. At noon two more French ships could be seen from the fleet and seven more from the masthead.

Hood adjusted his line as he came in sight of the French after rounding the southern tip of Nevis. The damaged *Alfred* was exchanged with the *St. Albans* (64), but even in her new position the *Alfred* was not sailing well and might cause danger to herself and the fleet if she could not keep up with her next ahead.

With the sighting of the British fleet, de Grasse put to sea. He believed that Hood's purpose was to set supplies and reinforcements ashore by anchoring under Brimstone Hill. The lack of transports must have told him that the troops, if any, were carried in the ships of the squadron and that to land them would mean bringing the whole squadron to anchor. The British were also between the French and their base at Martinique, and de Grasse was expecting reinforcements of four ships of the line to join him. Once at sea, he proceeded under easy sail to the southward in the general direction of the British fleet.

There was no chance of the two fleets coming to action that day after the delay Hood had suffered. As sunset came on, the French were seen now well under way but close in to land. Conditions were better on this night than the previous one, and in the brilliant moonlight the French fleet was seen again at 2 a.m.

The options now open to Hood were vastly different from those he had hoped for. Instead of attacking by surprise an unready French fleet at anchor, he had the French, in superior force, at sea and heading towards him. With de Grasse at sea, Hood faced a commander who had shown himself able to bring about the sort of action he desired, an engagement on the lines of Martinique and the Chesapeake. To achieve his objective of relieving the garrison of Brimstone Hill and saving St. Kitts, Hood had either to defeat the French or drive them away from the island.

For Hood the challenge of defeating the French at sea contained several imponderables. Could he expect the French to await *his* attack if he should have the weather gauge? Could he position his fleet to deliver an attack on only a portion of the French line, thus overcoming the French superiority in numbers? Would the French attack him? Could he rely on the quality of his ships and his captains?

The tactic that Hood eventually used successfully, of taking the French fleet's position in Basseterre Roads, could not have been carried out without prior discussion. Once the original intention to attack the French at anchor was frustrated, there was no opportunity for a conference of all captains and flag officers at the time of the collision between the *Alfred* and the *Nymphe*. But the contingency had always existed that, in unforeseen circumstances, the French might be encountered at sea. The idea of seizing the anchorage that the French had just vacated must therefore have been the subject of previous discussion, perhaps following the suggestion of a similar maneuver at the Chesapeake. Such a maneuver would require that Hood's subordinates instantly understand his intentions.

By the evening of the twenty-fourth the French were well out to sea and to the northwest of Hood. The British still held the windward gauge. While the French were making their way out, Hood took the opportunity to dress his line, but at 8 p.m. he signaled to make sail. Initially the fleet stood to the northward, but Hood then brought his ships onto the same tack as the French, standing out to sea. To the French it must have appeared that the British had given up their attempt at relief and were retiring.

At dawn the next day the two fleets were some seven miles apart, with the French still northwest of the British. At around 6 a.m. Hood again reformed his line, the ships at one cable's length. The French were still to leeward of the British, and Hood calculated that they were now far enough out from St. Kitts that he could to enable him to seize their former anchorage of Basseterre Roads. Hood was familiar with that anchorage, and he intended to take a position along a narrow ledge beyond which the water deepened so sharply that the French could not anchor alongside his ships. The attempt would require precision, and Hood signaled to the various parts of the fleet to keep the line well formed. At 8 a.m. the *St. Albans* was ordered to make more sail, at 8:15 to steer two points to starboard, and an hour later three points to starboard. At 9:31 the signal was made for the fleet to bring to, and for just over an hour Hood went through the process of reforming his line and getting everything ready for his run to the anchorage. At about 10:45 am the fleet stood on again.

To ensure that the fleet anchored where he wanted, Hood sent a pilot to the *St. Albans*, the leading ship now that the damaged *Alfred* had been transferred to the rear of the line. With professional expertise to lead the fleet in, Hood hoped that the *St. Albans* would be able to drop anchor so close to the shoal that de Grasse would not be able to pass inside the British line. Despite this, the *St. Albans* was not as close to Green Point as Hood wished when the fleet finally came to anchor, and he later adjusted her position as he strengthened the line after the initial French attack.

At 11:15 the *Barfleur* signaled to the van to make more sail, and the race to the anchorage was on. When the French commander saw the British standing to the northward, he did not at first realize what was happening. De Grasse brought his fleet around onto the northward tack, all ships carrying out this maneuver together to save time.

Hood signaled for all his ships to prepare springs on their anchor cables so that they could alter their line of fire while at anchor by adjusting their anchor cable.

The British, to keep a compact line and not to leave any gaps for the French to exploit, had to travel at the speed of the slowest ship. This gave the French their chance of catching up, and they were slowly gaining ground on the British.

The British frigates were positioned on the inside of the fleet, away from the French and nearest to the shore. This was to prove fatal to the *Solebay*, which ran aground during the race for the anchorage. Passing by the hills of Nevis, the British line led by the *St. Albans* crossed the narrow strip of water separating that island from St. Kitts. Hood relied on the commanders of the van and rear to be responsible for their own ships, particularly the rear division encumbered by the slow-sailing *Alfred* and *Prudent*.

The British plan was for the van to come to anchor first, covered by the center and rear, and then for the fire from the van ships to protect the center and rear as they too entered the anchorage. The whole operation was critically balanced and rested on the ability of the rear ships to withstand the attack of the French until they could be assisted by the fire of the already anchored van and center.

The French came within range of the rear ships at about 2 p.m. William Cornwallis in the *Canada*, the fourth ship from the rear, began to fire on the French van at 2:10. The *Barfleur*, in the center, records firing at 2:30. Now was the time of greatest danger, with the French ships making attempts to cut off some or all of the rear ships and generally disrupt the British line. In the rear division the danger point was the *Prudent*, which sailed very badly. When a noticeable gap opened between that ship and her next ahead, the *Canada*, de Grasse made for it with the *Ville de Paris*, hoping to cut off the *Prudent*, *Montagu*, and *America*, the last three British ships. This would have been a coup for de Grasse and a disaster for the British, but the attempt was foiled by Cornwallis throwing the sails of the *Canada* and placing himself in the path of the *Ville de Paris*. The raking fire of the *Canada* into the bows of the *Ville de Paris* was enough to force de Grasse to abandon his attempt to break through. It had been a close-run thing, for the jib boom of the *Ville de Paris* had been seen poking through the British line.

At about 3:30 p.m. the leading British ships began to anchor, undisturbed by the fire of the French who were engaged with the ships of the center and rear. As the *St. Albans* did not drop anchor as close to the shoal as Hood wished, he later anchored two more ships at the head of the line in a general strengthening of his position.

The British rear ships were under most pressure, but as the arcs of fire of the van ships were cleared by the center and rear divisions moving to their positions, the French were engaged by the van. Edmund Affleck, commanding the rear, thought that de Grasse had not pressed his attack hard enough and that he had had a good chance of cutting off some or all of the squadron. In his report Hood gave full credit to Affleck, Cornwallis, and Lord Robert Manners in fighting off the French attack.

As the last of the British ships anchored, the French wore and stood out to sea, leaving the British in possession of the anchorage. Hood had won a tactical victory, but the strategic initiative still lay with the French. The British could not disrupt the operations of the French against Brimstone Hill because of lack of troops. It has been suggested that Hood should have anchored nearer to Brimstone Hill, which would have placed him between the French fleet and army. The success of the whole operation depended on the British garrison being able to outlast the French will to continue the siege. If Brimstone Hill did not hold out, the position of the fleet would be very precarious, with a superior fleet at sea and a victorious army on the land.

The judgment of Hood's contemporaries on the achievement was one of universal acclaim. Lord Robert Manners wrote after the whole operation, including the successful escape, that the taking of the anchorage was "well judged, well conducted and well executed" and the "most masterly manoeuvre I ever saw." He told his brother, the Duke of Rutland, that if Samuel Hood was given half the credit at home that the French gave him, he "would stand very high" in public estimation. According to Manners, the French set no bounds to their praises, particularly the land officers. Hood's own protégé Captain Inglefield described the exploit as "one those wonderful things which has seldom been done by the greatest sea commanders."[5]

Historians have almost universally praised the achievement of Hood at St. Kitts, but it must be borne in mind that the ultimate objective of relieving St. Kitts was not attained and Hood eventually had to retire from the scene with the French triumphant. What he accomplished had been done in a very professional and competent manner, speaking volumes for Hood's ability. Without the troops to defeat the French on land, however, the end result was unlikely to be favorable to the British. George III saw this immediately when he was told of the operation, remarking that there had been some fine maneuvering but very little else and he expected to hear bad news come through about St. Kitts.

During the night Hood rearranged and strengthened his line to resist the attacks he knew would come. The rear ships in particular were in something of a cluster, and he ordered some ships from there to go and strengthen the van. He also reduced the intervals between the ships to prevent any chance of the French passing through and attacking from both sides. The *Barfleur* was the fifteenth ship in the line, after which the line turned sharply northwards, enabling the British to cover all possible angles.

The following day the French fleet was seen standing in towards the bay with the obvious intention of attacking. The attack was intended to fall on the van, and Thomas White, who later wrote his recollections thought that the French were trying to get through between Green Point and the leading British ship, thereby doubling the British line. This might well have been accomplished had Hood not rearranged his line during the night. As it turned out, the wind as the French rounded Green Point made it impossible for them to head for the start of the British line. They ended up alongside the fourth ship in the line but had to suffer the fire of the other ships as they came within range.

The *Pluton*, commanded by d'Albert de Rions, was the leading ship and accordingly received the most damage from the first broadside of each ship she passed. When the *Pluton* emerged from the action, she was so shattered that she had to leave the fleet and bear away for St. Eustatius (now in French hands). The *Ville de Paris* set the example for the day by slowing her passage through the water to allow a longer time to engage the British ships. Nothing that was tried, however, broke the formation of the British line. The French attack was over by 11 a.m. and de Grasse took his fleet out to sea. The French bore in again in the afternoon, but this time they concentrated on the center and rear of the British line. This attack began at about 2:30 p.m. but it was not pressed in the same manner as that of the morning, and the British had no difficulty in beating it off. When the French again stood out to sea, there could be no doubt that the honors lay with Hood. This was the final attack the British had to withstand. De Grasse decided that his advantage lay in time. The operations on shore were still continuing, and from his position Hood was unable to interfere with them. The British did land their troops, but it was obvious that they were too few in number, and they were soon reembarked.

While the French repaired their damages Hood was confident that it was impossible for the enemy to dislodge him. In a letter home he said that he had made preparations to counter a fireship attack, should the French decide to launch one. On board the *Resolution* Lord Robert Manners was also confident in the current position, but he hoped that the British reinforcement would precede that of the French, which he assumed was Hood's expectation too.

On 29 January it looked as if the French fleet was about to attack again, but after standing in for a little way to just within range, the French retired again. Later reinforcements increased the French fleet to thirty-two sail of the line, but even with this vast superiority de Grasse did not care to dispute the possession of the anchorage with Hood. The morning of the thirty-first revealed a small British vessel slipping through the French fleet to join Hood. It was Saumarez in the *Tisiphone* with dispatches from Kempenfeldt. He had been chased by the *Triomphante* and the *Terrible*, survivors of de Guichen's squadron, during the previous night but had eluded them.[6] It is possible that the *Tisiphone* was not the only ship to join Hood while he was anchored at Basseterre, for he is reported to have received replenishments of powder and shot as well as provisions shipped in from Antigua.

Operations continued on land, and Saxton recorded "a great deal firing and bombs flying at Brimstone Hill." When Hood had first arrived, General Fraser commanding at Brimstone Hill sent a message to Christie that, though he was glad to see him, he had no need of assistance. As the siege continued, however, such bravado became unrealistic as supplies of ammunition and food decreased and the French bombardment took its toll.

On 12 February General Fraser and the governor of St. Kitts, who had retired to the fort with the garrison when the French attacked, opened talks with the French about terms for surrender. De Bouillé was eager to get the matter over with and accepted the terms proposed. There had been rumors among the officers of the fleet that de Grasse had given de Bouillé a deadline to capture the fort or he would withdraw the fleet. The eagerness of the French to agree to terms may lend credence to the rumor. Hood, who had been unable to establish direct contact with the garrison, learned of the surrender only on the afternoon of the thirteenth when a flag of truce came aboard the *Barfleur*. Two officers of the 13th Regiment told him that the fort had surrendered at 8 a.m. Hood knew that he now had to withdraw the fleet before the French forces ashore could make the anchorage untenable. The problem for Hood was how to get his fleet out of the anchorage without being forced into an action with the superior numbers of de Grasse. For the sake of future operations, the fleet had to be kept intact to join up with the reinforcements being brought out by Rodney.

Hood signaled for Drake and Affleck to come on board the *Barfleur* and it was agreed that the escape would be dependent on circumstances, the position of the French fleet being the most important. A signal was arranged of a Spanish ensign at the main topgallant masthead, upon which all ships were to take up their stream anchors, hoist in their boats, and be ready to sail at short notice. The signal for getting under sail would be the Spanish ensign at the fore topgallant masthead. The ships were to sail out in the order in which they were anchored. In the event that daylight did not present an opportunity to escape, all ships were to prepare dummy lights to leave in their anchorage and cut their cables at exactly 11 p.m. The captains' watches were synchronized by setting them upon the firing of the eight-o'clock gun. Thus each ship should be able to get under way at the same time.

At 8 p.m. the French came to anchor off Point Nevis, and Hood guessed that they had anchored for the night. They were "very far out" according to the log, which gave Hood his chance to escape. All lights in the ships were extinguished as the crews worked to leave the false lights to fool the French commander. All captains had written instructions. After the cutting of the cables at precisely 11 p.m., in about fifteen minutes the *Alfred* was to make all plain sail and the succeeding ships to do likewise in succession and to maintain a distance of two cables' length from the ship ahead. The captains were to keep a watch on the ships astern, and if anyone was seen falling behind, the ship immediately ahead ship should shorten sail to maintain the distance. Hood wished to keep the line as compact as possible for security should the French be in a position to intervene. The leading ship was to steer west-by-south out of the anchorage. This was the way it happened, with no interference from the French and no hitches whatever. Absolute silence was preserved as the cables were cut and the ships began to glide out of the bay. The following day de Grasse was astonished to see an empty anchorage but for the hospital ship, which Hood had left behind with the more seriously wounded and sick. The French admiral had his own problems, as well as being balked of his prey. His fleet was very low on provisions and he had to leave almost immediately to restock for the forthcoming campaign.

The safe departure of the British fleet from St. Kitts was a dangerous operation carried out without trouble and with the utmost discipline and cohesion. Rodney would now have a full-strength fleet with which to engage de Grasse when the time came, but this did not stop him complaining that the departure of Hood during the night was disgraceful behavior and no British fleet ought to have fled from the French in such a way. The comment says a lot more about Rodney than it does about Hood! He also had the more valid comment that the loss of so many anchors would be a serious inconvenience in an area like the West Indies where there was a shortage of naval stores.

The Battle of the Saintes, 9 and 12 April 1782

The Franco-Spanish-American Alliance had two objectives left in the Western Hemisphere of the conflict: the capture of New York, which was a project that had long appealed to Washington, and the capture of Jamaica, which was an object much desired by the Spanish. An attack on New York would have to wait until the French fleet came north again when the campaigning season in the West Indies ended.

Unknown to the men on the spot, the fall of the North government, following the surrender of Yorktown, would take place a short time after Rodney arrived back in his command. The new Whig government under Rockingham had determined to end the American War as soon as possible. As part of this policy New York was to be surrendered should it be attacked, and it was to be agreed with the attacking force to evacuate all British forces from the area. So New York was a plum waiting to be picked as soon as the Franco-Americans could muster their forces. It was left to Middleton to point out that such a policy would require a vast number of transports, which could not be supplied instantly on demand.

Meanwhile there was the capture of Jamaica to pursue, which occasioned the initial French moves leading to the battle of 12 April. The taking of Jamaica was a Spanish war aim, and the French cooperated as repayment for Spanish assistance the previous autumn. The British had long feared an attack on Jamaica, and Rodney promised Sir Peter Parker immediate assistance with his whole force should the island be attacked.

The French too were expecting reinforcements and supplies from Europe but, as we have seen, these were virtually destroyed by the action of Kempenfeldt and the subsequent storm. Hood received his orders on the thirteenth of March and sailed on the sixteenth. The British ships had meanwhile had to refit, with particular emphasis on making up the anchors cut loose at St. Kitts. Hood's orders were to cruise five to ten leagues to windward of Point Salines until joined by Rodney with the remainder of the fleet. He was not happy with his station, thinking it too far south to be suitable for intercepting any French force from Europe. He complained to his brother that Rodney had been vacillating over the stationing of Hood's squadron and had changed his orders several times.[7]

Rodney joined Hood on 20 March and gave orders for the cruising ground to be stretched further to the north, though not far enough to satisfy Hood. Hood tried to stretch even further north but was recalled by his chief. However, all was in vain, for the French convoy that had been put together to replace the one destroyed by Kempenfeldt had got into Fort Royal on the day that Rodney and Hood united.

As soon as Admiral Parker heard of Rodney's arrival, he had written to him underlining the threat that was facing Jamaica now that the French armament had arrived in Fort Royal. He told Rodney that intelligence from various sources indicated the intention of the French and Spanish to keep the British fleet occupied in the Leeward Islands while a force of French and Spanish troops covered by naval forces landed at various parts of Jamaica. Parker and the commander of Jamaica's land forces, General Campbell,[8] both expected that the naval force available to the French and Spanish would be superior to the four sail they could muster, and that before word could reach Rodney the island would have been taken. He hoped Rodney would detach as many ships as he could spare to reinforce the squadron already under his command. The inhabitants of Jamaica, he assured Rodney, rejoiced in his tenure of the command with such a powerful fleet to windward, but they could not help "dreading the consequences of a descent which ought if possible (be)prevented by a Naval force."[9]

Hood thought that Rodney could have sent five or six sail of the line to convoy a regiment to Jamaica. To cover this move, he urged the bold step of appearing off Fort Royal with the remainder and offering battle to the French, stating that he would "be happy to meet the noble Count with a line of battle of thirty three."[10] Rodney declined, as he wished to keep his force united and to meet the French with every ship he possessed. It remained only to await the moves of the French, for the British commander could not anticipate an attack on Jamaica and take his fleet there before the French arrived. The prevailing winds meant that, once there, the British would struggle to get southward again should the French not come after all.

Relations between Hood and Rodney seem to have been good on the surface, but the correspondence of Hood to his friends back home is full of complaints about the uncertainty and vacillation of his chief. Hood seems to have been ill at this time and confined to his cabin, so his contact with Rodney was only by letter and what he heard from other officers, but Rodney did visit him once in the *Barfleur*, which must be taken as a great compliment and even a gesture of friendship from a man such as Rodney who did not place much value on subordinates. Perhaps it shows that he appreciated the qualities of Hood and the advice he gave, even if he did not always feel able to accept it.

Rodney was still far from well and missing his wife and family, but he was positive about where his duty lay. Once, when Hood remarked on the possible dangers to the Leeward Islands from the French concentration, Rodney burst out that Jamaica was of "ten times of more consequence than all of them put together."[11] He was convinced that the decisive battle "for the Empire of the Ocean" would be off Jamaica or Santo Domingo. He had no doubt that he now possessed the fleet to win such an encounter.

Intelligence was received from Fort Royal that de Grasse had 9,000 troops on board and a force of thirty-five sail of the line. It was anticipated that he would sail on either 7 or 8 April and that the destination was Jamaica.

The French in fact sailed on the morning of 8 April, watched by the frigates that Rodney had stationed off the port. When the news reached Rodney in St. Lucia, he at once got to sea. De Grasse, his progress hampered by the presence of the convoy, would not be able to outsail the British ships, so he decided to maintain a course along the chain of French islands, in any of which the convoy could seek safety if the British attacked.

The British sailed at midday with thirty-six of the line. The two least seaworthy ships, the *Intrepid* and the *Shrewsbury*, were to accompany a convoy to Jamaica. For the first time the British now had a numerical superiority over the French, thirty-six to thirty-five, though de Grasse included two 50-guns ships in his strength. By 2:30 p.m. the frigates signaled that the French had been sighted, and Rodney ordered a general chase. At 6 p.m. the French were in sight from the main body of the British fleet. As darkness descended, the British kept watch on the French by means of a chain of frigates with signal lights and were rewarded next morning by finding themselves appreciably closer to the French, who were forming a line under the lee of Dominica.

De Grasse, recognizing that his convoy was a hindrance, ordered it to make for the safety of Guadeloupe. The French fleet had become rather scattered by morning—the effect of being under the lee of Dominica. As the van passed out from shelter, it again got the trade winds and began to draw ahead. Meanwhile the van of the British fleet, commanded by Hood, was slowly closing on the rear of the French fleet.

The bulk of the French were north-northeast to east of the British, but during the night, two had got to the northwest, and as Hood advanced they were threatened with being cut off. De Grasse, having got rid of his convoy, now depended on the superior handling qualities of his ships to outsail the British and draw them away from the area. He then intended to work his way back to rejoin the convoy and proceed to his junction with the Spanish. The two French ships crossed the path of the British fleet in order to rejoin de Grasse, but neither side fired.

It was now the British turn to feel the effects of the calms that had disturbed the order of the French fleet. Hood in the van squadron, eight sail of the line, eventually emerged from the calms and was somewhat separated from the rest of the fleet. This offered de Grasse the choice of defeating this small detachment or continuing on his course and trying to outrun the British. He opted for an attack on the British van ships by a force under Vaudreuil. Fifteen French ships were brought to bear on Hood's squadron. Some commentators, including Hood, thought that this was a missed opportunity and that a far larger force could have been brought to bear while the rest held Rodney at bay. The defeat of the British van, even at the expense of serious damage to some of his own ships, would have given de Grasse the initiative and left Rodney at a serious disadvantage.

Vaudreuil took his division down until he was about level with the rearmost ships of Hood's force, then turned to the north and stood along Hood's line. Hood reduced sail so as not to increase the distance between himself and Rodney, and the French swiftly overhauled him. The British ships were now widely fitted with carronades, a very effective weapon at short range. The French were well aware of the potential of the new weapon and chose not to engage too closely but to maintain the range that enabled the long guns to be effective. But British gunnery was now much improved, and even without the assistance of carronades Hood was sure that the gunners on his ships could maintain a superior rate of fire.

As the British were almost stationary, Vaudreuil used the same tactic that Hood had intended to use at St. Kitts, with the attackers continually returning to attack along the British line. This went on for about forty minutes until the leading British ships of the center division began to emerge from the calms and come up with the embattled van ships, threatening to cut the French detachment off from the remainder of the fleet. De Grasse then ended the attack and signaled for Vaudreuil to withdraw and rejoin the main body.

Having reunited his fleet, de Grasse decided to try another attack on the British van while it was still largely separated from the main body. The danger for Vaudreuil was now not so great, as the rest of the French ships were now much closer and would be able to intervene if necessary. The renewed attack began at about 12:15 p.m., and again the French stayed out of carronade range. The British van had by now been reinforced by the *Royal Oak* and the *Warrior*. By 12:30 the leading ships of the British center also began to fire on the rearmost ships of the attacking force. This went on until about 1:45 when de Grasse once again terminated the attack and recalled Vaudreuil in order to preserve the integrity of his fleet. The British ships were not damaged seriously enough to have to leave the fleet, which is a commentary on the effectiveness of the French fire.

In the French fleet the *Caton* was badly damaged and was sent into Guadeloupe. Hood's comment on the whole business was short and pithy:

> had De Grasse known his duty, he might have cut us up, by pouring a succession of fresh ships upon us as long as he pleased, but we handled them very roughly, and they being to windward hauled off.[12]

Captain Bayne of the *Alfred* died of his wounds during the action. He was much criticized by both Rodney and Hood for opening fire at too great a distance. The British mode of battle was always to try and get close to an opponent where possible so as to inflict more damage.

Hood wrote to Rodney that the *Alfred* had expended so much of its powder in the action that only ten rounds of powder and shot per gun remained. The damage the *Alfred* had suffered, Hood thought, could be repaired in the fleet, and the deficiency of powder and shot could be made up by allocating munitions from the ships in the fleet that had been little engaged. Rodney concurred and said that he was appointing Captain Symons,[13] then serving as second captain of the *Formidable*, to be captain of the *Alfred*. The place of Symons on the *Formidable* would be taken by Lord Cranstoun.[14]

Thus ended the first phase of the action that became known as the battle of the Saintes. Neither side had suffered too severely, but de Grasse had missed the chance that was offered him to defeat the isolated British van. The French commander could now only rely on the ability of the French ships to outsail their British counterparts. William Cornwallis later commented, for his biography in the *Naval Chronicle* of 1802, that the French ships were in terrible condition and that virtually none were coppered and consequently their bottoms were extremely foul. The performance of the French fleet next day seems to give the lie to this statement, as it demonstrated an ability to gain distance on the British fleet that might have been enough to avoid action if the accident to the *Zélé* had not forced a change of course on de Grasse.

Rodney ordered Hood and Drake to change places in the line, giving Drake's squadron the van position and putting Hood's damaged squadron in the rear. It was important to have intact ships with unimpaired sailing powers in the van squadron in a "chase" such as Rodney contemplated. Rodney assured Hood that, the moment his ships had been put in a good state of repair, the dispositions would be reversed again.

Daybreak on the tenth showed the French fleet to be about fourteen miles to windward. Rodney ordered a general chase again to allow the best ships to exploit their qualities. The British chased to windward all day, but the French were able to hold their own and even gain on their pursuers. By the close of the day the distance between the leading British ships and their opponents had increased. The French ships were again demonstrating their superior rate of sailing compared with the majority of their opponents. During the night of 10–11 April, Hood reports, the fleet lay to. This is uncertain, but it may have happened in order that Rodney could reform his fleet into a more coherent body.

Dawn of the eleventh showed the French once again outsailing their opponents, but not everything was well with them. During the night the *Jason* and the *Zélé* had collided, and the former was so badly damaged that she had to be sent back to Guadeloupe for repairs.

The *Zélé* was commanded by the chevalier de Gras Préville, who had been appointed to her in 1781. There were doubts as to his professional experience when he was first promoted to the rank of *capitaine de vaisseau* five years earlier. Since then, however, he had served some frigate time with d'Estaing and had been flag captain to the comte de Sade under de Guichen. The *Zélé*, his first line-of-battle ship, had been involved in a number of collisions under his command. According to Tornquist, the *Zélé* had fourteen collisions in thirteen months, including her final fatal collision with the *Ville de Paris* early on the morning of 12 April.[15]

The *Zélé* conducted running repairs at sea and remained with the fleet, but it became clear that her sailing performance had been affected and she was dropping to leeward together with another ship, the *Magnanime*, which had been damaged in the action on 9 April. Both ships were losing ground to the leading British ships, and unless de Grasse went to their assistance, forfeiting all the distance he had gained, they would be taken by the British. However, he was saved from having to make this decision by the two ships getting themselves sufficiently seaworthy to rejoin the fleet.

During the night of 11–12 April there was a further mishap when the *Ville de Paris* collided with the unfortunate *Zélé* during a change of course. The *Zélé*, which lost her foremast and bowsprit and suffered other damage, could not continue with the fleet, and the frigate *Astrea* was detailed to tow her to Guadeloupe. The final loss of the *Zélé* after those of the *Caton* and the *Jason* reduced the French fleet to thirty sail of the line, while Rodney, having repaired all damage at sea, still had thirty-five.

The collision between the *Ville de Paris* and the *Zélé* took place at 2 a.m., but for some reason there was delay in getting the tow under way, and at daylight the whole situation was clear to the British as they were presented with the sight of the *Astrea* and the *Zélé* only five or six miles away. This was the moment that Rodney needed. It was inconceivable that de Grasse could leave these ships to be overwhelmed by the British. He would have to go to their assistance. Rodney signaled for four of Hood's division to steer to intercept the crippled *Zélé* and then for the rest of the fleet to form in line of battle. Hood detached the ships *Monarch, Valiant, Centaur,* and *Belliqueux* to chase the *Zélé* and its towing frigate. It was just after 6 a.m. and the whole day lay before him, ample time to bring on the action he so desired.

De Grasse saw the move by the British to cut off the *Zélé* and signaled for his fleet to turn to her assistance. The four British ships did not leave off their chase until the French admiral was so committed that a battle could not be avoided. The French fleet had only one course open to it. Because of the proximity of the Iles des Saintes, a group of small islands south of Gua-deloupe, de Grasse could not take his fleet to windward. To go to leeward would give the advantage to the British. He therefore chose the only option left, which was to form in line ahead standing to the south-southeast on the starboard tack. The British were heading in the opposite direction, also on the starboard tack. The time was about 6:15 a.m. The approach of the fleets was a very slow affair, as the winds were light. The wind was, as usual in the morning in that area, from the southeast. It usually altered later on, but this morning it persisted from the southeast for longer than usual. It eventually changed to east-southeast, which gave a slight advantage to the French in the race to achieve the windward position.

Although the British ships were sailing as close hauled as possible, it was soon obvious that the French would now cross the head of the British line and retain the weather gauge. This would give the French the option of re-stricting the engagement to just an exchange of broadsides as the two fleets sailed past each other.

Rodney wished to make the action as long and as close as possible and would therefore work to retard the progress of his ships once they came into contact with the French line. The French wished at least to keep out of range of the British carronades and to maintain their line and fleet intact with a view to completing their mission to Jamaica. The British were by now in good order sailing north-northeast, while the French ships were observed to be somewhat scattered and confused. It was later reported by Cornwallis that the French ships passed the British line in groups of five or six.

The opening shots of the action were fired at about 7:45 a.m. from a ship of the French van at the leading British ship, the *Marlborough*, which was heading for the ninth ship of the French fleet at about 400 yards from the

French line Captain Penney put his helm up and began to steer slowly along the French line. In order to bring his whole fleet into action, de Grasse signaled his leading ships, which had passed without firing, to alter course and close with the British line.

In his turn Rodney signaled to his leading ships to close more with the enemy, and each British ship sailed as near the wind as possible. The signal for close action, which Rodney flew from approximately 8 a.m., was the last contribution he could make to the battle in its present form. Each British ship was striving to close the distance on the French line and sailing as slowly as possible.

In this type of contest, though the French had the choice of distance, the British had advantages in certain gunnery improvements that increased the destructive power of the British ships. Several ships of the fleet— *Formidable, Duke,* and *Arrogant*—now had wider gun ports and could swivel their guns through an arc of 90 degrees rather than the usual 45 degrees, allowing fire to be directed ahead and astern for longer periods. In addition, some ships now had flintlock firing, which was faster and more reliable than the slow-match method previously used. Together with better fire discipline and the presence of the carronades, which were fitted to sixteen ships of the fleet, these changes enabled certain individual British ships to deliver a more destructive broadside than any they received, and more often.

As the two fleets slowly sailed past each other, de Grasse was fully aware that the ships of his van, on passing the rear of the British fleet, would be entering the lee of Dominica. There they would be virtually immobilized, while Rodney would have the sea room to maneuver and carry out another attack. At 8 a.m. de Grasse ordered his leading ships to bear away slightly to get them out of the area of calms and to align them with the British ships that were still entering the battle. At 8:15 he signaled his fleet to wear together and run north—that is, on the same course as the British and parallel with the British line. This would enable him to keep the British van engaged.

Although de Grasse signaled his intentions, starting with the rearmost ship to turn first, that ship was so closely engaged that it did not dare to turn and offer the British an opportunity for a raking fire. Vaudreuil, the commander of the rear division, likewise did not repeat or obey the signal. Seeing that his signal was not obeyed, de Grasse substituted one for the fleet to haul to the wind together and then later to wear in succession from the leading ship. This would have brought his van level with the British center and rear and again parallel and on the same course. This maneuver still exposed each ship to being raked as she turned onto the new course, and this time it was the leading captain who refused to obey.

By 9 a.m. the leading ships of the British van had passed the rearmost ships of the French line. Drake stood on for a while to enable his ships to make some repairs before turning to follow the French, but two ships of his division, the *America* and the *Russell*, turned immediately and sailed down the weather side of the French line, though the *America* reversed course again on not yet seeing a signal from Drake.

About this time there was a change in the wind from easterly to southeasterly. The French ships were immediately forced to try and fill their sails by steering more to starboard. The change had no effect on the British line, which was already sailing off the wind.[16] The first British ship to take advantage of the confusion in the French line was the *Duke*, commanded by Alan Gardner. The *Duke* had been among the leading ships of the British line and suddenly found the French *Conquérant* on her port bow. Gardner passed through the gap between the *Réfléchi* and the *Conquérant* but was not followed by any of the ships immediately astern of him.

As the *Formidable* approached the rear squadron of the French line, it was noticed that the *Diadème* had been taken aback by the change of wind, leaving a gap in the French line just at the moment when the British flagship was in a position to take advantage of it. Rodney led the way through, followed by the *Namur*, *Canada*, *St. Albans*, *Repulse*, and *Ajax*, each ship firing her broadside into the stern of the *Glorieux*, reducing her to a wreck. Further back Affleck in the *Bedford* likewise led the ships of the rear division through the French line—an act of his own initiative, as the rear division had only just entered the action and the ever-present clouds of smoke would have prevented him from seeing what was happening ahead. Following Affleck through the line, Hood in the *Barfleur* opened fire at 9:25 a.m. and continued engaging for another hour or two.

By noon the majority of the French fleet was to leeward of the British with their line irreparably shattered, leaving the British to dictate the course of events. Then the wind dropped and the ships lay still on the water. The mass of the French ships were now to leeward, but three dismasted or badly damaged ships, the *Glorieux*, the *Hector*, and the *César*, remained close to the British fleet.[17] These ships would be the object of British attention when movement became possible. Rodney pulled down the signal for the line, leaving his ships to take their own initiatives.

On seeing that the signal for the line was no longer flying, Hood had his flagship towed around and set what sail he could to head towards the enemy. The French fleet was in three groups which roughly corresponded to the divisions in which they had fought the battle. The *Ville de Paris* had six ships gathered around her, including her immediate seconds the *Languedoc* and the *Couronne*. Vaudreuil's division was about four miles to the north of the *Ville de Paris* and to leeward, while Bougainville was to windward by about two miles. The battle was now decided, and it remained only for the British to gather in the fruits of their enterprise as one by one the most shattered French ships—*César, Glorieux, Hector, Ardent*—were forced to lower their colors. Finally de Grasse in the *Ville de Paris*, who had been trying unsuccessfully to call the van and rear divisions to rally round the flagship, was forced to surrender to the *Barfleur*. The resistance of the *Ville de Paris* was outstanding, and for some time she contested against as many as nine British ships. By the time de Grasse surrendered to Hood, nearly all the powder in the magazines had been used.

In the opinion of Hood, more might have been done to exploit the victory, but Rodney called off the pursuit and lay to to secure the prizes. Hood spoke of twenty prizes being taken if the pursuit had been properly pressed, telling a friend that "we should most probably have been peaceably at home . . . in the course of another year." If the initial victory had been followed up, the French would "never have risen again this War," America would have broken off the alliance with the French, and Spain would have withdrawn from the war.[18] Very high-flown sentiments indeed! As it was, enough had been done to save Jamaica and to enable the new Whig government to negotiate good peace terms. The failure of his subordinates to support de Grasse caused as big a controversy in France as the Keppel and Palliser affair had done in Britain. The victory had cost the British 243 killed and 816 wounded (including those killed and wounded on 9 April). Two British captains, Blair and Bayne, died in the battle, and Lord Robert Manners, who lost a leg, died of his wounds on the way home. The French loss was not accurately assessed, but Dr. Gilbert Blane thought that there were 300 killed and wounded on the *Ville de Paris* alone and general casualties were likely to be higher than the British, with six French captains being killed. Adding to the French loss was a number of the 5,000 troops that the ships had been carrying for the invasion of Jamaica.

Blane gave his opinion on the prizes and the French officers and men who had manned them. He declared that the ships were neither "disciplined, commodious nor even decent" and that in "the art of signals and tactics" the French officers might surpass their British counterparts but "practical seamanship is not suited to their genius." French crews he thought tended to go to pieces in close action.

On 17 April Hood was given permission to pursue and immediately made for the Mona Passage between Puerto Rico and Santo Domingo, where a small force was sighted comprising the *Jason* and *Caton* and three frigates. Both the battleships were taken and two of the frigates. These were really the last shots of the battle.

By June Rodney, though not yet advised of his recall, was feeling unwell, and he left to Hood much of the detailed and hard work of refitting the fleet at Jamaica. Hood believed that Rodney wanted to go home to recover his health and speculated on whether Pigot or Harland would come out to relieve him. The increasingly leaky state of some of the ships was becoming obvious, and Hood told his brother that the *Invincible* was being readied for a passage to England, with the *Ajax* and the *Shrewsbury* to follow.[19]

While at Jamaica, Hood heard that £1500 had been collected among the merchants of the colony to provide a banquet for the officers of the fleet. He told Alexander that the money would have been better spent in procuring necessaries for the seamen of the fleet who "stood in great need." Hood commented sourly that "the foolish vanity of one" (Rodney) and "the passion for feasting of the other" (the Jamaican commercial classes) did not allow his suggestion to be accepted.[20]

By the middle of the year the French had been able to put their fleet back together and, with a Spanish contingent of fifteen, could now amass a force of forty sail of the line. Jamaica was still under threat while this force existed, but no further actions were fought. In July 1782 Rodney had been superseded by Sir Hugh Pigot. Rodney had for long been a favorite Aunt Sally of the opposition (now the government), and Keppel as the new First Lord of the Admiralty recalled Rodney only to hear the news of the successful action of 12 April.[21] Frantic efforts were made to cancel the recall but it was too late and Pigot proceeded to his command. He was a strange choice for commander in chief. He had not been to sea for many years and had never flown his flag at sea in any capacity. He was said to have gained his position through gambling debts owed to him by various members of the government.[22]

Hood got on well with Pigot, but he recognized that he was not the man to command a major fleet and attempted to guide operations in the direction he thought they should take. In a letter to Alexander he wrote that if Keppel had been honest he would have said that Pigot had not been at sea for over twenty years, never hoisted his flag, and never commanded any squadron whatever! He would need, Hood concluded, "the cordial advice and assistance of every officer under his command."[23]

Fortunately for the British, there were no further active operations to undertake, though Hood made strenuous efforts to find and engage the enemy. On the news of the Saintes, Rodney was made an English peer and Hood an Irish peer (his wife chose the title Hood of Catherington rather than Hood of Butleigh), while Drake and Affleck became baronets. Finally Hood would seem to have achieved his full potential.

There was to be no further chance of action for Hood during the rest of the war. At the end of the 1782 campaigning season he again took the fleet to North America, and it was there that he first met Horatio Nelson. Hood was impressed with the young captain and persuaded Digby to transfer him from the North American Command to his own command. Nelson was with Hood in the dying days of the war while the British fleet under Hood was seeking a final battle to end operations on a successful note. The French and Spanish fleets had no desire to meet him, and the war eventually came to an end.

It is remarkable that, during the time since the action off the Chesapeake, Hood had met three officers who were to play prominent roles in the succeeding wars: William Cornwallis, who looked on Hood as a friend and admired him for his professional abilities; James Saumarez, who had been given command of the *Russell* by Hood in recognition of his ability, though he was never a protégé in the sense that Nelson was; and finally Horatio Nelson, who seems to have made an immediate impression on Hood and whom Hood was to bring into prominence during his time as commander in chief in the Mediterranean. These men held important commands: in the Channel Cornwallis, the man on whom the whole campaign to defeat the French invasion threat of 1803–5 pivoted; in the Mediterranean Nelson, who delivered the finishing stroke at Trafalgar; and in the Baltic Saumarez, whose diplomatic abilities during the period 1809–12 kept a critical situation in balance and left the way open for Sweden and Russia to reenter the war against Napoleon.

Hood came home with his reputation high. George III declared him to be the "most brilliant officer of the war." Compared with Graves, who had spent the time since the Chesapeake as second in command at Jamaica, he was a naval hero. He had the admiration of the king and the friendship of the prime minister. His opinions mattered, and just as his comments on Rodney had become known, so had his comments on Graves and the action of 5 September. Both of his fellow admirals lost reputation because of it.

Hood spent the ten years between the wars in various ways. At the request of Pitt he became a Member of Parliament for Westminster, in a contest that was one of the most close-fought, and hence tumultuous, of the century. He attended Parliament but was never a good speaker and confined himself mainly to service matters. As an Irish peer, he was able to sit in the House of Commons.

The involvement in politics began to rapidly exhaust his monetary resources. He pressed the government for appointment as major general of marines, but as with his appeals to Lord Sandwich while he was commissioner at Portsmouth, he was unsuccessful.

He was commander in chief at Portsmouth in the period 1786–88, and when Lord Howe resigned as First Lord of the Admiralty in June 1788, Hood was considered as a successor. If the decision had been left to Pitt alone, he would probably have got the post, but Pitt consulted his colleagues, and Lord Grenville was of the opinion that Hood was not popular in the Commons and had been indiscreet in his remarks there, which would leave him open to attack by the opposition. Pitt eventually appointed his brother Lord Chatham,[24] and Hood was made a member of the Board of Admiralty, a post he held until his dismissal from service in 1795.

The possibility of an active command appeared in 1787 when he was intended as commander in the West Indies should a crisis lead to war with France, as appeared likely. However, all was settled amicably and his services were not called upon. He also appeared as commander of the projected Baltic Fleet during a crisis with Russia in 1791, but again the affair did not degenerate into war and Hood had to wait until 1793 when war with Revolutionary France gave him his chance at last to command in chief. He went to the Mediterranean, taking Nelson with him in the *Agamemnon*.

The command that Hood now held was the last and by far the most difficult of his career. It not only entailed a watch on the French at Toulon—though they were considered unlikely to come out—but also extensive diplomatic responsibilities, including most importantly the support of Britain's main allies in the area, Spain and Austria. Spain had been asked to put its fleet under the command of Hood but had refused.[25] The arrival of the British fleet in the Mediterranean was delayed slightly by manning problems, and potential allies delayed their formal alliance until British policy was clear. In this period there was considerable French activity at Toulon, with Admiral Trogoff being pressed to attack the Spanish fleet before the British arrived.[26] Trogoff declined, as he was unsure of the quality of his crews.

With the arrival of the British fleet under Hood, the diplomatic situation

improved. Hood arrived off Toulon on 16 July, having been delayed by contrary winds, and was almost immediately presented with a stroke of good
fortune when he was approached by representatives from Marseilles. The
Marseillais had sought an alliance with Toulon, but the authorities there
hesitated, and therefore the Marseillais approached Hood direct. They
were ostensibly seeking to get Hood to authorize free passage of eight grain
ships to feed the city, whose supplies from the interior had been cut off by
the Revolutionary Armies. In reality they wished to negotiate terms with
Hood. They declared themselves in favor of the restoration of the monarchy—which was not a British war aim—and Hood on his own responsibility drafted a proclamation urging this action and promising an alliance for
their protection. In the course of these negotiations, however, the resistance
of Marseilles collapsed.[27]

While the abortive Marseilles negotiations were going on, delegates from
Toulon arrived seeking British protection from the Revolutionary Armies
now approaching the area. The envoys told Hood that they would support
a Bourbon restoration on the lines of the constitution agreed in the Estates
General discussions of 1789.

An offer for the Allied forces to occupy Toulon was not something the
British Government had thought about when writing the instructions to
guide Hood's actions during his command. Protection of trade was a high
priority, as was cooperation with the Allies and protection of their coasts.
The possibility that Hood might have to occupy Toulon was a burden the
government had not catered for, and it would leave them scrambling to
include it in their plans.[28]

Before matters could proceed further, Marseilles was occupied by the
Revolutionary forces under General Carteaux. The Jacobins, pursuing their
policy of revenge on monarchist and other elements, carried out a mass
killing of the dissidents. This encouraged the Toulon authorities to urgently
press Hood for terms of the handover, and he accepted their offer of an alliance to defend the port against the advancing Republicans. It was definitely
not a surrender, so Hood was constrained as to what he could do about
the French fleet.[29] He issued a declaration that the Allies were fighting for
a restoration of the monarchy on the lines proposed and that the fleet in
Toulon and the forts protecting the port would be handed back at the end
of the war. There were some problems with this. The declaration made by
Hood was not in line with British war aims, but, as he said to the government in his dispatch, though he might have exceeded his authority in the
matter and his declaration might not be totally correct, he felt that he could

not lose time in consulting with the government where a decision of such critical strategic and political importance was presented to him.

The divided loyalties of the French ships then in the harbor reflected the divided opinion of the town itself as to aligning itself with the Allies. There were seventeen sail of the line in the outer road of the port. Eleven were known to be for the Republic, and the position of the rest was on a knife edge. The royalist-leaning commander, Admiral Trogoff, was deposed by the crews and replaced by Rear Admiral Saint-Julien. At one time it looked as if there might be a fight between the British and French fleets, but eventually discussions were held and the various sides agreed that the French ships would retire into the inner harbor and crewmen from the west of France would be given safe passage home. With the situation stabilized, Hood and the British fleet were able to enter the port and the Spanish fleet was soon seen in the offing. The first Allied troops landed early in the morning of 28 August 1793.[30]

The possibilities of exploiting the occupation of Toulon were infinite, and some historians believe that it might very well have led to the defeat of the Jacobin regime.[31] The political problems posed by the declaration could be overcome, but what could not be overcome was the shortage of troops to occupy the base and hold it against the Jacobin armies. A successful defense would require a force of 50,000 men, but at no time did the defenders—a mixed force of British, Spanish, Neapolitans, and other allies—exceed 17,000 men, while a French force of 34,000 opposed them.

As far as British troops were concerned, none were available in the quantities needed. The Duke of York had taken an army to campaign with the Allies in the Netherlands, and many more regiments had been sent to the West Indies to undertake a colonial campaign, the traditional way of conducting a war with France. By capturing the French sugar islands, Pitt thought to inflict a severe financial blow on the Jacobin regime. It was a campaign based on the successes of his father and the successes of previous wars, but compared with the possible consequences of a successful occupation of Toulon, the troops were being wasted in sideshows.

While it lasted, the operation at Toulon occupied a lot of Hood's attention, though not to the exclusion of naval affairs. He was active in pursuing the diplomatic and naval objectives of his command. He managed to get Genoa closed to French trade, but the French retaliated with pressure of their own on Genoa, which resulted in the port being closed to all trade. Thereby he lost a useful port for providing men and supplies to Toulon.

Hood also tried to play agent provocateur. In a plan to get the French to violate the neutrality of the North African ports, he sent a couple of frigates there in anticipation that the French would attack them. Unfortunately, for security reasons he had not confided in the senior officer of the squadron, and that officer successfully avoided contact with the superior French forces, thereby negating his admiral's plan. If the French had attacked the squadron, it would have given Hood the excuse he needed to sweep all French shipping out of neutral ports.

Relations with Spain were difficult. The Spanish were wary of the establishment of any British force in the Mediterranean and were unwilling, when the time for final evacuation came, to destroy the French fleet lying in Toulon for what they saw as the benefit only of Britain. Hood was overoptimistic in believing that he would be able to hold the port with the troops that he had and the small numbers that he could beg from the other Allies in the area. Napoleon had been confident all along of defeating the occupying forces and had submitted a plan to the authorities for the assault. The final French assault, in which Napoleon Bonaparte commanded the artillery, was made early in the morning of 17 December 1793. Against the desires of Hood, the evacuation was decided on that afternoon, of the Allied forces and those civilians who wished to go. The destruction of the French fleet of thirty of the line was a hasty, botched affair entrusted by Hood to Sir Sidney Smith,[32] who had volunteered for the task despite having no formal position in the fleet. Smith's knighthood was a Swedish title reflecting the time he had spent in the service of Sweden after the end of the American War, where he had served with Rodney. More recently he had been serving with the Turkish navy, but he took immediate steps to return when he heard of the outbreak of war between Britain and France. Smith had bought a small vessel and manned it with stranded British sailors at Smyrna. He then left in search of the British fleet and found it at Toulon.[33]

Though valiant efforts were made, the Spanish were less than wholehearted in their cooperation. Three sail of the line were carried away, and one 74-gun ship had been removed earlier by the Allies. A further fourteen ships, including nine battleships, were burnt and some of the port facilities destroyed. The loss to French naval power was significant and exceeded that inflicted by Howe at the Glorious First of June six months later. However, there was a feeling in the fleet that more could have been done, and a lot of the blame was placed on the shoulders of Sir Sidney Smith. In a private letter to Smith, Hood told him: "You *must* burn every French ship you possibly can."

The occupation of Toulon has been called by Bernard Ireland "the last opportunity to stop the French Revolution." Whether this was so or not is difficult to say. The main area of operations against the Revolutionary Armies was in northern Europe, and Toulon remained somewhat of a sideline. It called for an officer of great vision to seize the moment and the opportunity that was offered. Hood was that man. He did not hesitate to accept the responsibility of negotiating the terms of the occupation, although he must have realized that the declaration for restoring the French monarchy was not a British war aim. Hood could not neglect the chance to occupy what Nelson called "the strongest place in Europe" because of the chances it offered to the Allied war effort. In view of the threat the town faced, it required far more troops than Hood was able to scramble together to garrison and defend it.

The reasons for the offer of Toulon to Hood and the British fleet were mixed. There was never a majority royalist movement that wanted to restore the old monarchy. The authorities in the city could see that the forces of the Revolution were slowly advancing. They seized on British and Spanish protection as a last chance to save themselves, but the gesture was never supported by a large movement of people coming forward to support the announced royalist cause.

Hood's conduct during the occupation displayed some of his best and some of his worst characteristics. His determined optimism at all times was one of the main bulwarks behind the defense of the port against the approaching Jacobin armies. He maintained this spirit even when events did not really support it. It led him to ignore the advice of the British and Spanish governments to prepare for evacuation and the removal of the French fleet in case the worst should happen and the Republican forces should breach the defenses of the port. Consequently, when this did happen, the whole operation had to be extemporized and not enough could be done to remove the French ships. One officer who was extremely critical of the management of the evacuation was Cuthbert Collingwood. Not an admirer of Hood, he spoke of "gross mismanagement" and lack of preparations to destroy the French ships, which he said should have been loaded with ballast and holes made to ready them for sinking. He had no words of praise for Sir Sidney Smith, "as bad hands as could be found."

On the negative side, the occupation brought to light once again his combativeness in his dealings with military officers. His thrusting and optimistic nature clashed with their more realistic view of the chances of holding the port with the forces available. He was once again scathing in his denunciations of the military officers with whom he came in contact. This feud was carried on with vengeance during the operations in Corsica, and Nelson seems to have adopted the same attitude to army officers as his patron. Against this must be set the good relations that Hood generally maintained with the Spanish admiral Lángara and especially his immediate subordinate Gravina. He despised the Neapolitan commander as "the proudest, most empty and self sufficient man I ever had anything to do with . . . who is fond of having as many Nepolitan Flags daily to look at as he can."[34]

With the loss of Toulon, Hood needed another base in the Mediterranean, and he decided that Corsica fitted the purpose. Here he was able to work with the Corsican independence movement in negotiations to place the island under British suzerainty. The operations necessary to conquer the island proceeded with a good deal of acrimony between Hood and the military commander, General Sir David Dundas. In the American War, Hood seems to have been on reasonable terms with both Vaughan and Christie, but in the Mediterranean he displayed a strong antiarmy bias for what he deemed their lack of thrust and initiative. Sir John Moore, who was as difficult and as prickly a character as Hood himself, felt that Hood was impossible to work with.

It was while operations were continuing on Corsica that the French made a sortie from Toulon with a force of seven of the line. Hood pursued them as soon as he heard they were at sea. The French were sighted and pursued on 10 June, but they ran for the shelter of Gourjean Bay. With thirteen of the line, Hood was well placed to completely destroy the French squadron, but the wind failed at the critical moment. Hood had planned to attack five of the French ships with ten of his own, mooring two per objective. Two more British ships were to attract the attention of the two French batteries at the mouth of the bay, while a further 74-gun ship and the frigates were to attack the five French frigates. Hood reckoned that the remaining two French ships of the line would also surrender if the main attack was a success. All seemed set for the decisive battle that Hood still needed to seal his reputation, but the British were becalmed for two days, in which time the French commander had mounted more guns on shore and manned gunboats to deter fireship attack. Reluctantly Hood came to the opinion that the French were now too strongly posted and withdrew. Fireships had been prepared, but even this form of attack was thwarted by the strong French defenses.

As it turned out, this was the last chance Hood would have to command in a fleet action. Five months later he took home a portion of the fleet for repair and refit. He was also feeling some effect on his health, and it has been said that he did not wish to return to his command. In the spring of

1795, however, he was ready to sail again. During his period at home he had been promoted to Admiral of the Blue and his wife made Baroness Hood of Catherington. Still, he was unhappy with the force he was to take back. The navy was hard pressed to find ships enough to meet its worldwide commitments, and Hood felt that his force was insufficient to carry out the task he had been given. He wrote the prime minister a strong letter of protest, which the new First Lord of the Admiralty, Lord Spencer,[35] felt was unacceptable conduct. With the approval of the king, he was ordered to haul down his flag and was dismissed from his command.

If Lord Chatham had still been First Lord, the situation might have been handled differently, but Lord Spencer was not a personal friend and took a strong line. There is some reason to believe that Spencer did not relish Hood's manner of plain speaking and, being aware of the difficulties Hood had had with the army commanders in the Mediterranean, he seized the opportunity to dismiss an admiral who was unpopular with the army and was obviously not likely to alter his manner. Hood's credit with the king had also decreased since a contretemps with the Duke of Clarence over an officer Hood had appointed to be his "minder," so any support from that quarter was less likely. Hood made an effort to appeal to Pitt and Dundas for support, but Spencer held all the cards and Hood's career was over.

In 1796 his old friend Sir Hugh Palliser died and Hood was appointed in his place as governor of Greenwich Hospital. He had applied for the post based on past promises and his need to achieve the financial means to live in relative comfort and to provide for his wife should he predecease her. As it happened, his wife died in 1806, and the last years of his life saw his family and friends gradually dropping away. His brother Alexander died in 1814 and his cousin and namesake died as commander in chief in the East Indies in the same year. Spending less time at Greenwich and more at Bath, he died there in Queens Square in January 1816, the last surviving flag officer of the action off the Chesapeake, the action in which his action, or inaction, had done so much damage to the British cause.

APPENDIX 1

The British Fleet Commanded by Thomas Graves at the Battle of the Chesapeake, 5 September 1781

Alfred	74 guns	William Bayne
Belliqueux	64 guns	James Brine
Invincible	74 guns	Charles Saxton
Barfleur	98 guns	Rear Admiral Sir Samuel Hood (flag), Alexander Hood
Monarch	74 guns	Francis Reynolds
Centaur	74 guns	John Inglefield
America	64 guns	Samuel Thompson
Resolution	74 guns	Lord Robert Manners
Bedford	74 guns	Thomas Graves
London	98 guns	Rear Admiral Thomas Graves (flag), David Graves
Royal Oak	74 guns	John Ardesoif
Montagu	74 guns	George Bowen
Europe	64 guns	Smith Child
Terrible	74 guns	Hon. William Finch
Ajax	74 guns	William Charrington
Princessa	70 guns	Rear Admiral Sir Francis Drake (flag), Charles Knatchbull
Alcide	74 guns	Charles Thompson
Intrepid	64 guns	Anthony Molloy
Shrewsbury	74 guns	Mark Robinson
Adamant	50 guns	Gideon Johnstone
Santa Margarita	36 guns	Elliott Salter
Richmond	32 guns	Charles Hudson
Solebay	28 guns	Charles Everitt
Nymphe	36 guns	Hon. Charles Fitzgerald
Fortunée	40 guns	Hugh Christian
Salamander	fireship	Edward Bowater

APPENDIX 2

The French Fleet Commanded by Vice Admiral François-Joseph Comte de Grasse at the Battle of the Chesapeake, 5 September 1781

Pluton	74 guns	d'Albert de Rions
Marseillais	74 guns	de Castellane de Majastre
Bourgogne	74 guns	de Charitte
Réfléchi	74 guns	de Boades
Auguste	80 guns	de Bougainville (flag), de Castellan
Diadème	74 guns	de Monteclerc
Saint-Esprit	80 guns	de Chabert
Caton	74 guns	de Framond
César	74 guns	Coriolis d'Espinouse
Destin	74 guns	Dumaitz de Goimpy
Ville de Paris	104 guns	comte de Grasse (flag), de Vaugirault de Saint-Cézaire
Victoire	74 guns	d'Albert Saint-Hippolyte
Sceptre	80 guns	de Vaudreuil
Northumberland	74 guns	de Briqueville
Palmier	74 guns	baron d'Arros d'Argelos
Solitaire	64 guns	de Cicé Champion
Citoyen	74 guns	comte d'Ethy
Scipion	74 guns	de Clavel
Magnanime	74 guns	Le Bègue
Hercule	74 guns	Turpin de Breuille
Languedoc	80 guns	de Monteil (flag) Duplessis Parscau
Zélé	74 guns	de Gras-Préville
Hector	74 guns	Renaud d'Aleins
Souverain	74 guns	de Glandèves

The French North American Squadron under the Command of the Comte de Barras

Neptune	74 guns	de Medine
Duc de Bourgogne	80 guns	comte de Barras (flag)
		baron de Durfort
Conquérant	74 guns	de La Grandière
Provence	64 guns	Lombard
Ardent	64 guns	Bernard de Marigny
Jason	64 guns	Chadeau de la Clocheterie
Eveillé	64 guns	Le Gardeur de Tilly
Romulus	44 guns	de Villebrune

Notes

Where original manuscript material has been used, the following abbreviations indicate the source:

Add. MSS	Additional Manuscripts (BL)
ADM	Admiralty Records (NA, NMM)
BL	British Library, St. Pancras
GRE	Papers of Sir George Grey (NMM)
HOO	Papers of the Hood Family (NMM)
MKH	Papers of the Hood Family, Mackinnon Donation (NMM)
NA	National Archives, Kew
NMM	National Maritime Museum, Greenwich
PRO	Public Record Office (now National Archives)
PRO 30/8	Papers of William Pitt, 1st Earl of Chatham (NA)
PRO 30/20	Papers of George Brydges Rodney, 1st Baron Rodney (NA)
SAN	Papers of John Montagu, 4th Earl of Sandwich (NMM)

Note: The Sandwich Papers now in the National Maritime Museum were, when consulted, still held by the Montagu family, and access was by courtesy of the late Victor Montagu. Similarly, the Thomas Smith Papers were seen at Hagley Hall but are now split between United States collections, the Worcester Record Office, and the surviving family's collection.

Introduction

1. Thomas Graves (1725–1802): lieutenant 1743; commander 1754; captain 1755; rear admiral 1779; vice admiral 1787; admiral 1794; wounded while serving under Howe at the Glorious First of June; not employed again on account of age and injuries; Irish peer 1794.

2. Francis Samuel Drake (1729–1789): lieutenant 1749; commander 1756; captain 1756; rear admiral 1780; Admiralty commissioner 1789; MP for Plymouth 1789.

3. François-Joseph-Paul, comte de Grasse (1722–1788): entered the French navy in 1738; served in the Seven Years' War under Galissonière and d'Aché; was with de Guichen's fleet in 1780; was imprisoned following defeat at the battle of the Saintes but released on parole; carried British peace proposals to Paris; demanded inquiry into actions of subordinates at the Saintes, not upheld; retired to his estates until his death.

4. George Washington (1732–1799):After militia service in the Seven Years' War, entered politics until called on to lead the Continental Army in 1775; elected president of the new United States, served two terms from 1789 before retiring in 1797.

5. George Brydges Rodney (1719–1792): lieutenant 1740; captain 1742; rear admiral 1759; vice admiral 1762; admiral 1778; MP for Saltash 1751–54, for Okehampton 1759–61, for Penryn 1761–1768, for Northampton 1768–1774, and for Westminster 1780–82; baronet 1764, English peer 1782.

6. Richard Howe (1726–1799): lieutenant 1745; captain 1746; Admiralty commissioner 1763–65; rear admiral 1770; vice admiral 1776; admiral 1782; First Lord of the Admiralty 1783–87; Admiral of the Fleet 1796; MP for Dartmouth 1757–82; Irish peer by inheritance 1758; English peer 1782.

7. Jean-Baptiste-Charles, comte d'Estaing (1729–1796): served in the Army in India in the Seven Years War, was captured at the siege of Madras and again while returning to France in 1760, then settled into a naval career; vice admiral 1777; commander of North American Fleet 1778 but failed to defeat Howe or take New York; fought Byron at Grenada and inflicted serious damage; took the islands of St. Vincent and Grenada but failed to retake St. Lucia from Barrington; returned to France 1780; out of favor at court until 1783; commander of Franco-Spanish fleet at Cardiz, but peace treaty precluded further operations; commandant of the National Guard at Versailles 1789; spoke in favor of the king and queen; after execution of Marie Antoinette was executed as a "reactionary" on 28 April 1794.

8. Nelson in letter to Rev. Dixon Hoste, 22 June 1795.

9. Morriss, *Blockade of Brest*, 62.

10. Charles Hardy (1714–1780): lieutenant 1737; commander 1741; captain 1741; rear admiral 1756; vice admiral 1759; admiral 1770; MP for Rochester 1764–68, for Plymouth 1771–80; knighted 1755.

11. Francis Geary (1709–1796): lieutenant 1734; captain 1742; rear admiral 1759; vice admiral 1762; admiral 1775, Baronet 1782.

12. Hon. John Byron (1723–1786): lieutenant 1746; commander 1746; captain 1746; rear admiral 1775; vice admiral 1778.

13. Hannay, *Letters of Sir Samuel Hood*.

14. PRO 30/20/26 Keppel to Rodney 10 November 1780.

15. George Anson (1697–1762): lieutenant 1716; commander 1722; captain 1724; rear admiral 1744; Admiralty commissioner 1744–51; vice admiral 1746; admiral 1748; First Lord of the Admiralty 1751–56, 1757–62; Admiral of the Fleet 1761; MP for Hedon 1744–47; peer 1747.

16. For the Nelson quote, see Dorothy Hood 154. Nelson to Rev. D. Hosté, 22 June 1795. Tunstall, *Naval Warfare in the Age of Sail*, 197.

17. Edward Hawke (1705–1781): lieutenant 1729; commander 1733; captain 1734; rear admiral 1747; vice admiral 1748; admiral 1757; First Lord of the Admiralty 1766–71; MP for Portsmouth 1747–76; peer 1776.

Chapter 1. Hood's Early Career

1. Dorset Record Office parish registers for South Perrott and Mosterton. Register for Butleigh by permission of the rector, Rev. A. F. Synge.

2. Thomas Smith (d. 1762): lieutenant 1727; dismissed 1729; captain 1730; rear admiral 1747; vice admiral 1748; admiral 1757.

3. Duffy, "Samuel Hood," 249. The late Oliver Warner once told the author that an officer "posting" from Plymouth would not go near Butleigh. However, if Smith had been going from Plymouth to his home at Hagley he would likely have gone through or near the village.

4. Hood, *The Admirals Hood*, for the Hood family history and Admiral Smith connection.

5. Rodger, *The Wooden World*, 252–73.

6. Thomas Grenville (1719–1747): lieutenant 1740; captain 1742; MP for Bridport 1746–47.

7. Charles Watson (1714–1757): lieutenant 1734; captain 1738; rear admiral 1748; vice admiral 1756.

8. Duffy, "Samuel Hood," 250–51.

9. Hon. Augustus Keppel (1725–1786): lieutenant 1744; commander 1744; captain 1744; rear admiral 1762; Admiralty commissioner 1765–66; vice admiral 1770; admiral 1778; First Lord of the Admiralty 1782–83; MP for Chichester 1755–61, for New Windsor 1761–80, for Surrey 1780–82; peer 1782.

10. Hon. Samuel Barrington (1729–1800): lieutenant 1745; commander 1746; captain 1747; rear admiral 1778; vice admiral 1779; admiral 1787.

11. Hugh Palliser (1722–1796): lieutenant 1741; commander 1747; captain 1746; comptroller of the navy 1770–75; rear admiral 1775; Admiralty commissioner 1775–79; vice admiral 1778; admiral 1787; MP for Scarborough 1774–79, for Huntingdon 1780–84; governor of Greenwich 1780–96; baronet 1773.

12. Marriot Arbuthnot (1711–1794): lieutenant 1739; commander 1746; captain 1747; commissioner at Halifax 1775–78; rear admiral 1778; vice admiral 1787; admiral 1793.

13. Hon. Edward Boscawen (1711–1761): lieutenant 1732; commander 1737; captain 1742; rear admiral 1747; Admiralty commissioner 1751–61; vice admiral 1755; admiral 1758; MP for Truro 1742–61.

14. Charles Holmes (1711–1761): lieutenant 1734; captain 1742; rear admiral 1758; MP for Newport 1758–1761.

15. Baugh, "Sir Samuel Hood," 292–93; Duffy, "Samuel Hood," 251; *Naval Chronicle* 2:4.

Chapter 2. The Frigate Captain

1. Thomas Saumarez (1713–1766): lieutenant 1744; commander 1747; captain 1748.

2. Charles Saunders (1715–1775): lieutenant 1734; captain 1741; treasurer of Greenwich Hospital 1754–56; comptroller of the navy 1755–56; rear admiral 1756; vice admiral 1759; First Lord of the Admiralty 1765–66; admiral 1770; MP for Plymouth 1750–54, for Hedon 1754–75.

3. PRO ADM 2/525.

4. Hyde Parker (1714–1783): lieutenant 1745; commander 1747; captain 1748; rear admiral 1778; vice admiral 1780; baronet by inheritance 1782; drowned en route to India.

5. George Darby (ca. 1720–1790): lieutenant 1742; captain 1747; rear admiral 1748; vice admiral 1779; Admiralty commissioner 1780–82; MP for Plymouth 1780–84.

6. NMM MKH/C/1/C, miscellaneous correspondence.

7. Spinney, *Rodney*, 151–60.

8. John Stuart, 3rd Earl of Bute (1713–1792): Groom of the Stole to George III when Prince of Wales; later helped maneuver Pitt out of government over war with Spain; First Lord of the Treasury 1762–63; remained a confidant of the king but, having lost influence after George III married in 1761, withdrew from political life; prominent botanist and patron of the arts.

9. Duc de Choiseul (1719–1785): after military and diplomatic careers, served variously as minister for foreign affairs, war, and the marine; dismissed and exiled from court in 1770; a driving force behind the move to revenge the humiliating peace inflicted on France in 1763.

Chapter 3. The Commodore

1. Duffy, "Samuel Hood," 253.
2. *Oxford Dictionary of National Biography*, s.v. Bernard, Francis.
3. NMM ADM/L/R199, *Romney* log.
4. Alexander Hood (1758–1798): lieutenant 1777; commander 1781; captain 1781.
5. John Linzee (1743–1798): lieutenant 1761; commander 1771; captain 1777; resigned 1791.
6. Robert Linzee (d. 1804): lieutenant 1761; commander 1768; captain 1770; rear admiral 1794; vice admiral 1795; admiral 1801.
7. NMM ADM/L/R199, *Romney* log.
8. Gwyn, "Royal Navy in North America," 142.
9. PRO ADM 1/483, Hood to Stephens, 28 July 1767.
10. PRO 30/8/44, Hood to Lady Chatham, 20 September 1767.
11. PRO ADM 1/483, Hood to Stephens, 20 December 1767.
12. PRO ADM 1/483, Hood to Stephens, 28 July 1767.
13. Francis Bernard (1712–1779): practicing lawyer 1737–58; governor of New Jersey (1768–70) and Massachusetts (1760–69); baronet 1769. Initially successful and popular, he antagonised the influential Otis family by not appointing James Otis as lieutenant governor. Subsequently relations with the colonists deteriorated, and after publication of some of his correspondence to the government he was recalled.
14. PRO ADM 1/483, Hood to Stephens, 12 February 1768.
15. Thomas Gage (1720–1787): entered army 1741; fought at Fontenoy and Culloden; served under Braddock, including unsuccessful assault on Ticonderoga; Commander-in-Chief in North America 1763–73; martial law governor of Massachusetts 1774–75; commanded army at Bunker Hill, then returned to Britain.
16. Benjamin Hallowell, later surnamed Carew (1760–1834): lieutenant 1783; commander 1790; captain 1793; rear admiral 1811; vice admiral 1819; admiral 1830.
17. PRO ADM 1/483, enclosure in Hood to Stephens, 14 June 1768.
18. Hood to Grenville 15 October 1768. See Stout "The Royal Navy in North America" 1760–1775.
19. PRO ADM 1/483, Hood to Stephens, 14 June 1768.
20. The Boston Assembly was an elected body, as opposed to the Council, which was a nominated body. Both were concerned with running the town.
21. Henry Panton (d. 1769): lieutenant 1759.

22. John Adams (1735–1826): during Revolutionary War, American representative in France and the Netherlands; helped negotiate 1783 peace; U.S. vice president 1789–97, president 1797–1801.

23. James Bowdoin (1726–1790): of Huguenot stock; elected to Colonial Assembly 1753; delegate to Continental Congress 1774 but too ill to attend; president of Massachusetts Convention 1779; ardent naturalist who had papers read to Royal Society in London; largely responsible for creation of American Academy of Arts & Sciences. See Stout for relations between Hood and Bowdoin.

24. James Gambier (d. 1789): lieutenant 1744; commander 1746; captain 1747; commissioner of the Victualling Board 1773; commissioner at Portsmouth 1773–78; rear admiral 1778; vice admiral 1780.

Chapter 4. The Commissioner

1. The *Royal William* was the oldest ship in the navy, having been built as the *Prince* in 1670 as a 100-gun first rate under the auspices of Samuel Pepys. Renamed in 1692, she was not broken up until 1813.

2. PRO 30/8/41, Molly Hood to Lady Chatham, 25 December 1771.

3. PRO 30/8/41, Hood to Lady Chatham, 10 July 1776.

4. PRO 30/8/44, Hood to Lady Chatham, 12 February 1778.

5. Syrett, "Home Waters or America?" 368.

6. Ibid., 372.

7. Ibid., 365.

8. Fortescue, *Correspondence of King George*, George III to Lord North, 13 May 1778.

9. Rodger, *Command of the Ocean*, 341–42.

10. Hon. Robert Digby (1732–1815): lieutenant 1752; captain 1755; rear admiral 1779; vice admiral 1787; admiral 1794; MP for Wells 1757–61.

11. Rodger, *Command of the Ocean*, 337.

12. Samuel Hood (1762–1814): lieutenant 1780; commander 1782; captain 1788; rear admiral 1807; vice admiral 1811; baronet 1809.

13. Rodger, *Command of the Ocean*, 340–41.

14. Ibid., 341.

15. BL Add. MSS 35193, Samuel Hood to Alexander Hood, 3 July 1779.

16. Rodger, *Command of the Ocean*, 341.

17. BL Add. MSS 35193, Samuel Hood to Alexander Hood, ? March 1780.

18. NMM SAN, Hood to Sandwich, 23 March 1780.

19. NMM SAN, Sandwich to Hood, 24 March 1780.

20. NMM SAN, Hood to Sandwich, 25 March 1780.

21. NMM SAN, Hood to Sandwich, 26 March 1780.

22. Ibid.

23. BL Add. MSS 35193, Samuel Hood to Alexander Hood, 12 April 1780.

24. NMM SAN, Sandwich to Rodney, 14 July 1780.

25. Baugh, "Sir Samuel Hood."

26. NMM SAN, Sandwich to Hood, 15 September 1780.

27. NMM SAN, Hood to Sandwich, 16 September 1780.

28. NMM SAN, Hood to Sandwich, 18 September 1780.

29. NMM SAN, Hood to Sandwich, 20 September 1780.

30. PRO 30/20/26, Sandwich to Rodney, 25 September 1780.

31. PRO 30/20/26, Rodney to Sandwich, 24 December 1780.

32. Rodney to Hood, 4 January 1781, quoted in Spinney, *Rodney*, 359.

33. Quoted by Spinney, 359.

34. PRO 30/20/26, Keppel to Rodney, 10 November 1780.

35. PRO 30/8/44, Hood to Lady Chatham, 21 October 1780.

36. PRO 30/29/26, Rodney to Stephens, 10 December 1780.

Chapter 5. The Other Side of the Channel

1. Charles-François, comte de Broglie (1719–1781): after an army career, served as a member of the Secret de Roi, the private diplomatic service of Louis XV.

2. Patterson, *The Other Armada*, 7.

3. Jean-Frédéric, comte de Maurepas (1701–1781): Secretary of the Household to Louis XV; minister of the marine, called upon to meet the challenge of a British navy revitalized and expanding under Anson;. much involved in French affairs in Canada and North America; banished from court after attacking madame de Pompadour; recalled by Louis XVI, to whom he remained a councillor until his death.

4. Anne-Robert-Jacques Turgot (1727–1781): leading economist of eighteenth-century France; friend in Paris in the 1760s of Adam Smith, whose *Wealth of Nations* he greatly influenced; left a Church career for government service; believed that civilization moved in cycles, in which entrepeneurs were a force for good; accurately forecast eventual break of American colonies from the British Crown.

5. Charles Gravier, comte de Vergennes (1717–1787): diplomat, longtime ambassador to the Ottoman Empire, recalled in 1768 because Choiseul did not believe him clever enough to provoke war between Russia and the Ottomans; after the fall of Choiseul, promoted French interests in Sweden and ensured the succession of Gustave III; as foreign minister to Louis XVI, maintained friendly relations with the Hapsburg monarchy but opposed Britain to gain revenge for humiliation in the Seven Years' War; aided independence of the American colonies from Britain and took part in peace talks in 1783; underestimated France's postwar financial straits and had Necker removed as finance minister, believing him a dangerous influence.

6. Antoine de Sartine (1729–1801): minister of the marine from 1774; ably built up the French navy despite severe financial constraints but failed to achieve concomitant administrative reforms; also failed (unlike his contemporary Lord Sandwich) to use naval power well, producing generally negative results; dismissed in 1781 after a financial scandal; succeeded by the marquis de Castries.

7. Louis Guillouet, comte d'Orvilliers (1708–1792): transferred from army to navy 1728; commanded a ship against Byng off Minorca 1756; vice admiral 1764; commanded the French fleet against Keppel in the Channel in 1778; commanded the combined Franco-Spanish force in the Channel in 1779, when sickness among the crews contributed to failure; resigned command and retired from public life.

Chapter 6. The Flag Officer

1. Hon. John Vaughan (1738–1795): served in Germany in Seven Years' War; present at capture of Martinique; commander in chief of Leeward Islands 1779–95; died at Martinique.

2. Tunstall, *Naval Warfare in the Age of Sail*, 157.

3. Tilley, *Navy and the American Revolution*, 237–38.

4. Ibid., 238.

5. Walter Young (d. 1781): lieutenant 1765; commander 1779; captain 1779.

6. PRO 30/20, Rodney to Hood, 15 March 1781.

7. Francis Reynolds, later surnamed Reynolds-Moreton (1739–1808): lieutenant 1758; commander 1760; captain 1762; superannuated captain 1785; MP for Lancaster 1784–85; peer (Lord Ducie) by inheritance 1785.

8. NMM HOO/101, Hood to Henry Shales, 12 February 1781.

9. NMM HOO/1, Rodney to Hood, 25 February 1781.

10. NMM HOO/11, Hood to Rodney, 10 March 1781.

11. NMM HOO/11, Rodney to Hood, 15 March 1781.

12. Mahan, *Types of Naval Officers*, 225.

13. Peter Parker (1721–1811): lieutenant 1743; captain 1747; rear admiral 1777; vice admiral 1779; admiral 1787; Admiral of the Fleet 1799; MP for Seaford 1784–86, for Maldon 1787–90; baronet 1783. See Mahan "Types of Naval Officers" 225.

14. PRO ADM 1/314, Rodney to Stephens, 26 March 1781.

15. NMM HOO/5, Rodney to Hood, 15 March 1781.

16. PRO ADM 1/311, Rodney to Stephens, 17 March 1781.

17. NMM HOO/5, Hood to Rodney, 23 April 1781.

18. PRO ADM 50/122, entry for 13 February 1781.

19. Clowes, *The Royal Navy*, 3:487. Quoting Chevalier and Beatson.

20. NMM HOO/1, enclosure, Parker to Sandwich, undated.

21. NMM HOO/101, Hood to Shales, 4 May 1781.

22. Tunstall, *Naval Warfare in the Age of Sail*, 172.

23. NMM HOO/1, Hood to Middleton, 4 May 1781.

24. NMM HOO/1, Hood Papers; PRO 30/20/9, Rodney to Hood, March 15, 1781; Clowes, *Royal Navy*, vol. 3, 483.

25. NMM SAN, undated enclosure.

26. Tilley, *Navy and the American Revolution*, 241.

27. NMM HOO/101, Hood to Shales, 3 June 1781.

28. Ibid.

29. PRO ADM 1/313, Rodney to Stephens, 9 June 1781.

30. BL Add. MSS 35193, Samuel Hood to Alexander Hood, 9 June 1781.

31. NMM MKH/B/3, Hood to Jackson, 24 June 1781.

32. Edward Tyrrell Smith (d. 1824): lieutenant 1778; captain 1781; rear admiral 1801; vice admiral 1805; admiral 1812.

33. Probably John Davall Burr (ca. 1746–1784): lieutenant 1775.

34. Hon. Alexander Cochrane (1758–1832): lieutenant 1778; commander 1780; cap-

tain 1782; rear admiral 1804; vice admiral 1809; admiral 1819; MP for Stirling Burghs 1800–1802.

35. Hood, *The Admirals Hood*, 64.

36. BL Add. MSS 35193, Samuel Hood to Alexander Hood, 22 June 1781.

Chapter 7. The Chesapeake: The Forces Gather

1. Larrabee, *Decision at the Chesapeake*, 150.

2. Jean-Baptiste-Donatien de Vimeur, comte de Rochambeau (1725–1807): served in French army in War of the Austrian Succession and Seven Years' War; fled France during Revolutionary period but returned under Napoleon.

3. Charles, Lord Cornwallis (1738–1805): entered army in 1756; at Minden as aide-de-camp to the Marquess of Granby; served in America from 1776, operating in the Carolinas and then Virginia; besieged at Yorktown and forced to surrender; in India 1786–94, conducted operations against Tippoo Sultan; sent to pacify Ireland in 1798, resigned in 1801 after failing to secure Catholic Emancipation; led British negotiating team for Treaty of Amiens; died at commencement of second term in India.

4. Marie-Joseph Gilbert du Motier, marquis de Lafayette (1757–1834): strongly hated the British following death of father at Minden and humiliation of France in treaty ending Seven Years' War; early sympathiser with American Revolution, volunteer in American War from 1776; sympathetic to ideals of French Revolution but forced to flee France; imprisoned in Austria as a republican until grudgingly released by Napoleon.

5. Nathanael Greene (1742–1786): American military commander considered by some a better general than George Washington.

6. Quoted in Larrabee, *Decision at the Chesapeake*, 152–53.

7. Quoted in Center of Military History, U.S. Army, "The Sea Battle off the Capes of Virginia," www.hmsrichmond.org/degrasse.htm.

8. Francis, Lord Rawdon (1754–1826): heir to the Earl of Moira; raised volunteers in Ireland for the American War; commanded British forces at Savannah and Charleston; captured while returning home for health reasons.

9. *Rutland Papers*, 3:43, Lord Robert Manners to Duke of Rutland, ? July 1781.

10. Chadwick, *Graves Papers*.

11. BL Add. MSS 35193, Samuel Hood to Alexander Hood, 2 August 1781.

12. Tilley, *Navy and the American Revolution*, 242.

13. Spinney, *Rodney*, 378.

14. Thomas Wells (d. 1811): lieutenant 1780; commander 1781; captain 1782; rear admiral 1804; vice admiral 1808.

15. Edmund Affleck (1725–1788): lieutenant 1746; commander 1756; captain 1757; rear admiral 1784; MP for Colchester 1782–88; baronet 1782.

16. PRO ADM 2/1339, Admiralty to Arbuthnot, 22 May 1781.

17. Chadwick, *Graves Papers*, Graves to Stephens, 20 August 1781.

18. BL Add. MSS 35193, Samuel Hood to Alexander Hood, 2 August 1781.

19. Ibid.

20. PRO ADM 1/483, enclosure in Hood to Stephens, 30 August 1781.

21. Bicheno, *Rebels and Redcoats*, 214–215

22. Larrabee, *Decision at the Chesapeake*, 82.

23. George Collier (1738–1795): lieutenant 1754; commander 1761; captain 1762; rear admiral 1793; vice admiral 1794; knighted 1776; MP for Honiton 1784–90.

24. Banastre Tarleton (1754–1833): most effective British light cavalry leader of the war; accused by the Americans of brutality; not employed again after the war.

25. Gabriel Christie (1722–1799): served in Canada and West Indies.

26. Mackesy, *War for America*, 420.

27. Laughton, *Papers of Charles, Lord Barham*, 1:121–22, Graves to Hood 28 August 1781.

28. Jacques-Melchior, comte de Barras de Saint-Laurent (ca. 1719–1793): with d'Estaing in attack on Newport in 1778; commander in North America from May 1781; deferred to de Grasse at the Chesapeake; captured Montserrat in February 1782; ill health forced return to France in March 1782.

29. Chadwick, *Graves Papers*, Graves to Stephens, 20 August 1781.

30. Laughton, *Papers of Charles, Lord Barham*, 1:123, Hunt to Middleton, 29 September 1781.

31. Quoted in Chevalier, *Histoire de la marine*.

32. Tunstall, *Naval Warfare in the Age of Sail*, 172–73.

33. Padfield 263.

34. Mackenzie, *Diary*, 611.

35. Ibid., 616.

36. Ibid., 613.

35. Ibid., 616.

37. NMM GRE/6, Saxton, "Remark Book of HMS Invincible 1781–82."

38. Tilley, *Navy and the American Revolution*, 252–53.

Chapter 8. The Chesapeake: The Battle Joined

1. Thomas Graves (d. 1755): commander 1709; captain 1713; rear admiral, retired 1747; died 1755.

2. Samuel Graves (1713–1787): lieutenant 1740; captain 1744; rear admiral 1762; vice admiral 1770; admiral 1778.

3. Tilley, *Navy and the American Revolution*, 190.

4. Constantine John Phipps, later Baron Mulgrave (1744–1792): lieutenant 1762; captain 1765; Admiralty commissioner 1777–82; MP for Lincoln 1768–74, for Huntingdon 1776–84, for Newark 1784–90; Irish peer by inheritance 1775; English peer 1790.

5. *Rutland Papers*, 3:36, Lord Robert Manners to Duke of Rutland, 20 September 1780.

6. Details of French commanders supplied by the Musée de la Marine, Paris.

7. Barnes and Owen, *Sandwich*, 4:181–82, Graves to Sandwich, 14 September 1781; Hannay, *Hood*, 31, Hood to Sandwich, 6 September 1781.

8. Tunstall, *Naval Warfare in the Age of Sail*, 173.

9. Ibid., 174.

10. Talbott, *Pen and Ink Sailor*, 46–48, 105–11.

11. Ibid., 49–50, 53, 56, 104–10.

12. Ibid., 104.

13. NMM GRE/6, Saxton, "Remark Book of HMS Invincible 1781–82."

14. Larrabee, *Decision at the Chesapeake*, 200.

15. Barnes and Owen, *Sandwich*, 4:190, Hood to Sandwich, 6 September 1781.

16. Tornquist, *Campaigns of the Count de Grasse*.

17. Chadwick, *Graves Papers*, 62.

18. George Grey (1767–1828): lieutenant 1781; captain 1793; superannuated 1811.

19. NMM GRE/6, journal entry for 5 September 1781.

20. Sullivan, "Graves and Hood," 178–94.

21. Thomas White (d. 1833): lieutenant 1783; commander 1798; captain 1810.

22. White, *Naval Researches* 45.

23. See note 19.

24. Thomas Réveil Shivers (1750–1827): lieutenant 1777; commander 1782; captain 1790; rear admiral 1808; vice admiral 1812; admiral 1825.

25. NMM ADM/L/B/19, *Barfleur* log.

26. Quoted in Larrabee, *Decision at the Chesapeake*.

27. Chadwick, *Graves Papers*, 232.

Chapter 9. The World Turned Upside Down

1. Tunstall, *Naval Warfare in the Age of Sail*, 176.

2. Julian Corbett, quoted in Owen, Naval Review Vol. XIV 224. "Surrender at Yorktown."

3. BL Add. MSS 9343, Hood to Jackson, 13 September 1781.

4. Barnes and Owen, *Sandwich*, 4:189–90, Hood to Sandwich, 6 September 1781.

5. *Naval Chronicle* 8 (1802).

6. PRO 30/20/10, Rodney to Jackson, 19 October 81.

7. Mahan, *Major Operations of the Navies*, 184.

8. René de Kerallain, "Bougainville à l'armée du comte de Grasse, guerre de l'Amérique, 1781–83," *Journal de la Société des Américanistes de Paris* 20 (1928): 19, quoted in Larrabee, *Decision at the Chesapeake*, 215–16.

9. BL Add. MSS 9343, Hood to Jackson, 13 September 1781.

10. Ibid.

11. Hannay, *Hood*, 33–34, Hood to Graves, 10 September 1781.

12. Ibid., 34, Graves to Hood, 13 September 1781.

13. Ibid., 34–35, Hood to Graves, 13 September 1781.

14. Padfield, *Maritime Supremacy*, 269.

15. Bicheno, *Rebels & Redcoats*, 247.

16. See Breen, "Graves and Hood at the Chesapeake."

17. Mackenzie, *Diary*, 616.

18. Ibid., 629.

19. Ibid., 630.

20. Ibid., 636.

21. Syrett, *Royal Navy in American Waters*, 208.

22. Hon. William Cornwallis (1744–1819): lieutenant 1761; commander 1762; captain

1765; rear admiral 1793; vice admiral 1794; admiral 1799; MP for Eye 1768–74, 1790–1807, for Portsmouth 1784–90.

23. *Rutland Papers*, 3:37, Lord Robert Manners to Duke of Rutland, 27 September 1781.

24. Chadwick, *Graves Papers*, Graves to Stephens, 26 September 1781.

25. *Rutland Papers*, 3:37, Lord Robert Manners to Duke of Rutland, 27 September 1781.

26. Hannay, *Hood*, 37–38, Hood to Jackson, 14 October 1781.

27. Ibid.

28. Mackenzie, *Diary*, 653.

29. Hon. Charles Cochrane (1749–1781): son of the 8th Earl of Dundonald, killed at Yorktown on 19 October 1781.

30. Cornwallis-West, *Admiral Cornwallis*, 107.

31. *Rutland Papers*, 3:38, Lord Robert Manners to Duke of Rutland, 27 September 1781.

32. Mackenzie, *Diary*, 664.

33. Mackay, *Admiral Hawke*, 353.

34. Tunstall, *Naval Warfare in the Age of Sail*, 177.

35. Larrabee, *Decision at the Chesapeake*, 262.

36. Chadwick, *Graves Papers* , Graves to Stephens, 29 October 1781.

37. BL Add. Mss 9343, Hood to Jackson, 29 October 1781.

38. Barnes and Owen, *Sandwich*, 4:199–200, Hood to Digby, 31 October 1781.

39. Ibid., 4:200, Hood to Graves, 3 November 1781.

40. Hannay, *Hood*, 53, Hood to Digby, 10 November 1781.

41. Ibid., 54.

Chapter 10. The Rise and Fall of an Admiral

1. NMM MKH/B/3, Samuel Hood to Alexander Hood, 28 February 1782.

2. NMM HOO/101, Sandwich to Hood, 9 November 1781.

3. James Saumarez (1757–1836): lieutenant 1778; commander 1781; captain 1782; rear admiral 1801; vice admiral 1806; admiral 1814; knighted 1793; baronet 1801; English peer 1831.

4. *Rutland Papers*, 3:45, Lord Robert Manners to the Duke of Rutland, 14 December 1781.

5. NMM MKH/C/1/B, undated enclosure.

6. Ross, *Saumarez*, 1:59–60.

7. NMM MKH/B/3, Samuel Hood to Alexander Hood, 14 February 1782.

8. Archibald Campbell of Inverneill (1739–1791): POW exchanged for Ethan Allen 1778; major general 1782; governor of Jamaica 1782–85, of Madras 1785–89; MP for Stirling 1774–80, 1789; knighted 1785; buried in Poet's Corner of Westminster Abbey.

9. Syrett, "Countdown."

10. Mahan, *Major Operations*, 206

11. Barnes and Owen, *Sandwich*, 4:249, Hood to Sandwich, 3 April 1782.

12. Hannay, *Hood*, 101–2, Hood to Jackson, 16 April 1782.

13. John Symons (d. 1799): lieutenant 1755; commander 1761; captain 1771; rear admiral 1794; vice admiral 1795.

14. James, 8th Lord Cranstoun (1755–1796): lieutenant 1776; captain 1782.

15. Trew, *Breaking of the Line*, 155.

16. Ibid., 158–59.

17. NMM ADM/L/P/276, *Princessa* log, and ADM/L/C/78, *Canada* log.

18. BL Add. MSS 9343, Hood to Henry Shales, 12 May 1780. See Dorothy Hood, *The Admirals Hood*, 53.

19. NMM MKH/B/3, Samuel Hood to Alexander Hood, 21 June 1782.

20. NMM MKH/B/3, Samuel Hood to Alexander Hood, 8 July 1782.

21. Fortescue, *Correspondence of King George III*, Shelburne to George III, 21 April 1782; George III to Shelburne, 21 April 1782.

22. Ibid., Shelburne to George III, 18 May 1782; George III to Shelburne, 18 May 1782; Shelburne to George III, 19 May 1782; George III to Shelburne, 20 May 1782.

23. NMM MKH/B/3, Samuel Hood to Alexander Hood, 21 June 1782.

24. John Pitt, 2nd Earl of Chatham (1758–1835): First Lord of the Admiralty 1788–94; commanded land forces in the Walcheren Expedition 1809.

25. Rose, *Lord Hood and the Defence of Toulon*, 11.

26. Ibid., 11–12.

27. Ibid., 19–20.

28. Ibid., 12–13.

29. Ibid., 21.

30. Ibid., 22–23.

31. See Ireland, *The Fall of Toulon*, for this suggestion.

32. William Sidney Smith (1764–1840): lieutenant 1780; commander 1782; captain 1783; rear admiral 1805; vice admiral 1810; admiral 1821; in Swedish service 1790–93; MP for Rochester 1802–6.

33. Smith, *Knight of the Sword*, 30.

34. Hood to Sir William Hamilton, 21 November 1793, in Rose, *Lord Hood*, 152.

35. George John, 2nd Earl Spencer (1758–1834): Joined Pitt administration following outbreak of war with France; First Lord of the Admiralty 1794–1801; resigned with Pitt over Catholic Emancipation issue.

BIBLIOGRAPHY

Anderson, Fred. *Crucible of War: The Seven Years' War and the Fate of Empire in British North America, 1754–1766.* London: Faber and Faber, 2000.

Aspinall, A., ed. *The Later Correspondence of George III.* 5 vols. Cambridge: Cambridge University Press, 1962–70.

Barnes, G. R., and J. H. Owen, eds. *The Private Papers of John, Earl of Sandwich, First Lord of the Admiralty, 1771–1782.* 4 vols. London: Navy Records Society, 1932–38.

Baugh, Daniel A. "Sir Samuel Hood: Superior Subordinate." In Billias, *Washington's Generals and Opponents,* 291–326.

Beatson, Robert. *Naval and Military Memoirs of Great Britain, from 1727 to 1783.* 2nd ed. 6 vols. London, 1804.

Bicheno, Hugh. *Rebels & Redcoats: The American Revolutionary War.* London: HarperCollins, 2003.

Billias, George Athan, ed. *George Washington's Generals and Opponents.* New York: Da Capo Press, 1994.

Black, Jeremy, and Philip Woodfine. *The British Navy and the Use of Naval Power in the Eighteenth Century.* Leicester: Leicester University Press, 1988.

Breen, Kenneth. "Graves and Hood at the Chesapeake." *Mariner's Mirror* 66 (1980): 53–65.

Chadwick, French Ensor, ed. *The Graves Papers and Other Documents Relating to the Naval Operations of the Yorktown Campaign, July to October, 1781.* New York: Naval History Society, 1916.

Charnock, John. *Biographia Navalis; or, Impartial Memoirs of the Lives and Characters of Officers of the Navy of Great Britain from the Year 1660 to the Present Time.* 6 vols. London: R. Faulder, 1794–98.

Chevalier, E. *Histoire de la marine française pendant la guerre de l'indépendance américaine.* Paris: Librairie Hachette, 1877.

Clowes, William Laird. *The Royal Navy: A History from the Earliest Times to the Present.* Vol. 3. London: Sampson Low, Marston, 1898.

Corbett, Julian S. *England in the Seven Years' War.* London: Longmans, Green, 1907.

Corbett, J. S., and H. Richmond, eds. *The Private Papers of George, Second Earl Spencer, First Lord of the Admiralty, 1771–1803.* 4 vols. London: Navy Records Society, 1913–24.

Cornwallis-West, G. *The Life and Letters of Admiral Cornwallis.* London: Robert Holden, 1927.

Creswell, John. *British Admirals of the Eighteenth Century: Tactics in Battle.* London: Allen and Unwin, 1972.

Duffy, Michael. "Samuel Hood, First Viscount Hood." In *Precursors of Nelson: British Admirals of the Eighteenth Century,* edited by Peter Le Fevre and Richard Harding, 248–77. London: Chatham, 2000.

Dull, Jonathan R. *The French Navy and American Independence: A Study of Arms and Diplomacy, 1774–1787.* Princeton, N.J.: Princeton University Press, 1975.

———. *A Diplomatic History of the American Revolution.* New Haven, Conn.: Yale University Press, 1985.

Ehrman, John. *The Younger Pitt.* Vol. 2, *The Reluctant Transition.* London: Constable, 1983.

Ekins, Charles. *Naval Battles from 1744 to the Peace in 1814.* 2nd ed. London: Baldwin and Cradock, 1828.

Fortescue, John. *The Correspondence of King George the Third from 1760 to December 1783.* 6 vols. London: Macmillan, 1927–28.

Geddes, A. *Portsmouth during the Great French Wars, 1770–1800.* Portsmouth, Hants.: Portsmouth City Council, 1970.

Graves, W[illiam]. *Two Letters from W. Graves, Esq., Respecting the Conduct of Rear Admiral Thomas Graves, in North America, during his Accidental Command There for Four Months in 1781.* Pamphlet. London, 1783.

Gruber, Ira D. *The Howe Brothers and the American Revolution.* New York: Atheneum, 1972.

Gwyn, Julian. "The Royal Navy in North America, 1712–1776." In Black and Woodfine, *Use of Naval Power,* 129–47.

Hamilton, Richard Vesey, ed. *Letters and Papers of Admiral of the Fleet Sir Thos. Byam Martin.* 3 vols. London: Navy Records Society, 1898–1903.

Hannay, David. *Rodney.* London: Macmillan, 1891.

———, ed. *Letters of Sir Samuel Hood.* London: Navy Records Society, 1895.

Harvey, Robert. *A Few Bloody Noses: The American War of Independence.* London: Robinson, 2002.

Historical Manuscripts Commission. *The Manuscripts of His Grace the Duke of Rutland, G.C.B., Preserved at Belvoir Castle.* 4 vols. London: HMSO, 1888–1905. Cited as *Rutland Papers.*

Hood, Dorothy. *The Admirals Hood.* London: Hutchinson, 1941.

Ireland, Bernard. *The Fall of Toulon: The Last Opportunity to Defeat the French Revolution.* London: Weidenfeld and Nicolson, 2005.

James, William. *The Naval History of Great Britain.* Vol. 1. London: Baldwin, Cradock, and Joy, 1822.

James, William Milburne. *The British Navy in Adversity: A Study of the War of American Independence.* London: Longmans, 1926.

Jenkins, E. H. *A History of the French Navy.* London: Macdonald and Jane's, 1973.

Lacour-Gayet, Georges. *La Marine militaire de la France sous le règne de Louis XVI.* Paris: Champion, 1905.

Larrabee, Harold A. *Decision at the Chesapeake.* New York: Clarkson N. Potter, 1964.

Laughton, John Knox, ed. *Letters and Papers of Charles, Lord Barham, Admiral of the Red Squadron, 1758–1813.* 3 vols. London: Navy Records Society, 1907–11.

Lewis, Charles Lee. *Admiral de Grasse and American Independence.* Annapolis, Md.: Naval Institute Press, 1945.

Lloyd, Christopher. "Sir George Rodney: Lucky Admiral." In Billias, *Washington's Generals and Opponents,* 327–54.

Mackay, Ruddock F. *Admiral Hawke.* Oxford: Clarendon Press, 1965.

———, ed. *The Hawke Papers: A Selection, 1743–1771.* London: Navy Records Society, 1990.

Mackenzie, Frederick. *The Diary of Frederick Mackenzie.* 2 vols. Cambridge, Mass.: Harvard University Press, 1930.

Mackesy, Piers. *The War for America, 1775–1783.* London: Longmans, 1964.

Mahan, A. T. *Types of Naval Officers, Drawn from the History of the British Navy.* London: Sampson Low, Marston, 1902.

———. *The Major Operations of the Navies in the War of American Independence.* London: Sampson Low, Marston, 1913.

Martelli, George. *Jemmy Twitcher: A Life of the Fourth Earl of Sandwich, 1718–1792.* London: Cape, 1962.

Morriss, Roger, ed. *The Channel Fleet and the Blockade of Brest, 1793–1801.* London: Navy Records Society, 2001.

Mundy, G. B. *The Life and Correspondence of the Late Admiral Lord Rodney.* 2 vols. London: John Murray, 1830.

Owen, J. H. "The Navy and the Surrender at Yorktown, 1781." *Naval Review* 14 (1926): 18–33, 223–48.

———. "Hood at Saint Christophers, 1782." *Naval Review* 15 (1927): 496–518.

———. "Rodney and Grasse, 1782." *Naval Review* 16 (1928): 148–59, 213–38, 436–46.

Padfield, Peter. *Maritime Supremacy & the Opening of the Western Mind: Naval Campaigns That Shaped the Modern World, 1588–1782.* London: John Murray, 1999.

Patterson, A. Temple. *The Other Armada: The Franco-Spanish Attempt to Invade Britain in 1779.* Manchester: Manchester University Press, 1960.

Ralfe, James. *The Naval Biography of Great Britain: Consisting of Historical Memoirs of Those Officers of the British Navy Who Distinguished Themselves during the Reign of His Majesty George III.* 4 vols. London, 1828.

Rodger, N. A. M. *The Wooden World: An Anatomy of the Georgian Navy.* London: Collins, 1986.

———. *The Insatiable Earl: A Life of John Montagu, Fourth Earl of Sandwich, 1718–1792.* London: HarperCollins, 1993.

———. *The Command of the Ocean: A Naval History of Britain, 1649–1815.* London: Allen Lane, 2004.

Rose, John Holland. *Lord Hood and the Defence of Toulon.* Cambridge: Cambridge University Press, 1922.

Ross, John. *Memoirs and Correspondence of Admiral Lord de Saumarez.* 2 vols. London: Richard Bentley, 1838.

Rutland Papers. See Historical Manuscripts Commission.

Sherrard, O. A. *Lord Chatham: Pitt and the Seven Years' War.* London: Bodley Head, 1955.

———. *Lord Chatham and America.* London: Bodley Head, 1958.

Smith, William Sidney. *Knight of the Sword: The Life and Letters of Admiral Sir William Sidney Smith.* Edited by Lord Russell of Liverpool. London: Victor Gollancz, 1964.

Spinney, David. *Rodney.* London: Allen and Unwin, 1969.

———. "Rodney and the Saints: A Reassessment." *Mariner's Mirror* 68 (1982): 377–89.

Stirling, A. M. W. *Pages and Portraits from the Past: Being the Private Papers of Sir William Hotham.* 2 vols. London: Herbert Jenkins, 1919.

Stout, Neil R. *The Royal Navy in North America, 1760–1775: A Study of Enforcement of British Colonial Policy in the Era of the American Revolution.* Annapolis, Md.: Naval Institute Press, 1973.

Sullivan, J. A. "Graves and Hood." *Mariner's Mirror* 69 (1983): 175–94.

Syrett, David. *The Royal Navy in American Waters, 1775–1783.* Aldershot: Scolar Press, 1989.

———. "Home Waters or America? The Dilemma of British Naval Strategy in 1778." *Mariner's Mirror* 77 (1991): 365–77.

———. "Count-down to the Saints: A Strategy of Detachments and the Quest for Naval Superiority in the West Indies, 1780–2." *Mariner's Mirror* 87 (2001): 150–62.

———. *Admiral Lord Howe.* Annapolis, Md: Naval Institute Press, 2006.

Syrett, David, and R. L. DiNardo, eds. *The Commissioned Sea Officers of the Royal Navy, 1660–1815.* London: Navy Records Society, 1994.

Talbott, John E. *The Pen and Ink Sailor: Charles Middleton and the King's Navy, 1778–1813.* London: Frank Cass, 1998.

Tilley, John A. *The British Navy and the American Revolution.* Columbia: University of South Carolina Press, 1987.

Tornquist, Karl Gustaf. *The Naval Campaigns of Count de Grasse during the American Revolution, 1781–1783.* Philadelphia: Swedish Colonial Society, 1942.

Tracy, Nicholas. *Navies, Deterrence, and American Independence.* Vancouver: University of British Columbia Press, 1988.

Trew, Peter. *Rodney and the Breaking of the Line.* Barnsley, S. Yorks.: Pen and Sword, 2006.

Tunstall, Brian. *Naval Warfare in the Age of Sail.* Edited by Nicholas Tracy. London: Conway Maritime Press, 1990.

White, Thomas. *Naval Researches; or, A Candid Inquiry into the Conduct of Admirals Byron, Graves, Hood, and Rodney, in the Actions off Grenada, Chesapeak, St. Christopher's, and of the Ninth and Twelfth of April, 1782: Being a Refutation of the Plans and Statements of Mr. Clerk, Rear Admiral Ekins and Others.* London, 1830.

Willcox, William Bradford. *Portrait of a General: Sir Henry Clinton in the War of Independence.* New York: Knopf, 1964.

Wyndham, Maud Mary, ed. *Chronicles of the Eighteenth Century: Founded on the Correspondence of Sir Thomas Lyttelton and His Family.* 2 vols. London: Hodder and Stoughton, 1924.

INDEX

Colin Pengelly is a retired civil servant and amateur historian. His first book, *The First Bellero*phon (1965), was well received by both scholars and naval enthusiasts. *Sir Samuel Hood and the Battle of the Chesapeake* is based on a forty-year study of Lord Hood.

New Perspectives on Maritime History and Nautical Archaeology
Edited by James C. Bradford and Gene A. Smith

The Maritime Heritage of the Cayman Islands, by Roger C. Smith (1999; first paperback edition, 2000)

The Three German Navies: Dissolution, Transition, and New Beginnings, 1945–1960, by Douglas C. Peifer (2002)

The Rescue of the Gale Runner: *Death, Heroism, and the U.S. Coast Guard*, by Dennis L. Noble (2002; first paperback edition, 2008)

Brown Water Warfare: The U.S. Navy in Riverine Warfare and the Emergence of a Tactical Doctrine, 1775–1970, by R. Blake Dunnavent (2003)

Sea Power in the Medieval Mediterranean: The Catalan-Aragonese Fleet in the War of the Sicilian Vespers, by Lawrence V. Mott (2003)

An Admiral for America: Sir Peter Warren, Vice Admiral of the Red, 1703–1752, by Julian Gwyn (2004)

Maritime History as World History, edited by Daniel Finamore (2004)

Counterpoint to Trafalgar: The Anglo-Russian Invasion of Naples, 1805–1806, by William Henry Flayhart III (first paperback edition, 2004)

Life and Death on the Greenland Patrol, 1942, by Thaddeus D. Novak, edited by P. J. Capelotti (2005)

X Marks the Spot: The Archaeology of Piracy, edited by Russell K. Skowronek and Charles R. Ewen (2006; first paperback edition, 2007)

Industrializing American Shipbuilding: The Transformation of Ship Design and Construction, 1820–1920, by William H. Thiesen (2006)*Admiral Lord Keith and the Naval War Against Napoleon*, by Kevin D. McCranie (2006)

Commodore John Rodgers: Paragon of the Early American Navy, by John H. Schroeder (2006)

Borderland Smuggling: Patriots, Loyalists, and Illicit Trade in the Northeast, 1783–1820, by Joshua M. Smith (2006)

Brutality on Trial: "Hellfire" Pedersen, "Fighting" Hansen, and the Seamen's Act of 1915, by E. Kay Gibson (2006)

Uriah Levy: Reformer of the Antebellum Navy, by Ira Dye (2006)

Crisis at Sea: The United States Navy in European Waters in World War I, by William N. Still Jr. (2006)

Chinese Junks on the Pacific: Views from a Different Deck, by Hans K. Van Tilburg (2007)

Eight Thousand Years of Maltese Maritime History: Trade, Piracy, and Naval Warfare in the Central Mediterranean, by Ayşe Devrim Atauz (2007)

Merchant Mariners at War: An Oral History of World War II, by George J. Billy and Christine M. Billy (2008)

The Steamboat Montana *and the Opening of the West: History, Excavation, and Architecture*, by Annalies Corbin and Bradley A. Rogers (2008)

Attack Transport: USS Charles Carroll *in World War II*, by Kenneth H. Goldman (2008)

Diplomats in Blue: U.S. Naval Officers in China, 1922–1933, by William Reynolds Braisted (2009)

Sir Samuel Hood and the Battle of the Chesapeake, by Colin Pengelly (2009)